Modern African Writers
NADINE GORDIMER

Gerald Moore, General Editor

David Goldblatt

Nadine Gordimer

NADINE GORDIMER

Michael Wade

Evans Brothers Limited

Evans Brothers Limited
Montague House, Russell Square
London WC1B 5BX

Evans Brothers (Nigeria Publishers) Limited
PMB 5164, Jericho Road
Ibadan

First published 1978
Cover illustration by Colin Hawkins
Frontispiece photograph by David Goldblatt

Filmset in 11 on 12pt Ehrhardt type and printed by
BAS Printers Limited, Over Wallop, Hampshire
ISBN 0 237 49979 7 Limp
ISBN 0 237 49978 9 Cased   PRA 6330

Contents

Acknowledgements

The publishers are grateful to the following for their kind permission to reproduce the extracts in this book:
Nadine Gordimer for her works: *The Lying Days, Six Feet of the Country, Friday's Footprint, Occasion for Loving, Not for Publication, Face to Face* and Nadine Gordimer and Victor Gollancz Ltd for *The Late Bourgeois World*; Jonathan Cape Ltd. for *A Guest of Honour* by Nadine Gordimer, Victor Gollancz Ltd. for *A World of Strangers* by Nadine Gordimer; Faber and Faber Ltd. for *Little Gidding* and *Preludes 1* by T. S. Eliot.

Editor's Foreword

Considering her accepted status as a novelist, Nadine Gordimer has been the object of surprisingly little extended critical study. Is it that most of our critics are frankly scared by the complexity of moral vision revealed by the later work, from *The Late Bourgeois World* onwards? Or is it the *direction* of her work which has this effect on them; her increasingly frank recognition that the liberal attitudes which have been built into the tradition of the English novel wilt or collapse in the bitter air of South Africa?

Be that as it may, it is fortunate that Michael Wade, a fellow South African raised in the same liberal-Jewish metropolitan tradition, is peculiarly well-equipped for the critical task he tackles here. In earlier work, such as his study of *Peter Abrahams* (1973), Wade has already exposed the manner in which this liberal value-system, first evident in Olive Schreiner's *The Story of an African Farm* (1883), gradually declines into irrelevance, an irrelevance which matches that of public liberal stances in the age of Sharpeville and Soweto. But Nadine Gordimer's impressive development as a novelist gradually educating herself out of that tradition into one which accepts the inevitable failure of her romantic heroes (heroes as diverse as Toby, Max, Bray and Mehring), provides the best and most challenging means of tracing that decline. As Wade himself puts it:

> The orthodox presentation of the interplay of time and human character in the English novel is carried . . . on the same wave of radical optimism that bore the novel genre to the commanding heights of literary expression in English. That is, whatever tragic individual events may occur, the main tendency of development in human relations is ameliorative.

That faith in the ameliorative power of human relations has

nowhere come under stronger challenge than in South Africa, many of whose novelists clung to it with all the tenacity of the exile. That one of the strongest and surest voices in contemporary South African fiction now demands that we recognize the final collapse of this faith, that Bray the man of goodwill is finally as doomed and irrelevant as Mehring the cynic, is, ironically, itself an evidence that the illuminating power of art is greater than that of any tradition which may appear to contain and govern it. Nadine Gordimer has moved the South African novel into a new terrain, harsh and relentless in aspect, denying all reassuring resemblances to 'home'. That is the core of her achievement, and the reason why she deserves a place of honour in any list of writers who strive to define the African experience.

G.M.

The Author

Michael Wade grew up in South Africa. He came to England in 1964, and studied at the universities of London and Sussex. Since 1967 he has been lecturing in the departments of English and African Studies at the Hebrew University of Jerusalem. In the field of African literature he has published articles on Amos Tutuola, Peter Abrahams, and William Plomer.

Introduction

Nadine Gordimer was born in November 1923, in Springs, then a small mining and industrial town near the eastern tip of the Witwatersrand, the hundred-and-twenty-mile gold-bearing ridge that is the source of South Africa's wealth. Her father was a Russian Jew who married an English Jewess. She was a day-scholar at a convent, and later studied at the University of the Witwatersrand in Johannesburg. Nadine Gordimer began writing when she was nine, and her first adult story to be published, 'Come Again Tomorrow', appeared in *Forum*, a South African journal of current affairs, in November 1939, when the author was fifteen.

Nadine Gordimer has always lived in South Africa, remaining steadfast to her political, social and literary beliefs through difficult times, during which many other writers have chosen exile or had it thrust upon them. One of her novels has been banned in South Africa and the paperback edition of another may not be distributed there.

Nadine Gordimer has written six novels, charting South African and wider reality from 1953 to 1974. Like all serious South African writers, the reality she has had to scrutinize most closely has been that of politics. Indeed, the paradox is that when she was most concerned to write about the 'universal' processes of life and growth, the product was most relentlessly political, and as her political attitudes and responses matured and grew more sensitive, coming to occupy the centre of her concerns, so her novels were increasingly involved in the genuine issues of life and death.

Again like other contemporary South African writers of significance (there are not many), Nadine Gordimer is attracted to that most exacting of genres, the short story. Her novels are published after intervals during which she usually rehearses themes and preoccupations in a volume or two of the less extended form.

3

Thus her first novel, *The Lying Days* (1953)[1], was preceded by *Face to Face* (1949)[2] and *The Soft Voice of the Serpent* (1952)[3], two largely overlapping collections of stories, and a pattern is established between her first and second novels (one short story volume) which is repeated between her second and third, her third and fourth, and her fifth and sixth.

The emphasis of this book will be on the novels, and individual short stories will be treated at length only where they possess specific relevance to an issue arising out of our discussion of the novels.

It may be useful to situate Nadine Gordimer's career in relation to those of her leading South African contemporaries. Her first novel appeared when Peter Abrahams was already an established figure, having just published *Wild Conquest*, and Sarah Gertrude Millin was beginning to turn her corroded imagination to the sideshows of South African history. Dan Jacobson's career has been almost contemporaneous with Nadine Gordimer's, and shortly after *The Lying Days* appeared he produced the compressed, allegorical novelles *The Trap* and *A Dance in the Sun*.[4]

Of all the significant fiction being written at the time in South Africa, Nadine Gordimer's was at first the least ostensibly political. In some very important respects, however, it could be said to cast a much clearer light on the core of the political preoccupation of the South African novel – the relationships, in all their varied and stereotyped forms, between the different-coloured groups that form the population of South Africa – than any contemporaneous work. If Dan Jacobson's earlier South African novels could be said to occupy the 'middle ground' of interaction between white and black, Nadine Gordimer's first attempt at the genre stays solidly 'at home' in the world (or worlds) of the whites; but after this her work moves steadily towards becoming the most inclusive presentation we have of the multiracial totality of South African experience.

[1] *The Lying Days* (Victor Gollancz, London, 1953).
[2] *Face to Face* (Silver Leaf Books, Johannesburg, 1949).
[3] *The Soft Voice of the Serpent and other stories* (Victor Gollancz, London, 1953).
[4] D. Jacobson, *The Trap* and *A Dance in the Sun* (1955 and 1956 respectively).

1   The Lying Days

The Lying Days is the story of a young white girl from the almost symbolically representative background of the middle-level bureaucracy of the gold-mining industry. Her father is secretary of a gold mine in a small town on the Witwatersrand; he has worked there all his life, beginning as a junior clerk. They live in a staff house in the staff quarters of the mine, surrounded by other petty clerks and minor managers. It is a sort of enclosed suburbia, and the outlook on life of its inhabitants is a hothouse version of suburban attitudes in general.

The narrator of *The Lying Days* is its heroine, Helen Shaw. The essential structural components of the novel are three worlds, each apparently entirely separated from the other in the content of its experience: the mine, the seaside resort where she spends a long holiday, and Johannesburg in the early post-war years. They are linked, and a kind of unity is forged between them by the story of Helen's growing up.

This is what makes *The Lying Days* such a precarious undertaking, given Nadine Gordimer's technique of meticulous examination of detail in her tentative search for just assessments. It is possible to criticize the novel for being weighed down by evidence, as Arnold Abramovitz rather self-deprecatingly does in his article, 'Nadine Gordimer and the Impertinent Reader'.[1] He acknowledges, however, that her own recognition of the difficulty of providing the right answers goes a long way to negate his demand for them at the end of the book. His contention that South African writing had not produced the combination of artistry and social conscience that the society 'cries out for' is the more apt because it is made in connection with this novel, which, cast in the form of a journey from the outside inwards toward the heart of experience, is

[1] A. Abramovitz, 'Nadine Gordimer and the Impertinent Reader', in *The Purple Renoster* (Johannesburg), no. 1, September 1956, pp. 13–17.

itself the beginning of the necessary larger journey of discovery that will, in the end, lead to 'the pain . . . by which we recognize the depth of our own complicity in the plight of our brother and countryman.'[1] Mr Abramovitz, like many others, in assuming the nature of the goal, underestimated the difficulty of the journey itself; and although we may be letting the cat rather prematurely out of its bag, it will be the tendency of this study to suggest that however negative the effect may have been on some of her writing and in particular on the success of two of her novels – this one and *Occasion for Loving*[2] – Nadine Gordimer was merely recognizing the inevitable in adopting this technique. It is interesting to note, in passing, how her two 'serious' male contemporaries, Abrahams and Jacobson, were forced, each according to his own gifts and abilities, of course, to the same recourse, though in both cases after the unnecessary squandering of a certain amount of creative energy, and also in both cases in the wrong order. Jacobson reaches this point in *The Beginners* (1966), his fifth novel; and Abrahams in *Return to Goli* (1953) and *Tell Freedom* (1954), which are at the same time more directly autobiographical and more selective of the evidence than either *The Beginners* or *The Lying Days*. The point that is being made is that the South African novelist is unable to liberate himself sufficiently from the effects of his environment (that is, from a bewilderment of possibilities) to do artistic justice to any aspect of South African reality until he has undergone this experience, which is the experience of writing a book like *The Lying Days* or *The Beginners*. *The Beginners* is an accumulation of virtually all the evidence, a scrutiny as remorseless as it is subjective, and a partial submersion of the standard temptation of the novelist to 'tell the truth' until some sort of basis for an attempt to do so emerges from the welter of facts and feelings. It may well be impossible to make this attempt within the scope of the same work, and perhaps at least one novelistic failure is inevitable; but it is a failure that might be more than justified by its later rewards.

Thus *The Lying Days* sets out to record an unusual quantity of detail in the life and growth of Helen Shaw. We have said that it is cast in the form of a journey from the outside in, which illuminates the carefully-contrived pattern of reversal of appearance and reality that constitutes the design of the novel. It would seem, at least initially, that the centre of reality for Helen resides, or at least

[1] A. Abramovitz, *op. cit.*, p. 17.
[2] *Occasion for Loving* (Victor Gollancz, London, 1963).

should reside, in the comfortable conditions of life on the mine
estate, towards the smooth conduct of which her parents make such
an indefatigable contribution; and that all movements away from
the mine are explorations outwards from the heart of reality. Most
of the characters, in particular Helen's parents, simply assume that
this is the case, and in the absence of realistic alternatives, it is a
powerful assumption. The book opens with a hint of the limitations
of this assumption and an acknowledgment of its strength:

> One Saturday in late August when my friend Olwen Taylor's
> mother telephoned to say that Olwen would not be able to go
> to the bioscope because she was going to a wedding, I refused
> to go with Gloria Dufalette (I heard Mrs Dufalette's call, out
> of the back door in the next house – Gloriah, Gloriah!) or with
> Paddy Connolly. Paddy Connolly's little brother picked his
> nose, and no member of his family stopped him doing it.
> 'What'll she do, then?' asked my father.
> My mother was pinning her hair ready for her tennis cap,
> looking straight back at herself in the mirror. Up-down, went
> her shoulders. 'I don't know. She's not pleased with anything
> I suggest.'
> But her indifference was not real . . . . 'Helen! You must
> make up your mind what you want to do. You know I can't
> leave you on your own, the girl's out.' Yes, I knew that, an
> unwritten law so sternly upheld and generally accepted that it
> would occur to no child to ask why: a little girl must not be left
> alone because there were native boys about. That was all.
> Native boys were harmless and familiar because they were
> servants, or delivery boys bringing the groceries or the fish by
> bicycle from town, or Mine boys something to laugh at in
> their blankets and their clay spiked hair, but at the same time
> they spoke and shouted in a language you didn't understand
> and dressed differently in any old thing, and so were
> mysterious. Not being left alone because they were about was
> simply something to do with their mysteriousness.[1]

It is partly this quality of mystery that Helen waywardly sets out to
explore when her mother 'punishes' her for her recalcitrance by
leaving her behind:

> 'No, we're just going to leave her here, that's all,' said my

[1] *The Lying Days* (Victor Gollancz, London, 1953), pp. 13–14.

mother briskly and coldly. . . . 'The back door's open and she can just be left to her own devices. If something happens to her it's her own fault. I'm not ruining my afternoon for her.'

She had gone too far, and spoiled the effect. We all knew that her afternoon *was* ruined; that she was terrified and convinced that 'something' would happen to me; that her stride to the gate was a piece of bravado that cost her more than it was worth. (pp. 14–15)

Alone, Helen first enters the house, by the open back door.

In my bedroom I stood before the mirror that was the middle door of the wardrobe, looking at myself. After a long time, steady and unblinking, only the sound of my breath, the face was just a face like other people's faces met in the street. It looked at me a little longer. Suddenly I slammed the door, ran out of the passage which seemed to take up and give out the sound of each of my footsteps as if it were counting them, and through the kitchen which was noting each drip of the tap and the movement of a fly on a potato peeling. I went straight down the garden path and out of the gate into the road. (p. 15)

It may be that the fine observation and recording of detail is less than completely controlled, and as the later novels show, this is very much a matter of experience. But the technique is certainly not an end in itself. Up to this point, what has been recorded prefigures what is to come: the inherent conflict between mother and daughter, and the dominance of unexamined and unsubstantiated orthodoxy over the accepted system of choices, shown in the mother's moral bravado which is punitive in its essence, and the daughter's almost fearful rejection of her self-image as it is generated by those surroundings. When she is older, this develops into a deep anxiety over loss of identity, and the reaction is to be similar: an impulse to 'run away from home', to try to leave behind the guilty environment. The virtuosity of these early passages lies in the way they delicately begin to suggest how the dominant value system pervades the entire psychic universe of the characters. In the very gesture and mannerism of Helen's mother as she stands before the mirror, and in Helen's emulation of her, there are indications both of the kind of society they inhabit, with its value-structure based so meticulously on appearances that the mirror image becomes the reality, and of the hypnotic force with which the young are trapped into unwitting acquiescence.

At this point Helen leaves the house, and makes her way slowly out of the confines of white safety and respectability in a new direction:

> The red dust path turning off to the stores was somewhere I had never been. There were children in the Mine, little children in pushcarts whose mothers let their nursegirls take them anywhere they liked; go down to the filthy kaffir stores to gossip with the boys and let those poor little babies they're supposed to be taking care of breathe in heaven knows what dirt and disease, my mother often condemned. . . . I slowed. But to turn round and go back to the Mine would be to have been nowhere. (p. 18)

So she continues, and ventures into the new terrain, which is rendered with dreamy clarity, the parts bearing no familiar relationship to one another, not constituting a coherent unity, a confusion rather of the sordid and the exotic, the fascinating and the banal. The polarity between attraction and revulsion itself attracts her: she is fascinated, transported into a South African child's fairyland by a windowful of 'native medicines'.

> Not that these dusty lions' tails, these piles of wizened seeds, these flaking grey roots and strange teeth could be believed to hold tight, like Japanese paper flowers, magic that might suddenly open . . . But the dustiness, the greyness, the scavenged collection of tooth and claw and skin and sluggish potion brought who knows by whom or how far or from where, waiting beneath cobwebs and neglect . . . the shudder of revulsion at finding my finger going out wanting to touch it! (p. 21)

The confrontation between the 'traditional' Africa and the white child is charged with a highly indigenous kind of mystery: each is inscrutable to the other, fascinating and repulsive to the other. An obsolescent form of magic power confronts the child of its European supplanter, but there is neither knowledge nor meaning in their meeting. Helen's reaction is not what she expects it to be, perhaps because she recognizes half-consciously what is in any event an influence in her life, though ruled out as such by her parents: the black world, taken out of its artificial context of servants' quarters and kitchen.

This in itself does not amount to the kind of advance that leads anywhere in the life of a child, and the climax of the episode is

9

intensified, containing elements of surprise which again come from Helen's reaction:

> I crunched to the path and the road over burned veld that dissolved crisply in puffs of black dust round my shoes and I passed a Mine boy standing with his back to me and his legs apart. I had vaguely noticed them standing that curious way before, as I whisked past in the car. But as I passed this one – he was singing, and the five or six yards he had put between himself and the vendors was simply a gesture – I saw a little stream of water curving from him. Not shock but a sudden press of knowledge, hot and unwanted, came upon me. A question that had waited inside me but had never risen into words or thoughts because there were no words for it – no words with myself, my mother, with Olwen even. I began to run, very fast, along the tar, the smooth straight road. (p. 24)

And she returns to her parents in this way, along the white man's mastering artefact, joining them in their easy leisure at the Mine tennis courts. Disturbed by knowledge, she now retreats from it, for a time at least:

> I went there often on Saturday afternoons after that, accepted as one of them, but with the distinction of being the only child in the party. It was easy to be one of them because I soon knew their jokes as well as they did themselves and, beside my mother, sat a little forward as they did, waiting for each to come out with his famous remark. Then when they rocked and shook their heads at getting just what they had expected, I would jump up and down, clutching at my mother's arm in delight.
> I was quite one of them. (p. 25)

There is no doubt which of the two pictures is the more repulsive, the African urinating unconcerned in the veld or the falsely precocious white child sharing the inanities of Saturday afternoon adult humour at the tennis club. There is no doubt which deals the more telling blow to childish innocence. The first situation evokes a knowledge which is already there, and to flee from it is to choose the impossible. The second represents a voluntary insulation from glimpsed reality, a short cut into the corruption of adulthood, leaving the curiosity of innocence unsatisfied.

Nadine Gordimer has depicted two group scenes, each designed to contrast with the other – visually, kinetically and olfactorily – as starkly as possible, with the emphasis on colour – the gleaming tennis togs of the whites being, as it were, the joker in the pack. The child's identification with the white adults is, of course, inevitable, but not inevitably false, as the narrator authoritatively signals it to be, through the use of irony, in this instance. The falsity springs from the fake cosiness of the tennis-playing group. What seems to be a contrast is actually a continuity.

But this is the intended pattern of Helen's childhood. Inscrutable laws hedge her in from any sort of discovery, perception is relieved of its potential intensity, and such revelations as there are come cushioned to her senses. One Sunday there is a strike at the mine, and the African miners march on the manager's house, and take over his garden.

> Nobody trampled the stars of tight-packed pansies, nobody bent the mound of white lilies that gave out their incense as if convinced they honoured a grave. Though some sat beneath scythes of shade cast by the fronds of the palms, none leaned against the monster pineapples of the boles. An immense babble, like a tremendous tea party in full swing, filled the morning. (p. 36)

Helen and her father are ignored by the miners as they walk through the garden to the manager's house, and as the explanation of the events emerges, so does the irony of the tea-party image.

> The boys at the Compound didn't like the food they were given, and so they all came together to Mr Ockert's house to complain. Now they were going back to the Compound and they were glad because, although they had behaved badly, Mr Ockert wasn't taking their Sunday ration of kaffir beer away from them. Between the two men talking above my head I heard the word 'strike'; '– But it wasn't a strike, was it?' I said quickly. My father smiled down at me. 'Well, yes, it was, really. They didn't refuse to work, but they wouldn't eat; that's a strike, too.' He had told me often about the 1922 strike of white miners, when there were shots in the street of Atherton, and my grandmother, his mother, had stayed shut up in her little house for days, until the commando of burghers came riding in to restore order. To me the word 'strike' carried with it visions of excitement and danger; something for which, alas, I had been born too late.
>
> Those native boys sitting about making a noise the way

they liked to in the garden, and the lovely tea all ready in Mrs Ockert's beautiful lounge (the scones collapsed into hot butter; I should have liked one more) – *That* couldn't be a strike –?

Hunger was whistling an empty passage right down my throat to my stomach. – I twisted my hand out of my father's and ran on ahead, to bacon and egg put away for me in the oven. (p. 39)

The ironic technique used in this episode is so clear as to require little comment – the white child's hunger and innocent surety of immediate satisfaction, as she runs ahead to her bacon and eggs, in contrast with the helpless pangs of the miners. The illusion of security remains undamaged, as the whites, moving from island to authoritative island, seem to tread above the waters of experience. This problem comes to occupy a central position in Nadine Gordimer's work: what is the nature of the defect that retards perceptual development in this way, and in the way that appears in the following passage? Is it a disease, for which no blame can be attached to the sufferers? The problem of moral awareness is one that the author has had to work her way through, and it is not until her fourth novel, thirteen years later, that she is ready to regard the complexity as resolved.

As I came with my father and Mr Bellingan a little uncertainly on to the driveway, the way visitors come who are not too certain if they have come at the right time, a few of the boys looked up over their shoulders and then slowly swung their heads back again, like cattle. One was trying to catch a fly that kept flying on to his big mouth as he shouted. Another was not listening at all, quietly exploring his nose. Another one said something about us and laughed.

. . . My father shepherded us towards the house, through the standing groups who clotted more thickly round the verandah, slapping one another's chests and backs in emphasis of argument, shaking heads and turning this way and that in laughter and disbelief. But they moved aside to let us through, absently. As they moved their blankets stirred the smell of flesh and dust. (pp. 36–37)

The idea of this passage – an important one in Nadine Gordimer's early work – is that at the very least certain perceptual *mistakes* are being made, and that they constitute a part of the unconscious basis of the formation of judgment about everyday reality. The way in which the young girl sees the group of black miners suggests a herd of noisy but peaceful and docile animals.

The treatment of the whole of the hunger strike episode raises, through the mode of perception involved and the imagery deployed, the vital general question of validity of response. When Helen is a child, she sees as a child, understands and interprets as one. But from what vantage point is the reader to attest to the ironies, to measure the gap between mature and immature sensibilities? The major difference at this stage is in the way Helen's parents and the rest of their generation see the Africans who surround them. For Helen they are browsers, for the adults they are precariously tamed beasts of prey. Thus the basis for objectivity of judgment must be outside the characters themselves.

Is there a mature perceiver located somewhere in the text, at the end, perhaps, setting a standard of judgment against which to measure the perceptions and responses of the young and growing heroine? Is there a point in this story where time stops, as it were, and growth congeals into attitudes of permanent stability and validity? It is the same critical question that contains the key to (and is so frequently avoided in readings of) Joyce's *A Portrait of the Artist as a Young Man*. Critical approaches to this novel have generally foundered on errors relating to this question.

Helen Shaw is even less Nadine Gordimer than Stephen Dedalus is James Joyce; the child-Helen is not the same person as the adolescent or young adult or even the narrator of the book, who is again different from all these versions of herself. This creates a state of permanent ironic tension, technically almost identical with that which characterizes Joyce's book. The endings are also similar in the multitude of possibilities to which they point forward, because again neither Nadine Gordimer nor the 'mature' Helen Shaw is *present* at the ending to cast a final seal of stability, any more than Joyce emerges from behind a shower of falling fingernails at the end of *A Portrait*, or even produces a 'finished' version of Stephen Dedalus. (Another characteristic error committed by a reader of *The Lying Days* is to identify Helen with oneself, which is what Abramovitz does in his 'Nadine Gordimer and the Impertinent Reader'. (q.v.) To do this means either accepting oneself as permanently incomplete, as it were, or falsely postulating a known 'mature' version of Helen. Either way, the all-important irony is completely missed or misunderstood.)

Thus Helen Shaw's reaction to the Sunday morning demonstration over mine rations must be both accepted and rejected, understood in its time-context without being dismissed from some 'adult' vantage point ascribed to the 'mature' Helen – or, for that matter, to the author. This is not to say that such restraint has to be practised, that no value judgment should be imposed. Irony invites such judgments, even imposing its own. There is, for example, no acceptance of Helen's childish use of the phrase 'native boy', either by the narrator or the reader, except in that it is correct – the child Helen knows no other term. But this fact is in itself a kind of judgment – a judgment on the narrator's background, on the kind of person she herself may be as a result of it, on the very necessities that give rise to the judgment itself. Even Nadine Gordimer herself is judged, in a way, by this judgment, or the necessity of having to make it.

Thus Helen grows with her perceptions, which are the reader's only gauges. Her growth is neither simple nor steady, though at no point can it be said of her, 'This she *is*, now,' because the process is continuous. The importance of this realization to an understanding of the book is brought out by the repetition of incidents which tend to incorporate the half-grown Helen into the static finality of adult life on the mine. The power of this comfortable inertia is demonstrated by the attractions it seems to hold, initially, even for an intelligent and innately rebellious girl like Helen. The first section of the book ends with an extension of the false maturity adopted earlier in the description of the tennis parties, into the girl's adolescence, where it is significantly attached, again, to one of her parents' leisure activities.

At this time, too, my father was teaching me to play golf. When the hooter went at half past four I left my books open on the dining-room table and went into my room to put on rubber-soled shoes. My father came home with the air of expectancy of someone who is waiting to go out again immediately, and we were at the first tee just as the sun shifted its day-long gaze and glanced obliquely off the grass. Afterwards I sat on the veranda full of Mine officials at the club-house, drinking my orange squash at a rickety wicker table, with my father sipping his beer. Our heads were continually turned to talk to people; often two or three men screeched chairs over the cement to sit with us, others would swing a leg against the table while they paused to talk in passing. Even if their talk veered to channels that slowly excluded me, leaving me at some point gently washed upon the limit of my comprehension or interest, I rested there comfortably, hearing their voices rather than what they said, lulled by the warm throbbing coming up in my scarlet, blistered palms. I lolled my head back, put my dusty feet up on the bar of the table; the sky, swept clear of the day, held only radiance, far up above the shade that rose like water steeping the trees and the drop of the grass. Over at the water hole the whole world was repeated, upside down. It all seemed simple, as if a puzzle had dissolved in my hands. The half-questions would never be asked, dark fins of feeling that could not be verified in the face of my father, my mother, the Mine officials, would not show through the surface that every minute of every day polished. I rested, my foot dancing a little tune; the way the unborn rest between one stage of labour and the next, thinking, perhaps, that they have arrived. (pp. 43–44)

This is a sort of apotheosis of Mine social life, apparently Utopian in its leisurely simplicity. Images of smoothness and reflection abound, suggesting a whole and attractive surface. Helen herself is beginning to absorb something of the shininess of this surface appearance; her deeper responses are being lulled by the dreamlike cadences and rhythms of this existence. She sees no further than the most immediate reflections of her world; the reality and the mirror-image in the water of the (artificial) water-hole seem to constitute, together, a perfect, enclosed sphere, containing all experience, all possibilities within it. But this life is indeed a dream.

It is characteristic of the series of inversions of the generally accepted that mark the joints of this novel's structure, that Helen emerges from this dream-like state by entering upon a suspension of this unreality. She goes on holiday, away from her parents, to stay with her mother's widowed friend at the seaside. Instead of being suspended in holiday-amber, however, she emerges into a new world of genuine feeling. A symbolic passage close to the beginning of the novel prefigures the contrast in the quality of her life at home and by the sea. This is confirmed in the final stages, when she is about to take to the sea to free herself from the limitations of surroundings she has outgrown, and meets Joel, her one true but undiscovered love, and through him reaches a sort of *post facto* realization of her inland experience. The contrast between coast and hinterland is one of the structural analogues with Helen's growth.

15

> There was a smell of burning, and the faint intoxication of rotting oranges from the dustbins. I walked closer to the level line of fences, trailing the fingers of my left hand lightly across the corrugations so that they rose and fell in an arpeggio of movement. I thought of water. Of the sea – oh, the surprise, the lift of remembering that there was the sea, that it was there now, somewhere, belonging to last year's and next year's two weeks of holiday at Durban – the sea which did something the same to your fingers, threading water through them . . . like the pages of a thick book falling away rapidly rippling back beneath your fingers to solidity. The sea could not be believed in for long, here. Could be smelled for a moment, a terrible whiff of longing evaporated with the deeper snatch of breath that tried to seize it. Or remembered by the blood, which now and then felt itself stirred by a movement caused by something quite different, setting up reactions purely physically like those in response to the sea. (p. 16)

The sea is a natural force to which the human organism responds naturally, involuntarily, out of the sources of its life. The responses and activities of the hinterland mining community are as artificial as the central activity that governs them, as devoid of real meaning as the metal they mine lacks the value of usefulness.

So Helen's brief holiday with Mrs Koch at the coast is a period of intense, wakeful experience, in contrast to the dreamlike drift of her day-to-day reality. Nadine Gordimer's land-sea polarity, and choice of the sea as the pole of life, growth, and meaning, is neither arbitrary nor based on trite sentimentality, as we shall see demonstrated in the course of this discussion.

At the coast Helen meets Mrs Koch's son Ludi, who is a soldier on leave, ten years older than she. They fall in love, or she does with him, and they have a virginal affair. It is her first serious experience of sex, and the development of her emotional and bodily responses leads her to the recognition of things that operate below the surface she has always taken for reality. This realization evokes from her a calculated rejection of the vision of experience seen from the veranda of the golf club. After Ludi has caressed her breasts for the first time, as she takes off her clothes in her room and looks at her body in the mirror, she remembers the conventional answer she has given to Mrs Koch's question about whether she had enjoyed her morning.

> And I understood that almost all of my life at home, on the

Mine, had been like that, conducted on a surface of polite triviality that was insensitive to the real flow of life that was being experienced, underneath, all the time, by everybody. The fascination of the gap between the two came to me suddenly; I remembered, even out of childhood, expressions on faces, the tone of a commonplace sentence spoken unimportantly, the look of a person's back as she left on some unquestioned excuse. It was not the knowledge of a secret life beneath so much as the maintenance of the unruffled surface itself that was exciting. Now it seemed to me that every casual explanation might not conceal but simply float above, like the reflection of the sky which the water shows rather than its own depths, happenings as strange and wordless as the time I had just spent with Ludi. (p. 76)

The last sentence of this extract is in effect a precise rejection of the Mine's version of reality as expressed in Helen's musings on the golf-club veranda, especially those which close part 1.

. . . the sky, swept clear of the day, held only radiance, far up above the shade that rose like water steeping the trees and the drop of the grass. Over at the water hole the whole world was repeated, upside down. (p. 44)

What is now realized is that this is not the 'whole world', and the 'dark fins of feeling that could not be verified in the face of my father, my mother, the Mine officials', will at least now be felt and apprehended even if they do 'not show through the surface that every minute of every day polished.' (p. 44).

Ludi is not a conformist, and in peace-time he did not use his talents to 'settle down' in a conventional way. Early in her stay he shocks Helen by saying to her:

'I suppose you're going to go back and live there? – That life on the mine is the narrowest, most mechanical, unrewarding existence you could think of in any nightmare.' (p. 56)

The notion is entirely new to her. Ludi *is* conventional to the extent of being an old-fashioned romantic rebel who rejects urban life and commercialism, preferring to fish and swim among the coral reefs of the Pondoland coast.

'Look,' he said. 'I don't want to "get on". I'm happy where I am. All I want is the war to end so that I can get back here.'
'Shall you start up the chicken farm again?'

17

'It doesn't much matter. Any sort of a job would do so long as it brings in fifteen or twenty pounds a month. Just so's Mother and I can manage. She's got a small income of her own.'

I was embarrassed by my own reaction. I knew that in my face and my silence I showed a deep sense of shock and a kind of disbelief that timidly tried to temper it. (p. 57)

The difficulty of her acceptance on this level goes so deep that Ludi's embryonic political attitudes pass by as a part of the joke, without being noticed.

He made a noise of disgust. 'Grubbing under the earth in the dark to produce something entirely useless, and coming up after eight hours to take your place in the damned cast-iron sacred hierarchy of the Mine, grinning and bowing all the way up to the godly Manager on top, and being grinned and bowed at by everyone below you – not that there ever was anyone below me, except the blacks and it's no privilege to sit on them since anyone can.' (pp. 56–57)

Helen finds Ludi attractive, and she falls in love with the intense passion of the stifled adolescent. It marks one of the starting points of her conscious revolt against the values of her parents and the surroundings of her home life. (It is as much the general domestic atmosphere of easy intimacy and happiness in the Koch household as her infatuation with Ludi, that germinates the seed of dissatisfaction with her home within her.) It is much too early for her to realize the necessary extent of her revolt, or even that it is likely to erupt, but Ludi's passing inclusion of the blacks in his indignant caricature of Mine hierarchy is a significant portent of the scope of Helen's rebellion, when it does come.

At first, of course, the revolt is unconscious and its aim rather poor; she decides not to go to university, which is a blow to her father (who takes it very well) rather than to her mother. It may be that a general point is being suggested here: Helen's aim is poor because of the essentially, even inherently deceptive nature of the society she lives in. Its adherence to 'traditional' English bourgeois values is ostensibly very strong. In appearance, her father is the authority figure, and rebellion against authority would be directed against him, but Helen has much to learn about her own world still, and when the significant revolt does come, it is her mother who asserts the authority of the home, and who is Helen's major, if not only antagonist. At this stage she is still almost entirely undirected, feeling rather than knowing only that she rejects in a non-specific way parental values. This state of imprecision produces its own dissatisfactions, and after six months of spending a 'great deal of time reading', she wanders apparently with as much aimlessness as has characterized her behaviour since her return from the coast, into the university in the middle of the academic year, and decides to become a student.

The lack of direction in her life has been aggravated by her discovery, during the six months of inactivity, of Auden and Eliot, Pepys's diary and Smollett, Hemingway, Donne, D. H. Lawrence and Chekov.

> But in nothing that I read could I find anything that approximated to my own life; to our life on a gold mine in South Africa. Our life was not regulated by the seasons and the elements of weather and emotion, like the life of peasants; nor was it expressed through movements in art, through music heard, through the exchange of ideas, like the life of Europeans shaped by great and ancient cities, so that they were Parisians or Londoners as identifiably as they were Pierre or James. Nor was it even anything like the life of Africa, the continent, as described in books about Africa; perhaps further from this than from any. What did the great rivers, the savage tribes, the jungles and the hunt for huge palm-eared elephants have to do with the sixty miles of Witwatersrand veld that was our Africa? The yellow ridged hills of sand, thrown up and patted down with the unlovely precision that marked them manufactured as unmistakably as a sand castle; the dams of chemical-tinted water, more waste matter brought above ground by man, that stood below them, bringing a false promise of a river-greenness, cool, peace of dipping fronds and birds – to your nose as you sat in the train . . . We had no lions and we had no art galleries, we heard no Bach and the oracle voice of the ancient Africa did not come to us, was drowned, perhaps, by the records singing of Tennessee in the Greek cafés and the thump of the Mine stamp batteries which sounded in our ears as unnoticed as our blood. (pp. 96–97)

This is a crucial passage whose significance, important as it is to Helen's own development, only emerges fully when seen as the real starting-point for Nadine Gordimer's own vocation as a writer. It

19

echoes a theme that runs through William Plomer's writing on South African subjects; it is to be found in Jacobson, in highly mannered but nonetheless effective form in the symbolism of the house and its library and other contents in *A Dance in the Sun*, as well as more directly expressed in *The Beginners*. It develops into the attack on the values of the Mine community that emerges as the major theme towards the end of the book.

The passage contains both statement of intent and the formidable beginnings of a diagnosis, and it also signals the start of the author's search for a cure – even if this is confined in the end to the level of the individual. The passage comes to rest on the total lack of a worthwhile 'tradition', in roughly the sense T. S. Eliot uses the word, in South African society, particularly among the ruling white group, especially that part of it which is most advantageously placed in this respect by having command of English as a mother tongue. But in every respect, in every place where connections should flourish between the parent culture and its offspring, metropolis and cultural province, Helen is confronted with lacunae. These interruptions operate on as fundamental a level as the seasons themselves. The result for Helen is an absence of any relevant standard against which to measure the quality of the reality of her life, surroundings and aspirations. The need to find such standards is one of the impelling factors behind her late registration as a student at the university. It leads to a search which becomes a kind of duty and in the end dominates her behaviour. For Helen as for Nadine Gordimer herself the artistic search is not just for something to say, but for the *right* thing; not only the most telling and appropriate words and judgments but the correct spiritual vocabulary in which to frame them.

The problem is a complex one for South African writers, especially the white ones who write in English, and are thus part of a tradition that includes Forster and George Eliot, and insists on the values of European liberalism as at least a touchstone applicable to the situations that novelists attend to. This is a tradition that is peculiarly dear to the moral legislators of white South African society, to the mine managers' wives, government schoolteachers, and the like; but it is known to them in a strange version, barely recognizable next to the original article. Thus in the novels of Sarah Gertrude Millin, for example, again and again one comes across the assumption of a pure version of 'European' values that have become debased, usually by those who compromise themselves on the question of colour. 'Correctness' in this respect is made not merely to symbolize but to be the concrete manifestation of those values. Writers like Millin, peddlers of the conventional South African wisdom, seem to assume a monolithic value structure from which deviations may be inevitable but are doomed to fail or perish out of the evil inherent in the fact of their departure from the accepted norm. What such spokesmen further assume, without exception (and this is what makes them bizarre), is that they speak with the only genuine voice of Europe. In the passage quoted above, Nadine Gordimer's emphasis differs dramatically from this convention; it is concentrated upon the true absence of connections, rather than the false insistence on an 'English-pure' and 'South African-corrupt' association.

So writers like Nadine Gordimer start with the difficulty of being likely to be labelled freaks and deviationists by the self-appointed defenders of the tradition in which they write. This raises the vital problem for Gordimer, Plomer, Jacobson and others, of the precise nature of the relationship between Europe and Africa, or South Africa in all its depressing but undeniable particularity. To their credit, all these writers recognize their responsibility in relation to this question, but none is more assiduous than Nadine Gordimer in trying to make sense of it. The search for this particular meaning persists as the major unifying force throughout her work. It begins, at this stage, as a matter of self-examination, of examination of the immediate environment, and of coming to a diagnostic understanding of the possibilities of the situation.

Nadine Gordimer embodies her attempt at diagnosis in the development to maturity of Helen. This is accompanied by her often shrill critique of the life pattern of her parents and the society of the Mine at Atherton. (She, of course, is a victim of the same historic situation as her parents, and her shrillness comes out of a number of sources, among them a childish resentment that they haven't transcended their own moral and cultural isolation in what they make and expect of her.)

A good example of how an ugly situation turns them all ugly results from her parents' refusal to allow Helen's friend, the African student Mary Seswayo, to stay with them as examinations approach, so that she can have peace and quiet to study. Helen's idea is half-baked, patronizing but sincere, and her mother's refusal to entertain it leads to her departure from home to live in Johannesburg. But the corrosive combination of ubiquitous prejudices and anti-parental revolt produces an effect out of proportion to the ostensible causes.

21

My mother turned on me. 'No, you like to roll in the mud. Anything so long as it's not what any other reasonable person likes. You'd rather be seen running about with the son of a Jew from the native stores, that's much nicer, someone brought up among all the dirt and the kaffirs. *He* must be a finer person, of course, than anyone decently brought up by people of our own standing.'

A kind of thrill of getting to grips with real issues went through me. 'Ah, I thought that would come. You've had that on your chest a long time. And you've always pretended to be so polite to Joel. And all the time you're as bigoted as the rest. Worried because all the old crows of the Mine saw your daughter out with a Jew. Well, you can tell them to mind their own damn business, I'll be friendly with whom I choose. And I'm not interested in their standards or who they think would be suitable for me. You can tell them.'. . . 'Have him,' said my mother shrilly. The venom between us seemed like a race that we were shouting on. (p. 192)

But one of the results of Helen's upbringing, as she almost grasps in that moment, only to lose it again until much later, is her failure to bring to a consummation that which Joel is offering her. She feels uneasy in his house, with his East European Jewish parents, and she is scarcely welcomed within their modest gates. She discerns a particular contrast with the more salubrious (and pretentious) surroundings of her own home, which is part of her cumulative rejection of her own background. On the first occasion she goes into the Aaron home and meets Joel's mother, the uneasy atmosphere betrays her into a kind of revelation.

'Your father he's something on the Atherton Mine – and mummy? Your mummy's still alive?'

'Yes.' In an awkward burst I made some attempt to make my life real to her. 'We've always lived there. My father's Secretary. – I hate the Mine.'

She stirred slowly in her chair. 'So? It's your home, we all got to like our home.' (p. 117)

Helen has been offered, in this atmosphere of awkwardness, a sticky sweetmeat to eat.

'Would you like to wash?' said Joel, getting up. 'They leave you rather sticky, though my mother really does make them very well.' He put the dish of sweet biscuits away carefully in the sideboard.

I don't know why he surprised me; Joel was continually surprising me by ease when there might have been strain, a word where there might have been a vacuum. He said what he thought and somehow it was never what I thought he was thinking: his nature had for mine the peculiar charm of the courage to be itself without defiance . . .

Now I had been ready to make it easy for Joel; to show him that so far as I was concerned, he need not mind about his mother. This was quite a different thing from finding that *he* did not mind about his mother; that far from being apologetic of the peculiar sweetmeat which politeness had forced me to eat, he seriously commended her skill in preparing it. (p. 117)

This failure to cope fully with a social situation is the result of Helen's immaturity of perception which in turn stems from the restricted opportunities for emotional development afforded her by her childhood. When she leaves her parents' home over the row about Mary Seswayo, Joel finds her a place in a flat belonging to two 'progressive' young people, part of the set she has been moving in, called John and Jenny Marcus. This period in her life affords her an intense opportunity for perceptual development, and Nadine Gordimer is particularly successful in conveying Helen's initial reaction of over-excitement to the new possibilities that life with the Marcuses seems to hold.

Their friends were all people whom I knew; a kind of distillation of the acquaintances I had been meeting over and over again for some time. Like a school of fish these people appeared at Isa Welch's, at Laurie Humphrey's, disappearing into the confused stream of the city again, and then reappearing, quite unmistakably, known at once by the bond of species which showed them unlike any other fish and like one another, although they were big fish and little, tame fish and savage as if they had all worn a pale stripe round the tail or a special kind of dorsal fin. Now I was permitted to see what went on when they had whisked out of sight round the deep shelter of a dark rock; in this home water they swam more slowly and clustered, two or three, in a favourite shade.

I called them, along with John and Jenny, 'our kind of people'; and certainly I felt myself more closely identified with them than I had with any others who had looked in upon my solitude. – First Ludi, then Joel, in their different ways,

23

had stepped within its circle and been with me there, but this had not broken its transparent compass. It had still thrown me back like a sheet of glass that smashes a bird's head with the illusion of freedom. Now, quite undramatically, it melted, was suddenly simply not there: the way of life that I wanted seemed to be lived by these people with the acceptance of commonplace. Nothing could have been more reassuring . . . An almost physical expansion took place in me; I began to wear bolder clothes. I even sat and moved with an ease and assurance of my own. And the timidity fell away from my opinions; in the intoxication of company I spoke them, ill-considered or not, in emulation of the outspokenness of Isa . . . (pp. 208–209)

Helen is clearly almost bursting with ingenuousness, a quality which is generated by the very suggestive choice of imagery in this passage; by her use of the phrase 'our kind of people' (very much the same language used by her detested mother on disapproving of Helen's choice of friends), and even more surely by Isa's remark at the beginning of the next paragraph:

'My, but it's become a keen little scout . . .,' Isa broke in on an argument I had been having, one evening. (p. 209)

Helen is actually more flattered than punctured by the barb from one of the brightest members of her new-found circle, and the naïveté of her response is conveyed in the irony of narration. Other images, suggesting conformity instead of the accepted notion of the group's independent 'otherness' (such as the 'school of fish', the 'cluster') make the ironic distance between the narrator-Helen and the version of herself whose story she is telling, abundantly plain. The suggestion is that the 'transparent compass' of the 'circle' of her solitude has merely enlarged itself without any great modification of Helen's character. Indeed, she herself notes that 'Nothing could have been more reassuring,' which again inverts the stock notion of the excitement, vigour and independence that should characterize the life of the emancipated bourgeois intellectual. Reassurance, one would think, is the last thing anyone would hope for from this kind of group, but what has emerged clearly enough from Helen's earlier experience is that the values of Mine society, with their heavy emphasis on outer conformity with substanceless norms, leave little place for warmth and affection within the family circle. As a result of this, Helen, as she acknowledges to Joel much later, 'needed to be loved'; and 'our kind of people are prepared at least to accept her.

In other respects they come off less well, in some ways not even as well as her parents. They lack her father's tolerance, for example, or her mother's consistency. The episode with which her awareness of disillusion may be said to commence may be amusing, but it also shows in a harsh light the intolerance and inconsistencies of phoney idealism.

> I had been to town early and, on coming back, had thrown my parcels and coat and hat on John's and Jenny's bed. I went into the bathroom and when I came out and passed down the passage, I thought I saw, in the liquid flash of the mirror through the door, Jenny looking at herself. When I had been in the other room for the length of time it takes to smoke a cigarette, her silence in the room next door roused a faint curiosity. I got up lazily and wandered in on her. She was sitting on the edge of the bed with my hat on. With her back to me, she saw me first in the mirror, and, in the mirror, smiled, and with a little noise of embarrassment pulled off the hat as she turned round.
>
> 'It suits you better than me,' I said ruefully. 'But it shouldn't be so straight.' And I put it on her again, at more of an angle. We both looked at her, a pretty girl in the red hat. She put up her hand and touched at the side. 'The velvet's so soft,' she said. 'I saw a green one, not the same, but something like it, a dear, in town. So cheap, too. I'm dying to buy myself one, but John'd kill me.' . . .
>
> 'He won't' – I was going to say 'allow' but stopped myself at what was quite an unthinkable word between John and Jenny – 'he won't let you wear a hat? Oh nonsense –' I had to laugh to convince myself it was some kind of loverlike game between them. And I stood there forcing her with the laughter of unbelief. This was not John, either. For a second it was as if I caught a glimpse of two people who seemed very like, but were not them, could not be them. (pp. 213–214)

John and Jenny are substitute parents for Helen; she wallows in the apparent warmth, ease and freedom of their domesticity. She keeps her make-up on their dressing table, and lies at the foot of their bed on Sunday mornings, a possibility not suggested by her picture of home life in Atherton. Yet the difference between her mother and Jenny is significantly compressed into each one's attitude to her own image in the mirror. To Mrs Shaw, as the narrator demonstrates repeatedly, looking at her reflection is a vital act of reassurance, confirming that all is indeed as it seems to be, that the appearance and reality are one. Major statements are made while consulting her appearance in this way, as if to check that nothing has changed that would affect the values summed up in her reflection.

> 'Isn't she meeting people all the time at the University?' My father patronised her a little, smiling at me.
>
> My mother settled the pearls on her neck. She looked herself over in the mirror, shook out her gloves, looked again, herself and her mirror self challenging each other for correctness. 'I mean her own kind of people.' (p. 136)

Jenny's uncertainty before the glass, on the other hand, suggests a positive lack of confidence in the world of appearance combined with a hankering for a concrete sense of the real; but she lacks either the intellectual equipment or the basis in experience that would carry her over the gulf of self-doubt. Her suspicion of reality is a duty to fashion, a form of submission (and a very orthodox one) to her husband, an indication of her immaturity. Jenny doesn't possess the courage of her half-baked convictions; Mrs Shaw's may be completely raw, but she will stick to them to the bitter end. Thus Helen moves from one hypocritical pole to another, though of course her condemnation of the Marcuses is really a spyhole for the percipient reader into Helen's developing soul.

There can be no doubt, in the light of this, that one of the most important themes in this novel is the difficulty, the uncertainty of perceiving adequately the true nature of people and relationships. Nadine Gordimer suggests that one requires an adequate idea of oneself before one is able to proceed to just assessments of others, and it is a measure of Helen's aptitude in this direction that she chooses Paul, the most genuine member of her circle, to fall in love with, just as the eventual failure of their relationship is an indication that a gift for self-knowledge is only the beginning of the task of achieving it.

Paul is an anthropologist and a practical liberal who works during the day for the Native Affairs department of the Johannesburg municipality, in the housing division – a sort of hopeless, idealistic philanthropy – and at night hobnobs with black intelligentsia and politicians. The chasm between these two apparently related activities is irreconcilable, as is illustrated by Paul's directing volunteers to plant the grass for a township sports field which, he knows, his politician friends are urging the inhabitants to boycott. At first Helen finds a liberation in their relationship. They sleep together and afterwards live together. But the limitations of their environment inevitably impinge upon them; on Helen's side it is her parents' refusal to accept their living together (as well as Paul's insensitivity to the reality, for her, of this conflict): while on Paul's the murderous contradiction of the two versions of 'native affairs' he has caught himself up in is a sympathetic but unsparing examination of the well-known bourgeois liberal syndrome of wanting things at least both ways at the same time. So while their relationship may have foundered anywhere, in the event the determining causes are shown to be peculiarly South African versions of familiar kinds of modern conflicts and difficulties that frustrate the growth of love.

The one thing that Helen's upbringing seems to have given her is a keen, uncompromising and rather priggish moral sense, without the ability to evade distasteful applications which is usually supplied with the full kit. She very much wants to be someone she is not, but she equally strongly desires to be loved for what she is; and when she perceives that Paul is prepared, however unconsciously, to compromise himself in the conviction that his dual involvement with African affairs is a possibility, her love for him is shaken. Their lovemaking, which is at first expressed as a lyrical affirmation of faith in each other's commitments and ability to live up to them, becomes an over-frequent pacifying response to the pressures imposed on them largely from outside, but also intensified by the nature of their individual reactions to them. Helen is particularly dissatisfied by Paul's self-indulgent refusal to accept the con-tradiction between his two levels of involvement. Her desire for perfect truth to oneself is turned mainly on to him at this stage because she is faced by a crisis in which one of the main difficulties is her lack of insight into her own soul.

The sexual aspect of their relationship is used as a symbolic device which denotes the degree of internal freedom and balance each possesses within its framework. Significantly, one of the first withdrawals takes place soon after the Malan government begins to enforce legislation against mixed marriage and cohabitation across the colour line. Many people who possess long-standing re-lationships are threatened by this, and a wave of anxiety is set up in the coloured community, where confusions of racial identity are most likely to occur. One of the coloured clerks in Paul's office is worried because he has a rather light-skinned wife, though not sufficiently so to create ambiguity, and yet he has an obscure dread. As Paul points out, the same evening after work when he tells Helen the story:

'Out of a reversal of the very thing he fears now, he's liked to think her that much nearer the distinction of whiteness.' (p. 260)

That night they make love.

We lay there with my hand on him lax the way I liked to keep it after he had parted from my body, on the edge of making love a third time or going to sleep, each possibility as delightful as the other . . .
I took my hand away.
I took it away instinctively, in answer to some other withdrawal. Paul did not move, but with each wash of light I felt come into my mind through his own the real pain and strangeness of that conversation with the man Robert, and even the jokes of the others. And I knew Paul was thinking of it; feeling for himself the impossibility of a white man understanding these things out of his own security. (p. 261)

Thus their relationship is threatened in its most essential aspects, because of external events, that would be unthinkable outside South Africa; so its failure might be justly described as a local rather than universal one – though perhaps all the more serious for that.

This episode has an important conclusion.

Just as I went off to sleep I had one of those curious starts in my mind – the mental equivalent of the jump of a leg or an arm momentarily jerking your body back to wakefulness – that flips up a piece of past consciousness. I did not remember that incident of the Sunday afternoon I went with Joel to MacDonald's Kloof; for a moment I was *there*. The sun was down and the air smelt of dust and eucalyptus. I walked past the old Afrikaner packing up baskets and rugs. I called to Joel, Wait, there's something stuck to my shoe – and he picked up a little piece of twig and scraped at my heel. And the torn thing was there.

The only difference was that this time, unlike the real time that it happened, we were not safe from disgust. We got into

the car full of shame and I kept my face turned away from
Joel, although I seemed to see his face all the same, as you do
in a dream. And perhaps it was here that it all really became a
dream, and I was asleep. (p. 261)

This waking dream refers back to an episode when Helen goes for
a drive into the country with Joel instead of accompanying her
parents to a Mine braaivleis. The structural parallels with the
opening scene, in which Helen goes exploring her surroundings in
defiance of her parents, explicitly among the forbidden areas of the
world she knows, are clear. Certain areas of her relationship with
Joel fall under the same prohibition, and the afternoon they spend
together on a ledge halfway up a hillside, talking and sleeping, is a
chaste one. Their talk is random but not insignificant: Joel suggests
to her that she should get married:

'. . . I mean sometimes there are women with a kind of – how
can I put it – vivid feeling for life. They push it into things that
waste it; activities that could run on something colder. So it's
lost; they change. Because it's something for between men
and women.' (p. 143)

Although this offends Helen at the time, she realizes much later
how right he has been. The episode ends on a peculiar and
disturbing note; as they walk back to the car Helen notices

Something has stuck to my shoe – 'Just a minute –' I held on
to the door-handle of the car, balancing on one leg, laughing.
'Here' – Joel snapped off a twig and prised at the mess on my
heel. It fell away and it was a rubber contraceptive, perished
and dust-trodden, relic of some hurried encounter behind the
trees, inconsequent and shabby testimony. But between us at
this moment it was like a crude word, suddenly spoken aloud.
In dismay more than embarrassment, we ignored the
happening, jumped quickly into the car. Joel, encouraging the
reluctant kick-over of the engine, his hand over the gear-knob,
the frown with which men pay attention to engines drawing
down his eyebrows, was my reassurance. The finger of disgust
had hovered, but could not make its smudge on us. Again, I
did not know why. (p. 146)

Obviously, the episode and its dream repetition are intended,
together, to add up to something significant, though this has not
been critically elucidated. The South African critics Woodward

and van Heyningen[1] both react with well-bred, glassy-eyed horror to the first presentation. Woodward [1] quotes it and comments:

> I do not think that the accusation of vulgarity has to be proved any further: a writer who resorts to that kind of titillating melodrama to gain her effect is self-condemned.

To critics such as these, the possibility that reality itself may contain this or any kind of 'vulgarity' apparently has nothing to do with the writing of novels; in particular, such an attitude automatically debars them from having anything to say about the South African version, with its much grosser actualities. Neither Woodward nor van Heyningen makes any reference to the key dream-repetition, thus missing one of the essential links that forge the book's unity – no doubt owing to a super-susceptibility to titillation, which must have been taxed to the utmost by the passage in question.

It remains to establish the meaning of this dream-repeated image of ugliness. There is no doubt that the object itself poses a threat to Helen, who is still virginal and sexually repressed when she encounters the reality; somehow, at the time, being with Joel seems to preserve the purity of the moment. One level of the image's total significance emerges from its second occurrence just after Helen has made love with Paul. Again Joel, who has so carefully and considerately shown her the way to this new quality of freedom, is involved, but this time the effect is different. The difference lies in the context of Paul and Helen's conversation – the appalling personal insecurity arising from the state's ability to pry into the very marital bed, nay, the sexual act itself. No one can be safe; more than that, everyone is defiled, whether he knows it or not, by such a possibility, and even the purest relationships, like that between Joel and Helen, are smudged with disgust. Thus the society's most characteristic legislation becomes a symbolic statement about the status of individual freedom within it. The dream-sequence also illustrates the nature of Helen's journey. The nearer she comes to

---

[1] van Heyningen, Christina: 'Nadine Gordimer', letter to *Theoria* (University of Natal, Pietermaritzburg) no. 17, 1961, pp. 74–76. Miss van Heyningen's letter has nothing to add to Woodward's article in the previous number: she merely falls over herself in her eagerness to be associated with his judgments, in a peculiarly spiteful manner: 'The author's account of her [Helen's] love-making and of her attitude to her parents, for example shows her to be cold, vain and – yes, "vulgar" is the word (it is Mr Woodward's).' (p. 75)

the *reality* of the land she thinks of as her own, the more tenuous her control over herself becomes.

On the powerful level of particularity possessed by the book, the context of the search mentioned earlier is constituted by precisely this question: the nature of South African reality. Nowhere does the author's emphasis on uncertainty of perception fall more appropriately. One of the reasons for Helen's attraction to Paul is that he seems to be in a position at least to come to grips with the problem. In the end, he is reduced to stasis by his attempt to live some of the basic contradictions contained in that reality. Joel, on the other hand, possesses a different perspective. Significantly, during the height of Helen's relationship with Paul, he drops out of sight. Before he reappears Helen has to undergo a proving experience, one which brings her to a confrontation (that stops, of course, just short of contact) with an underlying, even fundamental level of that reality.

Helen's mother has forbidden her the family home on being told that she was living with Paul, but a reconciliation takes place not too long afterwards and Helen spends the weekend with her parents at Atherton. It is the weekend of the first of May, and as she returns to Johannesburg by train, she sees a newspaper poster from the window.

At this little station a newsbill stood against the wire fence, though apparently the paper boy had sold out his stock of papers and left. It was rucked up under the wire frame that held it to a board: STRIKE SITUATION: POLICE PREPARED FOR TOMORROW. Of course not – those were not rosettes: no wonder the men weren't dressed like a football team. Freedom Day badges. Yet I could not feel anything about the strike that was coming tomorrow, the strike that, the whole of the previous week in Johannesburg, we had talked of. Neither fear nor apprehension nor curiosity at the nearness of this threat – to ourselves? to the Africans themselves? – that would soon be here; soon now . . .

Nothing happened on Monday. I know. Not only because it was true in fact, the papers said so; but because I felt in the anticlimactic calm of that day a kind of guilty reflection of my own state. It seemed to me that the fact that nothing happened justified my lack of interest, made it excusable. (p. 312–313)

But something does indeed happen, to her as well as to others, the following night, the night of the strike. Paul is in one of the townships. Laurie, their barrister friend, telephones with news he is wary of giving. So he comes to fetch Helen to look for Paul, telling her that one of Paul's black political associates is in danger of arrest and that this could involve Paul himself. They drive in Laurie's superior English car to the location and stumble into a riot, escaping eventually unharmed, but Helen's reaction is significant.

> Laurie was sitting with his great heavy arm stretched out pressed back against me like a barrier, as if he were restraining me from jumping out of the car. Behind it I breathed like an animal that has been caught and is being held down for branding. I thought I should burst with horror. I do not think I was afraid. I had no room for fear because I was so mad with horror. Again I was overwhelmed by an emotion whose existence I had not ever thought about, every bursting blood-vessel pushed full with a racing blood I had not counted in the emotional scope of my life. Everyone fears fear; but horror – that belongs to second-hand experience, through books and films. (p. 325)

She sees a telephone-booth flung into the air, stones thrown, a man shot dead by the police. It is a moment of awakening for her, a highly personal experience.

> Laurie was afraid. He was not horrified, he was only terribly afraid. (p. 326)

And what remains of the experience is their safety behind the steel frame and armour-plated glass of Laurie's expensive English car – glass which lets in an awareness of *permanent* suffering and horror but at the same time confers on one the immunity of a spectator – like the glass of the train window through which Helen had seen the newsbill the previous night; the earlier image of the 'sheet of glass' which is the 'transparent compass' of Helen's solitude (p. 209) now acquires thematic force.

This safety, on a physical level, is clearly built into the situation for white South Africans. The 'Englishness' of the cultural vehicle symbolizes it. But it operates obviously on an emotional, even a spiritual, level as well. When Helen says of her parents and their society at the Mine: 'That was what these people did to everything in life; enfeebled it,' (p. 136), she is unaware how far she herself has been 'enfeebled' in her ability to make adequate emotional and moral responses to the reality lying all around her. Indeed, both perception and judgment are 'enfeebled', and Helen is a victim of her background. So, of course, is Paul. His acceptance of a life based on an impossible contradiction is a compensatory show of strength; a gesture to show that he has freed himself from the moral feebleness of his fellow whites. But even the death of his friend Sipho, shot by the police in the riots, cannot make him see the impossibility of his chosen situation. His perception *is* permanently impaired, 'enfeebled'.

Can any white South African escape or recover from this malady of experience? This is one of the central questions the book asks, and it continues to occupy Nadine Gordimer's mind as a novelist throughout her career. Next to the horror, the feebleness: because the riot scene was only a compressed version of an extended reality, for most South Africans. Does Helen's ringside seat help her to recover? Does it aid her in her search for self-knowledge? She reacts to the experience with a minor nervous breakdown, staying in the flat, and reading letters to the newspapers about the horror she has known.

> The old sense of unreality would come down upon me again. A calm, listless loneliness, not the deep longing loneliness of night, but the loneliness of daylight and sunshine, in the midst of people; the loneliness that is a failure to connect. I would pick up, in my mind, Atherton, Paul, Johannesburg, my mother and father; Paul. Like objects taken out of a box, put back. But in the end there was only myself, watching everything, the street, the workmen, life below; a spectator. (p. 332)

At the end of this period she suddenly perceives that the building opposite, a new apartment block, is complete. The building has been in the process of construction since the time she moved in with Paul, and she has seen it through the stages of its development.

> The building was in front of me, five storeys high, clean with fresh paint. On top, the chimney of the boiler-room crooked a finger. A row of gleaming dustbins waited to be put into the kitchens. I thought, when I came here with Paul the first time that Sunday afternoon, they were just beginning the foundations, you could see right out over the hill, you could see the Magaliesburg.
>
> And it came to me, quite simply, as if it had been there, all the time: I'll go to Europe. That's what I want. I'll go away. Like a sail filling with the wind, I felt a sense of aliveness, a sweeping relief. (p. 333)

33

Thus (as usual) the search becomes a journey becomes a quest. The nature of the quest and its goals is not obscure but well known, although perhaps difficult to define with precision. 'The loneliness that is a failure to connect' – Helen has to start one stage before her metropolitan mentors in her search for the liberal's 'good life', based on love and the development of human relationships: without a history, without a tradition she cannot begin the first stage of knowing herself on the relatively secure foundation of a moral code that has been tested, adapted to a historic series of situations in a particular place, and possessing the flexibility of long and familiar use. She has to discover for herself such a code before she can adapt it to her own situation; she also has to define this situation.

Perhaps the most glaring symptom of her emotional and perceptual enfeeblement is her failure to understand the nature of Joel's relationship with her. Joel is contrasted with Helen through his possession of a history and a tradition, and his ability to reconcile past and present. He is thus able to preserve his clarity of vision, to fall on his moral feet, so to speak, in the country where he chances to have been born. He is always aware of life as a journey or series of journeys lying ahead: he wants to go to England, walk through Europe, work in Israel. Though he has no ostensible political involvement, he tells Helen and a friend, as they sit in the cafeteria at the university:

> 'Look, if you're a native . . . you have to be exceptional to do ordinary things. You have to be one of four in ten who go to school at all, in the first place. You have to be able to concentrate on an empty stomach because you haven't had any breakfast, you have to resist the temptation to nip off and do a bit of caddying for pocket money you never get given to you, you have to persuade your parents, who can't afford to keep you, to go on keeping you after you're twelve or thirteen and could be a houseboy or a nanny and keep yourself. And that's only the beginning. That's what you've got to do to get to the point at which white kids only start off making an effort. Just to get through ordinary schooling you've got to be a very exceptional kid. And from then on you've just got to be more and more exceptional, although in your school life you've used up enough determination and effort to put a white boy right through to qualification in a profession. That's how it is.' He sat back, looking at us. (p. 134)

Joel's ability to present unflinchingly a political statement of such uncompromising clarity is in contrast to the rather ostentatious gestures in the direction of non-racialism like inviting Indian lawyers to supper on the 'girl's night off' or selling *The Guardian* (then the newspaper of the South African Communist Party) to Africans in the townships – the standard practices of Helen's 'our kind of people'. In its context, this statement of Joel's is also distinguished by being informed with love for Helen: it is a kind of gift to her, an answer to her need, her demand to know something about the situation she lives in. But Helen's perceptual ability is so weak at this early stage in her search for freedom that she does not understand that Joel loves her; and of course intuition has been stifled within her almost at birth. Spontaneity of reaction can only arise out of a background which possesses the accumulated potential for it, and this is a matter of history and tradition, which Helen lacks.

At the end of the book they meet in Durban, days before Joel is due to leave for Israel and Helen for England. It is a suitable culmination in that it re-establishes for Helen a sense of continuity of which she so acutely feels the lack. Joel is able to reconcile his present with the immediate past of his parents' generation, and is about to begin a new adventure in time, to attempt the reconciliation of his historic past with his living self. He is a link between Helen and both areas of experience she has come to reject – her life with Paul and their friends, as well as her parents and the Mine. His reassertion of continuity and the validity of the past, as well as his revelation of what she has known but failed to formulate consciously – his love for her – help her to reach a position of strength based for the first time in the book on a degree of self-knowledge that is, for her, permanently valid. Having gone to look for him aboard his ship, Helen invites Joel to supper at her hotel.

But while I was putting the finishing touches to my dress I realized something that put an edge of self-consciousness on my pleasure. I was assuming a right to Joel's time and attention which would follow from a similar claim on his behalf for mine in the normal course of our lives in Johannesburg. But this had not been so. We had not seen each other; I had let him drop out of my life when it suited me – now when it suited me to take him back into it again, I calmly did so. I remembered the acute shame that had swept over me that day outside the theatre booking-office, when I had met him and realized that I had forgotten his graduation. (p. 346)

35

The feeling of shame, of failed obligation, and the awareness of selfishness all suggest a maturing of Helen's emotions. This has come about through the disillusion and suffering of her break with her past, with Paul, and through the catalyst of Joel's analytical kindness and patience, and his as yet unrevealed love for her. At the end her need to understand and know how he achieves his relationship with the past emerges strongly (because it is such a felt lack in herself); and Joel helps her to realize in words the nature of her own past mistakes and their relevance to her present situation. His diagnosis takes into account the problem of tradition and history, but has an application beyond Helen; it is a summation of the most fundamental weaknesses of European liberalism in any of its South African manifestations.

'– You always set yourself such a terribly high standard, Helen, that's the trouble. You're such a snob, when it comes to emotion. Only the loftiest, the purest, will do for you. Sometimes I've thought that it's a kind of laziness, really. If you embrace something that seems to embody all this idealism, you feel you yourself have achieved the loftiest, the purest, the *most real*.' (p. 353)

The laziness grows out of assumptions which originate in the basic South African situation: that certain things are quite simply one's due, like the girl Helen's bacon and eggs waiting for her in the oven on the Sunday morning of the African miners' hunger strike. The armour-plated glass robs the individual of the necessity, as well as denying him the ability, to perceive, feel, touch, smell reality directly and immediately. And so he, or she, cannot grow, or does so only in a stunted fashion. Thus Helen's choice of Paul is reduced to the gesture of an atrophied limb, rather than the grasping of the full moral life. And Paul's choice of crucifixion, as Joel calls it, is meaningless in the context in which it is made, and of no good to anyone, including himself. It is another symptom of this 'kind of laziness', which is the result of a fundamental assumption that whatever fulfilment the individual chooses for himself will be there for the taking. Paul sticks obstinately to his chosen path, refusing to recognize inconvenient realities; laziness gives rise to suffering.

Joel's revelation of his love is about the only thing that can give meaning to Helen's desire for escape. It takes place on the ship on which he is to sail for Israel, in the hour before his departure.

He said, gently, still looking at me, 'But you've known always,

Helen.' And after a pause, 'There's nothing to be surprised about.'

But he could not possibly know what was going through my mind. I said to myself, 'It's the heat, the excitement, the drink and the stirring awareness of the occasion. Everyone here feels it in some way or another, that is why they laugh so much, are too talkative, or keep touching and fussing at their clothes. People only rise to the surface of their lives when there is to be change, a threat. You only say: I'm alive, when you see death. You only say: I'm here, when you're about to go.' But I could not calm the trembling that astonished me all through my body; I felt for a moment that my whole consciousness, resting, since I was born, on one side, had suddenly turned over, like a great stone on the bed of the sea, and shown an unknown world, a shining unseen surface, different, different utterly, alive with waving weeds and startled creatures pulsating on the coral. (pp. 363–364)

The ship sails, and Helen returns to her hotel, where she realizes or thinks she realizes (even at this late point, narrator-Helen is wary of character-Helen's perceptions) that, 'perhaps I had always loved him, always wanted him, and merely made do with others.' (p. 366.) This, together with their discussion a couple of nights before, the realization that an inhibition springing from racial awareness had once prevented consummation between them, in the context of the web of relations in which they are enmeshed – the Mine, the difference between their backgrounds, their differing perspectives on the 'emancipation' of the group Joel introduces Helen into – makes the failure of their love to come to fruition a South African tragedy, a loss attributable to a combination of circumstances in time and place. Helen realizes, at last, the three things that separate mature from immature perception of reality.

Of lovers and friends, he seemed the only one who had not discarded everything and found nothing. Unlike me, he loved his parents enough to accept their deep differences from him, and so he had not suffered the guilt of breaking the unreasoning ties of the blood. He had not placed upon any relationship with human beings the burden of the proof of an ideal. (p. 366)

She wakes up in the night, and hears and sees

. . . in the street below the huddled figures of some little native minstrels, singing as they padded along in the rain. The song was a popular dance tune of a few years before, 'Paper Doll', but they made it infinitely mournful, infinitely longing. I stood there quite still, for a minute or more. I shall never forget how I felt. A feeling of extraordinary calm possessed me; I felt I could stand there in full possession of this great calmness for ever. It did not seem to me that it would ever go.

My mind was working with great practicalness, and I thought to myself: Now it's all right. I'm not practising any sort of self-deception any longer. . . . Whatever it was I was running away from – the risk of love? the guilt of being white? the danger of putting ideals into practice? I'm not running away from now because I know I'm coming back here.

I was twenty-four and my hands were trembling with the strong satisfaction of having accepted disillusion as a beginning rather than an end: the last and most enduring illusion; the phoenix illusion that makes life always possible. (p. 367)

These concluding paragraphs are rather crudely and sentimentally contrived, in mood and emotional texture; they embody some of the characteristic faults of the book as a whole, including a sometimes embarrassingly intense self-consciousness, a self-satisfaction with 'clever' intellectual or emotional performances, a setting-up of situations for the superficially sharp perceptions of the immature Helen to bore into. But the intention at the end is to convey a stability of purpose, a sense of real, if limited, insight, a knowledge that the journey's true start has been reached.

One of the least satisfactorily explored areas of experience in *The Lying Days* is the terrain on which black and white do manage to meet on terms of normality. The reader is never brought face to face with Paul's African political contracts, or Jenny Marcus's 'pet' Indian, Nathoo Ram; Helen's relationship with Mary Seswayo is presented with admirable clarity, in all its awkwardness and gaucherie, but exclusively (though this does not mean advantageously) from Helen's viewpoint, in accordance with the new realizations it brings Helen; and it closes on a rather contrived note, with Mary apparently in possession of saintly resignation and Helen cast in the role of the uncompromising, if unrealistic, revolutionary. Mary is not a successfully realized character, not merely to the point of limitation one would expect from Helen's naïveté of perception; but also her casual disappearance from the novel constitutes a lapse in Nadine Gordimer's usually careful construction.

The point is raised because of the general limitation this area of failure imposes in the novel as a whole. The beginning of Helen's search – in other words the scope of the novel's plot – falls far short of the ambitious prefiguration with which the book opens. Helen is seeking a quality of self-knowledge sufficiently profound to constitute a basis for personal fulfilment, and she has the idea that an understanding of her society is at least an essential step in the right direction. But she explores less than half the society, using the attitudes of whites towards non-whites as a yardstick in her soundings. She does not appear to realize (and this, it seems to me, applies as much to Nadine Gordimer) that the whites cannot be understood from the inside, as it were, no matter how acutely and percipiently observed, unless the blacks are. The two are not separate; their apparent separation is a potent, convincing and dangerously misleading illusion. So Helen cannot understand her own group, nor arrive at a worthwhile degree of self-knowledge, without extending her search beyond the gates of the native location – with all the risks to personal identity that may seem to imply. The closing scene of *The Lying Days*, with the African child street musicians apparently setting the seal on Helen's knowledge that she will return to South Africa to pursue her quest, may suggest that the awareness exists, and the risk will have to be taken.

This seems to be confirmed by two stories in the collection *Six Feet of the Country*[1] which bridges the gap between *The Lying Days* and nadine Gordimer's next novel, *A World of Strangers*.[2] In the first, 'What New Era would that be?' Nadine Gordimer shows no mercy towards the 'liberal' pretensions of an emancipated young white woman from the Cape. The tone of the story seems to be a continuation of Helen Shaw's disillusion with the pretentious quasi-intellectual liberalism of Johannesburg's middle-class Bohemian set as it is depicted in the Marcuses and others in *The Lying Days*; but there is an important development. In 'What New Era would that be?' there is an attempt to write from the point of view of those at the receiving end: the black character who is a kind of centre of consciousness (though much vitiated by the ubiquitous and omniscient presence of the Gordimerian implied

[1] *Six Feet of the Country* (Victor Gollancz, London, 1957).

[2] *A World of Strangers* (Victor Gollancz, London, 1958; Penguin Books, Harmondsworth, 1962). Page references in the text are to the latter edition.

author). Jake is a stab in the direction of Steven Sitole in *A World of Strangers*. With him opens up a whole new field of awareness for the exercise of Nadine Gordimer's talents – and her judgment. The ultimate question is to what extent she will realize that the demarcation between this new area and the one she has already ploughed is illusory.

In 'What New Era would that be?' the non-white characters are intended to be human, natural and unaffected. It is Jennifer, the self-lacerating – or rather self-indulgent – bore, who cannot behave naturally in the situation, but imposes the contortions of her self-consciously 'liberal' guilt on it. She is a 'liberal' from Cape Town, visiting Johannesburg, who has been taken by an English journalist, Alister, to see one of Alister's black friends, Jake, a successful entrepreneur. They meet in a printing shop after hours, where Jake and some of his protégés are drinking together. One of these, a trade union organizer, tells how he and a left-wing white lawyer had been invited home to lunch by one of the employers with whom they had been negotiating, and how, after drinking beer together with the other men in the sitting room, he had been asked by the industrialist to take his meal alone on the verandah.

When Alister and Jennifer take their leave, Nadine Gordimer chooses to explode the pretence:

> Jennifer shook hands with Temba and Maxie, called 'Good-bye! Good-bye!' to the others, as if they were somehow out of earshot in that small room. From the door, she suddenly said to Maxie, 'I feel I must tell you. About the other story – your first one, about the lunch. I don't believe it. I'm sorry, but I honestly don't. It's too illogical to hold water.'
>
> It was the final self-immolation by honest understanding. There was absolutely no limit to which that understanding would not go. Even if she could not believe Maxie, she must keep her determined good faith with him by confessing her disbelief. She would go to the length of calling him a liar to show by frankness how much she respected him – to insinuate, perhaps, that she was *with* him, even in the need to invent something about a white man that she, because she herself was white, could not believe. It was her last bid for Maxie.
>
> The small, perfectly made man crossed his arms and smiled watching her out. Maxie had no price. (*Six Feet of the Country*, p. 96)

Jennifer Tetzel is one version of the sort of thing that can go wrong in a situation like Helen Shaw's, and she is an easy target. At this time Nadine Gordimer was enjoying quite a reputation for deflation, to the point of being regarded as a cynic. (It may be interjected that the trouble with South African readers and critics is their over-readiness to identify, or rather to feel that they have been identified, as members of one or other group in a very small society, and to react with a group loyalty that is almost ferocious – nearly all Gordimer's South African critics bear this out.) Not surprisingly, they failed to perceive Nadine Gordimer's drift, though the signals were out clearly enough in the last story of this collection, 'The Smell of Death and Flowers'.

In this story a very ordinary South African girl of twenty-two, endowed with considerable if 'two-dimensional' prettiness, finds herself almost accidentally at a multi-racial party in Johannesburg, and dances with a black man for the first time in her life. She is fascinated by Jessica Malherbe, an Afrikaans woman who has rejected her parental tradition, become involved in left-wing politics and trade union activities, and married an Indian. Jessica is one of the leaders of the Defiance Campaign and had been arrested for entering an African 'location' illegally. The girl, impossibly named Joyce McCoy (does the identity of initial letters suggest that there is on an individual level no difference between her and Jessica Malherbe?), goes up to Jessica and volunteers to join the next group attempt to march into a location, thus defying the statutory power of this division of humanity. She eventually does this, but not before a crisis of fear overtakes her, and almost forces her to escape. It happens in the house in Fordsburg, the run-down Indian and coloured area of Johannesburg where the marchers rendez-vous.

Jessica Malherbe's Indian husband sat down . . . he began to talk to her in his Cambridge-modulated voice . . . quite suddenly she began to be aware of the odour of incense. Sweet and dry and smoky, like the odour of burning leaves – she began to smell it. Then she thought, it must be in the furniture, the curtains: the old woman burns it and it permeates the house and all the gew-gaws from Birmingham, and Denver, Colorado, and American-occupied Japan. Then it did not remind her of burning leaves any longer. It was incense, strong and sweet. The smell of death and flowers. She remembered it with such immediacy that it came back literally, absolutely, the way a memory of words or vision never can.

41

'Are you all right, Miss McCoy?' said the kindly Indian, interrupting himself because he saw that she was not listening and that her pretty, pale, impassive face was so white and withdrawn that she looked as if she might faint.

She stood up with a start that was like an inarticulate apology and went quickly from the room. She ran down the passage and opened a door and closed it behind her, but the odour was there too, stronger than ever, in somebody's bedroom, where a big double bed had an orange silk covering. She leaned with her back against the door, breathing it in and trembling with fear and with the terrible desire to be safe: to be safe from one of the kindly women who would come, any moment now, to see what was wrong; to be safe from the gathering up of her own nerve to face the journey in the car to the location, and the faces of her companions, who were not afraid, and the walk up the location street. (p. 217)

In the bedroom she regains her nerve, realizing that what comes to her aid is 'the code of a well-brought-up child at a party': '*It would be terribly rude to run away now.*' (p. 218). But the controlling image is the smell of incense, of 'death and flowers' which is not unconnected with the 'colourless formula of good manners' that can serve to stifle fear as well as spontaneity. At the party, when Joyce hears that Jessica Malherbe is married to an Indian, a train of associations is set up in her mind.

> . . . suddenly she remembered that once, in Durban, she had talked across the counter of a shop with an Indian boy. She had been down in the Indian quarter with her sister, and they had entered a shop to buy a piece of silk. She had been the spokeswoman, and she had murmured across the counter to the boy and he had said, in a voice as low and gentle as her own, no, he was sorry, that length of silk was for a sari, and could not be cut. The boy had very beautiful, unseeing eyes, and it was as if they spoke to one another in a dream. The shop was small and deep-set. It smelled strongly of incense, the smell of the village church in which her grandfather had lain in state before his funeral, the scent of her mother's garden on a summer night – the smell of death and flowers, compounded, as the incident itself came to be, of ugliness and beauty, of attraction and repulsion. For just after she and her sister had left the little shop, they had found themselves being

followed by an unpleasant man, whose presence first made them uneasily hold tightly to their handbags but who later, when they entered a busy shop in an attempt to get rid of him, crowded up against them and made an obscene advance. He had had a vaguely Eurasian face, they believed, but they could not have said whether or not he was an Indian; in their disgust, he had scarcely seemed human to them at all. (p. 208)

Nadine Gordimer is anxious to weave a Freudian strand into the pattern of her story. Otherwise the second incident described would be completely superfluous; as it is, its aesthetic justification is dubious, and the attempt to emphasize the dual significance for Joyce of the smell of incense is heavy-handed and smacks of melodrama. Perhaps Nadine Gordimer wishes us to seek the reason for the mysterious and unlikely conversion to liberalism and political action of the emphatically ordinary white South African girl, who hasn't even enough conversation for the dance floor, on the level of the subconscious, where the repercussions of such incidents took place undetected. Joyce is very eager at the party to catch a glimpse of Rajati, Jessica's husband, the consummator with a white woman, in a framework of mutual consent, of the threat to her (white) femininity posed by her would-be molester who was (possibly?) Indian. And days later in the house in Fordsburg it is while speaking with Rajati that she is overcome with fear.

Artistically this is not a success although Nadine Gordimer is certainly deploying the conventional sexual bogeyman of the South African racial scene: the texture of the Freudian tapestry is too vague to be interpreted in such a logical series of causes and effects.

But there is a level on which the story 'works', and very effectively too, absorbing into its structure the rhythms and tensions set up by the smell of incense and its associations. The duality of incense and its connection with death provide the foundation for it. It is possible that the village where Joyce's grandfather died is in England; she has just spent five years living there. The incident in the Indian quarter of Durban is replete with peculiarly South African connotations. A link is thus established between a parent culture, the one which evolved the (as it turns out, decisive) code of good manners, and its remote offshoot. The association of the smell of incense with death comes through her grandfather, a figure embedded in and suggestive of the English tradition, as a component in Joyce's present, South African life. But the component, like her grandfather, is dead: what survives of it is the merest surface gloss, the code of good manners. However, in the offshoot culture, which possesses little depth of tradition as yet, this varnish is remarkably potent. Thus the smell of incense in the Indian house makes Joyce fearful because it symbolizes the death of what once might have enabled her to cope with this new situation – a certainty of values, coming from a sense of tradition. But the residue of this tradition, arbitrary as it is, and apparently fragile, in both ways like the prettiness of the flowers that constitute the other side of the duality of incense, is potent enough to save Joyce for a new flowering. Significantly, Nadine Gordimer locates this new flowering in an area that was problematic to the end for Helen Shaw in *The Lying Days*; after the marchers enter the location the police move in, arrest them and begin to take their names.

> Joyce stood waiting her turn, and her heart beat slowly and evenly. She thought again, as she had once before – how long ago was that party? – I feel *nothing*. It's all right. I feel *nothing*.
>
> But as the policeman came to her, and she spelled out her name for him, she looked up and saw the faces of the African onlookers who stood nearest her. Two men, a small boy, and a woman, dressed in ill-matched cast-offs of European clothing, which hung upon them without meaning, like coats spread on bushes, were looking at her. When she looked back, they met her gaze. And she felt, suddenly, not *nothing* but what they were feeling, at the sight of her, a white girl, taken – incomprehensibly, as they themselves were used to being taken – under the force of white men's wills, which dispensed and withdrew life, which imprisoned and set free, fed or starved, like God himself. (p. 233)

Suddenly the political gesture is validated, commitment becomes meaningful in an identity of newly-discovered feeling. For Joyce is discovering the ability to feel; and this is perhaps more important than the nature of the feeling itself. It is also strongly reminiscent of Joel's indictment of Helen (and white South Africans in general) for emotional laziness at the end of *The Lying Days*. There is another significant parallel in that Joyce's awakening, like Helen's to the horror of her moral surroundings, takes place within the forbidden reality of the 'native location'; but in Joyce's case the situation is more mundane and acceptable, less horrendously climactic, than Helen's; and Joyce is not shielded from the African spectators by glass. Thus she feels with them, not about them or for them; and this is the direction of the author's development.

Because Joyce is very much the other side of the Jennifer Tetzel coin, her very inability to feel seems to give rise to a painful, introspective honesty, an inner search involving all things on the road to the numb sources of feeling. Joyce is thus at once the logical development of Helen as she appears at the end of *The Lying Days*, the refutation of the charge of cynicism against her creator and the prelude and prefiguration of a new and dominating conviction leading up to commitment that emerges in Nadine Gordimer's next phase of development, which begins with *A World of Strangers*.

2 A World of Strangers

A World of Strangers is narrated by Toby Hood, a 'lucid reflector' who comes to South Africa to look after the Johannesburg office of the family publishing firm. Toby is young, British, the scion of an upper-class left-wing family; he is in a state of muted revolt against the liberal preconceptions and preoccupations of his uncle and mother. (His father, we are told, having participated in the Spanish civil war, died two years later in England of a kidney infection.) Toby is new to Africa, and in Johannesburg he gravitates first towards the social group surrounding a leading mining magnate, and then in the direction of the non-racial half-world inhabited by Bohemians, left-wing politicians and intellectuals, both white and non-white. He maintains a precarious balance between these two spheres for a time, but in the end it is an impossible feat, and the equilibrium collapses.

The novel is about love and friendship, loyalty and trust. Its emphasis on personal relationships is uncompromising, Forsterian. Toby himself is a somewhat Forsterian figure, full of little awkwardnesses over his dress, his manner, his style, and rather pleased about being slightly out of the swim; but nevertheless, a passionate follower after feelings and relationships. His very freedom from ideology, even the philanthropic Fabianism of his mother and uncle, reinforces this impression. Forster is quite a strong influence in the novel: major events such as the death of Toby's black friend and the marriage of his white mistress are handled in a way that smacks of Forsterian 'management', which is quite a departure from the scrupulous if rather passive scrutiny of detail that, one felt, often stood in the place of action in *The Lying Days*.

But there are also important divergences from the Forsterian mode. *A World of Strangers* is a much more compressed work than *The Lying Days*; and the material can be more neatly packaged and economically handled because, so to speak, it exists, whereas in *The*

Lying Days it had to be created and its identity established through the mists of an uncertain and immature perception. The South Africa of *A World of Strangers* is an established reality, and one of the technical reasons for choosing an outsider as its centre of consciousness is that a more concrete impression of this reality can be obtained through apparent objectivity and freedom from preconceptions. Indeed, as we have said, insofar as Toby has preconceptions they can be said to run counter to those of the 'committed' liberal, in relation to South Africa at least. He introduces himself to the reader, in the first sentence of the book, with the words:

> I hate the faces of peasants.
> I thought that the day the ship anchored at Mombasa, and
> I saw the Africans for the first time.[1]

The adoption of Toby as narrator also marks a technical innovation in the author's work which helps her to avoid becoming bogged down in the natural tendencies of short-story technique. If the technical faults of *The Lying Days* are to be characterized in a phrase, it may be said that the book suffers from too much omniscience about uncertainty. The short stories that appeared between the first two novels are replete with direct authorial intervention, omniscience, *post facto* irony and so forth, all things demanded by the genre. 'A Smell of Death and flowers' is the most novelistic, the most restrained, from this point of view. In *A World of Strangers* Nadine Gordimer solves the technical dangers at a stroke by using a familiar and acceptable tool of her trade – the mask. That Toby functions as a mask for his creator can be illustrated by juxtaposing the background and experience she ascribes to him with that she gives to Helen Shaw, always uncomfortably close to being an imitation rather than a version of the author herself. Toby is male, Helen female; Toby British, upper-class, self-confident, Helen South African, petit-bourgeoise, pathetically uncertain; Toby thinks of himself in the beginning as formed, Helen is externally almost shapeless and eagerly exposed to experience; Toby is an outsider, Helen an indigénée. The mask in literature, Yeats tells us, has the opposite characteristics to those of its user, the creator or artist. Apart from that, it has many practical virtues. Could any South African as central character have oscillated between such vastly separated extremes as Toby manages

[1] *A World of Strangers* (Victor Gollancz, London, 1958), p. 7.

to do? It would have been too great an unlikelihood to overcome, which just shows that truth is stranger than fiction.

Nadine Gordimer is at least firm enough with herself to disentangle the two – mask and creator – something her South African critics were, alas, unable to do. The book was well enough received, understood and appreciated abroad, but as each South African critic has his own version of *Hamlet* with himself cast as the prince, so the author could not have succeeded with them, no matter what she had made of her theme.

What she does is impressive, though not, in the end, fully successful. It is not so much arguable as certain that no white South African novelist (these dreary categories!) has ever succeeded so well in the presentation of a black character as Nadine Gordimer does with Steven Sitole, the raffish, feckless, charming man-about-Sophiatown who becomes Toby's closest friend. If Toby is the central character, Steven is the hero and Cecil (Toby's upper-class white girlfriend) the heroine; and these two meet only in Toby, in the strange world of this novel.

The author does her spadework carefully for Steven's character, which is beset with potential disaster for a white novelist (Steven could only have come to life through the eyes of an alien narrator, such as Toby); both in 'Which New Era would that be?'[1] and 'The Smell of Death and Flowers'[2] there are prototype characters. Jake Alexander in 'Which New Era would that be?' 'had decided long ago (with the great help of the money he had made) that he would take the whole business of the colour bar as humorous'[3], which approaches Steven's attitude of disgusted non-involvement in the whole business, especially from a political angle; and in 'The Smell of Death and Flowers', Eddie Ntwala, the natural, relaxed African who is the first black man Joyce has ever danced with, is presented to her by his friend in such a way that she knows:

> . . . that he must be someone important and admired, a leader of some sort, whose every idiosyncracy – the broken remains of handsome, smoke-darkened teeth when he smiled, the wrinkled tie hanging askew – bespoke to those who knew him his distinction in a thousand different situations. (p. 204)

Steven too possesses this charisma, and like him, Eddie Ntwala is

[1] *Six Feet of the Country* (Victor Gollancz, London, 1957).
[2] Ibid.
[3] Ibid., p. 89.

apparently non-political, since Joyce does not meet him again in the course of the story, during which the rest of her contacts with non-whites are political. The author treads warily and sparingly with Eddie Ntwala, making him first an object for Joyce to test her reactions on, then an amusing conversationalist, and lastly, as he explains the meaning of a song to her:

> He said as simply as a peasant, as if he had never danced with her, exchanging sophisticated banter, 'It's about a young man who passes and sees a girl working in her father's field.' (p. 209)

Steven is, of course, much more than the sum of Jake Alexander and Eddie Ntwala. he is meant to be a life principle, pitted not only against the vast weight of luxurious inertia of the High House, where Toby's mining magnate friends the Alexanders live and entertain, but also against harassment by a rapidly-increasing and encroaching swarm of customs, laws, petty regulations that are consciously designed to stifle his very sense of humanity; and against poverty, dirt, ugly surroundings and sheer physical in-security.

Steven and Toby first met at a party which Toby comes to through Anna Louw, who is Jessica Malherbe of 'The Smell of Death and Flowers' brought to life – the dedicated Afrikaner girl committed to left-wing political action, once married to an Indian but now divorced. (Nadine Gordimer's ability to take Anna seriously and treat her with respect represents a growth in maturity away from the callow cynicism about white liberals as a class evinced in her earliest stories.) The party is one of her well-known set pieces – indeed, throughout her fiction she uses parties as what might be called prototype aesthetic situations, composed of an overlay of artifice on a basis of fundamental human need, the artifice being an attempt to give the best possible setting for the realization of the need. Afterwards, Steven takes Toby to a township shebeen, where they become drunk and fall into deep agreement.

> He said, 'We like to read the Russians. You'll see, Africans want to read Dostoyevsky, man, they read lots of Dos-toyevsky.'
> I said, '*You* read that somewhere, Steven.' . . .
> He laughed in ready guilt. 'Anyway, a few do. They read Dostoyevsky because they want to feel miserable, to glory in another misery. I follow the racing page,' he added

swaggeringly. But even he didn't believe in himself, as a man of the world. 'The comics,' he said, putting on a serious, considering face, 'and the comics.'

'Trouble with me,' he went on, 'I don't want to feel miserable, I don't want any glory out of it. Sam and Peter and all those others, yap-yap all the time, chewing over the same old thing, this they've taken from us, that they've denied our children, pass laws, injustice – agh, I'm sick of it. Sick of feeling half a man. I don't want to be bothered with black men's troubles. You know that, Toby? These –' and he circled the noisy room with a movement of his slim black hand with the too-long fingernails and a signet-ring in which a piece of red glass winked, exasperated and distasteful.

'A private life,' I said. 'That's what you want.' He caught my arm. 'That's it,' he said. 'That's it,' while I nodded with the reiteration of a discovery. There it was, the truth. Created by drink or not, I had had few such moments in my life, even in my own country, among my own friends. We did not understand each other; we wanted the same thing.[1]

It is necessary to understand the deployment of the author's technique in this, one of the central passages in her prose fiction. She is at pains to document fully the discovery it contains, and she surrounds the incident with an intricate and dense tracery of detail. Abundance of detail combined with a shrewd eye for significance is, of course, a marked characteristic of her style, but I cannot think of another passage in any of her novels in which technique is brought to bear on the raw material of meaning with quite such laser-like intensity. The scene-setting commences with a list of impressions as the car enters black territory:

The street-lights ended. We went down, into the dark. There were shapes, darker against the darkness; there was the moon, half-grown, spreading a thin, luminous paint on planes that reflected her. A graveyard of broken cars and broken porcelain; an old horse sleeping, tethered, on a bare patch; mute shops patched about with signs you could not read; small, closed houses whose windows were barred with tin strips across the street; a solitary man stooping to pick up something the day had left; a sudden hysterical gabble behind a rickety fence, where a fowl had started up. (p. 98)

[1] *A World of Strangers* (Victor Gollancz, London, 1957), pp. 102–103.

The imagery expresses non-communication, a closed and barren-seeming world resisting the perceptions of the young white man, who was already felt in the car that 'I had neither recognition nor volition in its progress.' (p. 98). Steven, on the other hand, is 'at home in a dark and lonely street'; he 'went along with the happy ease of a man who could have found his way in his sleep.' (p. 99)

At this stage it is impressionistic and rather general; though individual images possess their share of precision, the total picture is unspecific. But the focus becomes clearer as the friends near their goal.

> 'Here.' We turned into an unlit yard, with two rows of rooms or cottages – each row seemed to be under one continuous roof, but there were four or five doors in the length of each. They were shut against the night as if they were deserted and empty, but our feet were sucked by mud round a tap that snivelled and drizzled, and there was a strong smell of rotting vegetables, and the general sourness of a much-used place. Beyond and slightly behind the end wall of the right-hand row, there was a small detached building with some kind of lean-to porch attached – a creeper grew over it like a fishnet draped to dry. Steven pushed me up three broken steps and knocked on the door. (p. 99)

The imagery is almost at the Wordsworthian level of 'I measured it from side to side.' There is a feeling of straining to get everything exactly right, so each detail not only tells, but interprets. Words like 'snivelled' and 'drizzled' evoke the squalid lives of the people who must live in these surroundings, but go beyond the surroundings themselves. The shebeen is located with the care of a police report. Though the dwellings are 'shut against the night as if they were deserted and empty', appearances are given the lie by 'the general sourness of a much-used place', which in turn refers to the meaning of the whole experience, supplied casually by Steven a few moments before: 'If the door's open, the place is shut; that's wrong.' (p. 99)

The suggestion is that under these circumstances life depends on massive, fundamental deceit, but as a result survives in an impaired form: '. . . that's wrong.' Such nuances constitute a sort of hedge between the climactic moment of shared consciousness which is about to occur, and life outside – the life Toby has lived and observed up to this time. But, consistently in terms of the author's argument, the hedge between white and black South Africa only

51

appears to enclose the one from the other, and in reality presents a whole series of opportunities or avenues or gaps through which communication does take place. Despite the desolate appearance of the township at night, the presence of an unusually intense mode of human existence is revealed in the imagery of rotting vegetables, trampled, muddy ground and 'a much-used place': the darkness and mystery provide the whites with their stereotype, but in fact conceal abundant life.

As Steven opens the door to the new apprehension of experience, the hedge goes on sprouting fresh details.

> – we went in, past a woman's face with a woollen scarf wrapped round the head, under the candle she held against the wall. I remember noticing that it was the swollen-looking face of a stupid woman. We went through a cave of a room where something smallish, probably a child, was asleep on an iron bed, and the candle caught, in passing, a bunch of paper roses and a primus stove, and then into a larger room with the walls painted olive green halfway up like the waiting room in a station, and an electric bulb with a celluloid shade hanging over a table where four or five men did not look up.

The implied contrast with the splendour and luxury of the High House is clear, but the point is to be clinched with one of Nadine Gordimer's characteristic little perceptual shocks.

> There was also another group, sitting on a bed, and they stubbed out their laughter, almost with relief, as if it had gone on too long beyond the merit of what had occasioned it, as we came in, and started talking in what, even in a language I didn't understand, I could recognise as the interrogatory tone of a change of subject. Everyone was drinking, but there were no bottles in sight. On the walls, a huge Coca-Cola calendar – a girl on a beach, in bathing costume and accompanied by a tiny radio and a carrier of Coca-Cola – hung with the look of inevitability of a holy picture given its niche. It was the barest room I had ever seen in my life; it depended entirely on humans. (p. 100)

The relative unimportance of 'humans', the preponderance of things, objects both decorative and 'useful', is emphasized in the description of Toby's first impression of the Alexanders' house.

> The entrance hall led away down a few broad shallow steps to

the left; I got the impression of a long, mushroom-coloured room there, with gleams of copper and gilt, flowers and glass. In the hall there was a marquetry table under a huge mirror with a mother-of-pearl inlaid frame. Further back, the first steps of a white staircase spread in a dais; carpet seemed to grow up the stairs, padding the rim of each step like pink moss. An African appeared soundlessly; I followed him soundlessly (I found later that the entire ground floor of the house was covered with that carpeting the colour of a mushroom's gills) past the mirror that reflected three new golf balls and a very old golf glove, sweated and dried to the shape of the wearer's hand, on the table below it, and through a large living-room full of sofas and chairs covered in women's dress colours, that led to a veranda. If you could call it that; a superior sort of veranda. The entire wall of the room was open to it, and it was got up like something out of a film, with a bar, a barbecue fireplace, *chaises longues*, glass and wrought-iron tables, mauve Venetian glass lanterns and queer trailing plants. (p. 49)

The general profusion of furnishings muffles human noise, making Toby's entry ghostlike and insubstantial; it diminishes the vitality of the 'burst of laughter' he interrupts, and surrounds every social gesture, every communication, with a framework of propriety, a contest of conventional comfort, or the comfort of convention, which is much less penetrable than the layers of detail which surround Toby's and Steven's instant of real human contact.

. . . the meal was at an end, and we all got up and went into the room I had caught a glimpse of from the front door. There was coffee and also old brandy and liqueurs, and the smell, like the smell of fine leather, of cigars; a warm fug of well-being filled the room, in which, in my slightly hazy state, I saw that every sort of efficient indulgence lay about, like in those rooms conjured up by Genii for people in fairy stories who always seem to wish for the same sort of thing, as if, given the chance, nobody really knows anything else to wish for: there were silver or Limoges cigarette lighters on every other table, as well as the little coloured matchbooks on which were printed 'Hamish' or 'Marion', silver dishes of thin mints and huge chocolates, jade boxes and lacquer boxes and silver boxes filled with cigarettes, silver gadgets to guillotine the cigars, even amethyst, rose, and green sugar crystals to sweeten the coffee. (pp. 61–62)

The profusion of needless objects baffles the imagination, takes the experience into the absurd. For what is this room trying to say? Such a heavily-wrought context presumably suggests something human behind it, an effort of thought, a series of conscious decisions; but no significant statement results; for Toby, in terms of rational discourse, in terms of ordinary human experience, needs and desires, the room is as communicative as a fairy tale. The 'reality' of the surrounding objects swamps the human reality.

The contrast between this room and the shebeen is brought into focus through the description of their respective wall decorations; and the aesthetic level, fittingly, clinches the argument.

Most of the guests were drawn to look at Marion Alexander's new 'find' – a picture she had evidently just bought. 'Come and tell me what you think of this,' she said, with the faintest emphasis, as if I didn't need any more, on the last word. It was a small and rather dingy Courbet, deeply set in a frame the colour and texture of dried mud. 'Interesting,' I murmured politely. 'They're not easily come by, I imagine.' 'Here!' she said. 'Can you believe it? I found it here, in Johannesburg!' I attempted to look impressed, although I couldn't imagine why anyone should want to find such a thing anywhere. 'How do you spell the name?' a woman asked me, quietly studying the picture. I spelled it. The woman nodded slowly. 'I love it, Marion, I think it's the most exciting thing you've bought yet!' said someone else.

'Well I can tell you I couldn't believe it when my little man told me there was a Courbet to be bought in Johannesburg,' Mrs Alexander said for the third or fourth time. (p. 62)

The contrast with the Coca-Cola advertisement on the wall of the shebeen could scarcely be more explicit. The advertisement 'hung with the look of inevitability of a holy picture given its niche.' (p. 100). The Courbet is rendered even more pretentious by its incongruity among the other pictures in the room, mostly 'in the Table Bay *genre*; the *genre* of the room, generally; not a discomforting brush-stroke in any of them.' (p. 62)

Not only is the Courbet dingy and ill-framed; in its singular ironic but unperceived appropriateness it is meaningless, and evokes insincere and foolish responses. It is merely further evidence of the Alexanders' ability to control things through money, another example of white man's magic. Whereas the Coca-Cola advertisement is not only appropriate to its surroundings, it implies a world of meaning to the people who see it – again in direct contrast with the Courbet. The advertisement suggests to its viewers that good world of object-induced comfort forever before their eyes but beyond their reach; and further, in the advertizing-man's symbolic summary of the values of his world, it states the contrast between the world, those values, and the life that is available to the drinkers in the shebeen, who are there in the first place as a result of the force of that contrast.

This contrast also has the significant effect of pointing up an overall technical strategy of considerable importance that the author employs throughout her works, and that seems to bear organic relationship to the growth and development of her ideas. This may be called the strategy of massive deceit. Its application is clear enough in a book about growing up like *The Lying Days*, where the span of change in the heroine's perceptions is necessarily vast. But its persistence into *A World of Strangers* suggests that Nadine Gordimer considers it to be more in the nature of things than a phenomenon specifically related to the maturation process. In other words, in the world of experience she writes about, people live in an atmosphere of sensual treachery, where the very objects in the visible world, let alone the mutable and labile sphere of personal relations, suggest a meaning to the most perspicuous of perceivers that is the opposite of true. Nothing can be trusted in this universe, least of all the evidence of the most refined senses. The truth can only be approached (one hesitates to say 'arrived at') through action of one kind or another, including the act of committing oneself to a particular vision or version of life. This emerges with increasing strength from the later novels, but it is something which is always there, and it sets Nadine Gordimer apart among South African novelists who write in English, because it takes her past the boundaries of liberalism, beyond the liberal-humanist norm. This process has its real beginning in *A World of Strangers*, and reaches a culmination that is both impressive and decisive in *A Guest of Honour*.

The strategy of massive deceit may be illustrated in action at this stage by considering Steven's remark to Toby as they reach the shebeen: 'If the door's open, the place is shut; that's wrong', (p. 99), and applying it to what happens to Toby when he visits the High House for the first time: 'The car dropped me at the front door, which was open ...' (p. 48). That door may stand permanently ajar, but the place behind it is as effectively shut to Steven as if the opening had been a thick chunk of metal sealed with a time-lock for a hundred years. This is not rhetoric; it is a point the author is evidently anxious to establish. Toby's best friend and Toby's mistress, despite their similarity in temperament, will never meet, because, it is stressed more than once, one belongs to the High House, the other to the milieu of the shebeen.

The nature of the insight that Nadine Gordimer has isolated with such rigour turns out to correspond with her governing strategy of technique. 'A private life' seems so trivial: the very choice of phrase is intentionally banal. But it is, in fact, the central issue, and all-important. The author suggests that the truth of the South African situation is not to be sought in the political sphere that it is not, primarily a 'political' situation, and that the truth (if not the remedy) should be looked for on the level of individual human existence. Neither Steven nor Cecil, the liveliest of the book's characters, makes more than a perfunctory gesture in the direction of what *seems to be* the overweening reality. Each in the end lives his life entirely on the individual level, and is defeated by circumstances mightier than himself, circumstances which are not intrinsically political but owe some proportion of their existence to a distortion in the political universe.

But the author is not yet ready to come to terms with such an extreme resolution of her chosen fictive situation; and through Toby, Sam (Steven's composer friend), and Anna Louw she attempts an honourable compromise, in which liberal optimism is left with a little space for manoeuvre. Perhaps it is only the ruling liberal ideology of the genre that impels her to produce this minute melioristic dilution – the (sometimes) unspoken assumption of the novel form that 'Life goes on'. From someone who is not a liberal, or can no longer conceive of a possible resolution of the grim South African enigma within liberalism's boundaries, the rejoinder might well be that that is the trouble; life must not go on under such circumstances, because it *does* not; and the hope that underlies the assumption just mentioned is offensively irrelevant in the context of this novel.

Nadine Gordimer now seems ready to go beyond the 'ethical' resolutions or moral attitudes that characterize most South African fiction on the side of the angels. *A World of Strangers* is not, from the liberal point of view, a comfortable book; indeed, it is about the breakdown of human relations, the failure of an ethical system (however loosely defined) that has been advanced as the total answer in the face of whatever horror is thrown up by the depths of the human soul. The author is willing to face failure, and to accept the final evidence of her senses: the dykes are down, there is no redeeming decency left, the lycanthropes innocently govern. The climactic passage ends: 'We wanted the same thing.' (p. 103). Well, the transcendent moment comes – and goes. Steven's doom is sure; Toby's is no less in the balance, but even if he achieves this 'thing' alone, it will be diminished, flawed and imperfect by virtue of the paradox that 'a private life' cannot be attained in isolation. A private life is an act of choice arising out of the necessary condition of freedom. Minutes after their shared instant of revelation, Steven and Toby are leaping out of the window of the shebeen, fleeing from the police; the threat of retribution follows closely on their moment of reckless metaphysical daring. Such is the quality of the freedom available.

From this point the texture of the novel becomes denser and more complex, though the direction of its development is straight-forward and not unpredictable. Toby becomes involved in a love affair with Cecil Rowe, an upper-crust (it is a little out of place to talk about class in relation to white South African society – see Nadine Gordimer's insistence in this novel on the absence of old buildings in Johannesburg) horse-riding girl who is divorced, whom he meets at the High House; he also spends much time in the company of Steven and Sam, Steven's quiet intellectual journalist friend with bourgeois aspirations. These two areas of his life are kept (apparently) completely separate. He also remains friendly with Anna Louw, through whom he met Steven in the first place.

Through Toby we are thus introduced into sections of South African society that are normally regarded as being isolated from one another: the white upper crust, the mostly white left-wing intelligentsia, and urban black society. Obviously Toby as an outsider may be assumed to be a relatively objective judge. He doesn't begin to judge, however, until immediately after the episode in the shebeen with Steven. Up to then he is very much the neutral, even polite observer, who quietly enjoys the luxury of the High House, visits Johannesburg booksellers, notes the similarity of facial expression between black workers in a bus queue and workers he has seen at home in Britain. But after his shebeen excursion he awakens to a new mode of consciousness: Steven finds him a taxi-driver who takes him home, he arrives at his flat in white Johannesburg at five in the morning, and sleeps.

... I will only say that when I woke, as I did with knife-stroke abruptness when the flat boy came in to clean, I seemed to have awakened from months-long sleep and heavy dreams. I had landed on a corrugated iron roof among the pumpkins, all that went before that – the ship plying south in warmer and warmer seas, the hotel, the parties and faces – seemed as exaggerated, high-coloured, and hallucinatory as the room in Sophiatown where I had been drunk with Steven. I felt as if I had just arrived in Johannesburg. I knew, in my bones, without opening my eyes to the room, where I was, that morning. Sick, shaky, insatiably thirsty, and with the restless aching in my hands and feet that I always get with a hangover, I was aware of the place as one would silently accept a familiar presence on a morning too hideous for speech or sign. (p. 107)

The moment of inner awakening is cleverly located among objects characteristically South African, equally familiar to black and white, a part of the landscape of both groups. As they give the police raiding the shebeen the slip, Steven and Toby have scrambled onto the corrugated iron roof of a low shed, 'among pumpkins put out to ripen'.

Steven put a pumpkin under his head, as you might use a plump quilted cushion for a sofa nap. We lay there panting and laughing in swaggering, schoolboy triumph.
All at once, it was morning. (p. 104)

Basic, prosaic, ordinary and ubiquitous, the pumpkin and the corrugated iron roof rise to the occasion to become symbols of the reality above which Toby has been floating dreamily and rather dangerously up to that moment. Thus Toby's awakening is located in an objectification (of a very deprecatory deflating kind) of South African life: 'You are welcome, sir, to Cyprus – goats and monkeys!'
The relationship between Steven and Toby takes time to get under way after this episode; its course is jarring and its end abrupt. Steven gives Toby a sense of the life of a place, which is a prerequisite for participation in it. The gift is communicated rather than given, and there is nothing conscious on Steven's side in the conferring. Nadine Gordimer's point is that Steven is an artist; his style of life is his medium, and as an artist, he communicates it through living. This is the distinction between Steven and his close friend, the quiet intellectual Sam Mofokensazi. Sam is a gifted

composer, who has adopted the manner of life of the white bourgeoisie as the acceptable standard, the appropriate aspiration. His composing is an analogue for his attempt to impose a chosen form on the messy material of black township life; his music must be mediated through a white 'patron' or 'collaborator'; he is bogged down in pretentious, provincial corruptions of 'European' forms, because in his music as in his life, they are the only models available for adoption. And he is involved in politics. He is committed in precisely the areas which Steven rejects because in accepting as desirable the white man's standards and style of living, Sam has automatically accepted the problem of the white man's authority and he can only attempt to free himself from it through the political methods of the white man, which are barred to him in practice. Steven cuts the Gordian knot by not accepting the categorizations of colour; by accepting only his need to live as the defining standard of his behaviour.

Most of this is understood by Toby as a result of his awakening into reality; but it lands him on the prickles of multiple dilemmas, which are only at first confined to the intellectual plane. With Cecil, the meaningful sexual relationship is struck the day after the night out with Steven; but Toby finds that Cecil, whom he had 'coveted jealously yesterday', actually 'belonged to the unreality through which I had fallen'. (p. 110). The seeds of trouble are here, of course, though they take time to germinate. On the level of human relations, Toby is compromising in a way which by his own standards can only be condemned. To this question we shall return, though it is not distinct from what follows.

Steven is, as I have said, the most successful evocation of a black character by a white South African writer up to the time the book was written. At the same time, however, he remains half-created, rendered through the perceptions of others; and in the end, as a character, colour disregarded, a partial failure. What we have are reactions to Steven, opinions of him, from other characters; and yet his quiet friend Sam Mofokensazi lives in his determination, his bitterness and gentleness more completely than the life-embodying Steven. This is because Sam comes to the reader relatively unmediated: he is not elevated into a principle, and is created on a more modest and manageable scale. Steven's death comes as a shock to the reader not so much because of the impression of vitality he has produced but because of a feeling that one has scarcely come to know him, that there must be a great deal more of him to be experienced before he is fully understood. The strategy is effective;

but it is partly accidental. That is to say, as a result, Steven remains too much of a symbol. Although he evades labelling, he can never descend to the matrix of literary realism. It is thus a paradox of this novel that in the character intended to define and embody life through his ordinary behaviour, turns into a symbolic essence rather than a living being, and is more dependent on the whim of the author than are the other characters.

The paradox and the failure emerge from the situation: the author is further from the type of experience she wishes to create in and through Steven than she is, even, from Toby; she has to work much harder to give him the semblance of life, and with correspondingly less effect. The suggestion that Steven's life possesses extraordinary intensity is conveyed together with a sense of swift motion, of difficulty in pinning down either the man or the impressions that he creates. So it is not surprising that Steven cannot come to be the focus of Toby's commitment. This role falls to Sam, whose inherent stability is an easier point from which Toby's confused emotions and moral guilt acquire the impetus for the action, however unclear, which Toby takes at the end of the book.

Steven's function in the book is indubitably a tragic one, and the contrast with Sam indicates the nature of his tragedy. Sam in his various social, political and artistic activities, is committed to action on a particular time-scale; he operates within the limits of the present, striving for a recognizably better future. Steven has disengaged himself from history, and thus cut himself off from redemption by time. This is a relatively early but powerful indication of the author's deep preoccupation with the process of time in relation to the individual in his social role. But there is an inhibiting factor, which prevents the development of this dimension of Steven's functioning in the book: the presence of that ubiquitous phenomenon in the South African novel, the extraneous level of reality like a thin and irritating echo just beneath the level of the fictive resonance, hemming it in, cutting its waves off from their full reverberation: the informational level, the great betrayer of authorial intention.

African writers in English write, or certainly at the time *A World of Strangers* was published, wrote, either for themselves or for a metropolitan audience. There is – or was – scarcely ever a halfway house. Often they write best when they write for themselves: *The Story of an African Farm*, some sections of Jacobson's *The Beginners*, and parts of Abrahams' *Tell Freedom*. When they don't, however, they are usually concerned to do their informing against an implied background of metropolitan cultural assumptions, which emerge either scathed or unscathed. In *A World of Strangers* Nadine Gordimer *is* concerned to inform and explain, and unfortunately she chooses the wrong character to bear the main burden of the enterprise. For although Toby stands nominally between the audience and the whole of South African society, almost all of what he has to say is transformed from mere information to a novelistically acceptable degree of imagined second-hand experience through Steven and there is a serious confusion of function between the two, because of the importance of Steven's other, tragic function. In a sense we learn most about South Africa through what Steven does, is, and suffers; but we learn most about Steven through the reactions of others and thus cannot discover what he really is. We have to take it on trust to a degree that does not immediately show that he lives in his own right. Yet his tragic function may be defined as an heroic opposition, inevitably unsuccessful, to the negation and evil immanent in the surroundings – in other words, to stand, like David Mercer's Morgan, for 'life and growth'. This contradiction is sufficient to reduce Steven's intrinsic possession of life to the point where he is little more than a sounding board.

These assertions are almost quantifiable. Steven is directly present to the reader on eleven occasions of varying degrees of specificity and length. Each of these situations is directed towards fulfilling the purposes of the 'informational level' of the action more than it is towards the functioning of Steven as an individual, even though this is what the book is ostensibly 'about'. After all, the 'climax' of the relationship between Toby and Steven is reached very soon: after their first meeting at the party they go on together to their moment of mutual revelation at the shebeen. During the party one learns, mainly from Anna Louw, a reasonable amount about Steven's background and appearance. We learn a little more later through Toby's rather unsatisfactory re-establishment of telephone contact (p. 112), and their brief encounter at Anna Louw's (p. 118), after Steven's failure to turn up for lunch. Characteristics such as egocentrism, disregard for convention, liveliness and charm emerge from these episodes, but they do not add up to a convincing rendition of a complete personality.

The whole of the sixth chapter is devoted to Toby's developing relationship with Steven, but, in fact, for ninety per cent of the time Steven is again used as a vehicle of information. In nine pages,

61

Steven utters thirteen sentences, all in the course of a single brief
conversation with Toby. It may be objected, however, that it is how
Nadine Gordimer uses those thirteen sentences that is important.
She does succeed in creating a counter-ideology, embodied in
Steven, but it is limited to Steven, and fails to permeate the texture of
people and places by which he is surrounded in the chapter. Toby and
Steven visit Sam and his wife Ella in the township:

> . . . when we walked . . . through the door that opened
> abruptly from two uneven concrete steps, I was bewildered. I
> might have stepped into a room 'done over' by some young
> couple in a Chelsea flat. Green felt deadened the floor
> underfoot. There was a piano, piled with music. A record
> player in what all cabinet makers outside Sweden consider to
> be Swedish style. A divan with cushions. A red lamp. All
> along one wall, a bookcase made of painted planks and bricks.
> At the window, a green venetian blind dropped its multiple
> lids on the township. Sam's wife, Ella, pretty and shy, served a
> roast lamb and potato dinner with a bottle of wine, and
> afterwards the four of us listened to a Beethoven quartet and
> to Sam, playing some songs of his own composition. (p. 132)

Afterwards Steven and Toby go on to a shebeen. Steven says:

> 'A place like Sam's is all right . . . but it costs too much.'
> 'His wife's got quite a well-paid job, too, I gather, so I
> suppose they can manage,' I said . . . I had already got over
> the bewilderment of the difference between what was well-
> paid for blacks and what was well-paid for whites . . . I, with
> my not-very-generous salary, and my flat all to myself, was a
> rich man when I was in the townships.
> 'I don't mean just money. The effort and trouble. Keep up
> a place like that in a location. All the dirt, the easy-going, all
> round you. Imagine the way the neighbours look at you;
> you're like a zoo! All the old women want to come and peer in
> the door to see what people do in such a house.' Like most
> exhibitionistic people, Steven was a good mimic.
> I laughed. 'Still, it's an achievement to manage to live that
> way, in a location.'
> 'Ah,' said Steven, 'that's it. It's a showplace.' He assumed a
> high falsetto, parody of some white woman's voice he must
> have heard somewhere: ' ". . . an oasis of culture, my dear!"
> Is it a king's house, a millionaire's house? Man, it's just an
> ordinary way to live.'

I saw what he meant. If living decently, following a modest taste for civilized things, meant living eccentrically or remarkably, one might prefer to refuse the right masquerading as a privilege.

'Why should I guard like a cave of jewels,' he said, changing his sharp-eyed fake ring from one finger to another, 'a nice little house that any other man can have anywhere he likes in a street full of such houses?' And he grinned at me with that careless aplomb, shrugging his shoulders and looking down his nose at himself, that gave him such an air, and always, wherever we went in the townships, drew the young bloods about him to hear what he would say next.

He was, without question, the most 'popular' person I have ever known. I put the word popular between the quotes of the suspect, because to me it connotes a man who gets the most votes in a presidential election at a golf club, and I don't mean that sort of popularity. Perhaps 'loved' would be a better word. But he wasn't exactly loved, either; he was too impersonal and elusive for that. I think they gloried in him, those hangers-on – they gloried in his white man's ways produced unselfconsciously in their company, like a parlour trick that looks easy enough for anyone to learn. (pp. 132–133)

I have continued the quotation somewhat beyond Steven's remarks because I believe that the extract as it stands exemplifies the major flaws in the treatment of Steven. The counter-ideology, as I have called it, is successfully established, and in turn establishes and reinforces certain ideas about the kind of person Steven is; but the interpolations so much outweigh in quantity this little patch of life, that one has the impression that the author is exploiting, with great delicacy and skill, but insufficient restraint, a very limited amount of material. That is to say, the reader has actually been given very few details about Steven. Nevertheless, the opportunity is seized to spread his presence thinly over diverse topics, such as comparative wage scales of whites and blacks in South Africa, contrasting attitudes to what is desirable in African aspirations, the falseness and condescension of white attitudes to Africans like Sam and Ella, what makes Steven tick for his followers, and what those followers themselves feel they lack. Steven is pretty nearly used up by the end of this. The author should not have to tell us, as she does later in the same paragraph, that Steven 'had not gone under beneath his correspondence college B.A. the way black men did, becoming crushed and solemn with education . . .' Either this is sufficiently evident from Steven's behaviour and attitudes, or she has been wasting time and opportunity. At this fairly advanced stage of Steven's development as a character, such explicit explanations should be unnecessary unless there is a sound strategic reason; and what *does* emerge is again that tinny echo of information directed at the metropolis.

Nadine Gordimer does with Steven in this passage what she does in most of the others in which he appears. An African character sufficiently original to stand out from an otherwise relatively anonymous group is used, through his originality, to illuminate that anonymity. The process leaves us with a strong impression of originality, and a weak one of Steven.

In the inner structure of the novel gaps predominate over relationships; hence the title *A World of Strangers*, and the link that is most obviously missing is that between Cecil, Toby's 'classy' girlfriend, and Steven. Initially, it seems paradoxical that he is introduced to Steven and his world through the serious and dedicated Anna Louw, rather than Cecil, whose zest for life parallels Steven's; but Toby quickly understands that the two will never meet.

> I heard her say, to some people with whom we were having coffee after a cinema, 'Toby does a lot of work among the natives.' Later, when we were alone, I asked her, 'What made you tell the Howards that I do a lot of "work" among natives?' 'Well, don't you?' she said, yawning. 'I never have', I said. She let it drop; she assumed that anyone who had anything to do with Africans was concerned with charity or uplift, and that was that – she wasn't going to quibble over what she satisfied herself could only be a matter of definition. And I, I left it at that, too. I had had my little flirt with danger by questioning her at all; thankfully, I hadn't had to take it any further.
>
> For I knew that if I told Cecil that my closest friends in Johannesburg were black men, and that I ate with them and slept in their houses, I would lose her. That was the fact of the matter. And I was damned if I was going to lose her. (pp. 163–164)

The passage indicates the existence of an area of blankness, of deadness of response, in Cecil's 'freedom', the quality that Toby suggests that she shares with Steven (p. 168). There is an implied attack on her entire social milieu here; but in the very rhetorical flourish which ends the quotation, Toby's essential dilemma is exposed. He is as much a victim of the situation as Steven or Cecil or anyone else – in a sense more so, because he thinks he can have the best of both worlds, which involves him in a personal betrayal whose magnitude and inevitability he only becomes aware of through the death of Steven. Indeed, only innocence of the real nature of his situation, or simple ignorance, could produce the almost childish defiance of reality evinced by his last statement, or by what follows.

> I knew that it was natural and unremarkable that I should sleep at Sam's, in the township, on Sunday night, and in Cecil's bed on Monday, since it is natural and unremarkable for a man to have friends and a woman to love. (p. 164)

But it is precisely this unremarkable state of affairs that is denied by the reality that Toby inhabits, and he gradually comes to realize this. His personal development in the course of the book is represented by, as much as anything else, this realization.

> Often I thought how well he and Cecil would have got on together, if they could have known each other. Their flaring enthusiasms, their unchannelled energy, their obstinately passionate aimlessness – each would have matched, out-topped the other. (p. 205)

Their fates, too, are similar, the essential distinction being dictated as always by the reality – the fact of colour. Steven dies suddenly, in a getaway car which crashes during a police chase; the crime the occupants had committed – drinking illicit liquor in a shebeen – being one of the many defined by colour alone. Thus for a reason of little worth, he loses that which he has loved most; but the immediate cause of his death is intimately related to the distorted world he has lived in, and its strange laws based on diabolic values. In this light his death, far from being arbitrary, is the very embodiment of the peculiar logic of that world.

Cecil capitulates to pressures no less inherent in the peculiar system she has unwittingly shared with Steven. Such limited possibilities of love as are afforded by *her* circumstances, those of the upper-bracket white divorcée, must be turned down, in her 'greed and fear' of life, in favour of 'Patterson' – 'the hero preserved in whisky'. (p. 261). Her 'greed and fear', apparently antithetical to Steven's easy generosity, are in fact the white expression of the

65

same love of life, and are thus closely related to Steven's qualities, springing as they do from the same roots in the same South African soil. She survives, stripped of that inconsequential freedom that has been her unique quality, into a living death, a loveless life in a world of strangers; Steven dies, but at his funeral he is surrounded by hosts of those who knew him and loved him because of his ability to show that life was worth living. Cecil's surrender is at once avoidance and betrayal of Steven: a dramatic, particularized version of what happens every minute of the South African day.

Nadine Gordimer inserts the dimensions of Cecil's future skilfully, by sending Toby off on a hunting trip in the bush with a group of his High House acquaintances. One of the members of the group is Patterson, Toby's rival (though he is not yet aware of this) for Cecil's hand. Patterson's personal situation is relevant in view of the persistent preoccupation in the book with the relationship between metropolitan and provincial cultures. (Like Toby, he is English. He is also a war hero, a fighter pilot, and is now director of one of Hamish Alexander's companies.) He asks Toby, in his pre-war Cambridge drawl, ' "D'you believe these black chaps could ever be the same as us, Hood?" I heard Steven's voice, mimicking him perfectly.' (p. 243). But Steven dies during the same week-end, and Cecil makes up her mind to marry Patterson, for the security he will give her. Her image of Toby is at least partly damaged by the gossip she hears from Patterson that Toby receives black visitors in his flat.

The hunting interlude includes an episode in which Toby is lost in the wilds with an African bearer; the descriptive work is finely evocative, but the symbolism creaks. What rings much truer is the obsessive bloodthirstiness of one of the members of the party; and the white-hunter stereotype relationship with the country is effectively demolished. The equilibrium in Toby's own relationship with the world of strangers is maintained partly through Anna Louw, who functions as a kind of interpreter of the land and the changes it has wrought upon him. At first he is antagonistic to her, seeing in her a South African version of the English do-gooding liberal he rejects, or alternatively dismissing her as a 'committed' leftist, seeing life in political terms. She performs her first significant function early enough, by introducing him to Steven; and soon after that they state their respective positions in a long conversation that has Steven for its ostensible subject. Actually, it bears on issues that are more far-reaching in terms of Nadine Gordimer's development as a novelist – the metropolitan-provincial polarity among them.

'I'm glad to hear that you're not too down on Steven's romantic view of life – although I'm not sure, yet, that I agree about it being romantic.'

'It's romantic, all right,' said Anna, sending tomatoes seething into a hot pan, 'and I am down on it. I understand the need to be romantic in some way, but I'm down on this way. It's a waste of energy. You won't catch Steven working with Congress or any other African movement, for that matter. He never defied, either – I'm talking about the defiance campaign, the passive resistance movement of a year or two back. The only defiance he's interested in is not paying his bills, or buying drink. He's got this picture of himself as the embittered, devil-may-care African, and believe me, he's making a career of it. He doesn't care a damn about his people; he's only concerned with his own misfortune in being born one of them.' The sizzling of the tomatoes in butter spat angrily around her.

'Why should Steven *have* to be involved in these movements and congresses and what-not?' I said. 'I must admit, the whole idea would fill me with distaste. I'd run a mile at the thought.' . . . 'He wants the results of that political action, doesn't he?' she called, over her shoulder. 'He wants to be free of the pass laws and the colour bar and the whole caboodle? – Well, let him fight for it.' She laughed, indignant in spite of herself.

All the old, wild reluctant boredom with which I had borne with this sort of talk all my life was charged, this time, with something more personal; a nervous excitement, a touchiness. I felt the necessity to get the better of her; to punish her, almost, 'My dear Anna, you're so wrong, too. The private liver, the selfish man, the shirker, as you think him – he's a rebel. He's a rebel against rebellion. On the side, he's got a private revolution of his own; it's waged for himself, but quite a lot of other people may benefit. I think that about Steven. He's muscling in; who's to say he won't get there first? . . . But, most important of all, he's alive, isn't he? He's alive, in defiance of everything that would attempt to make him half-alive . . .' (pp. 121–124)

Toby states a position which has become not merely respectable, but obligatory, in English fiction since the advent of Forster, if not of George Eliot; and which has, in a curious way spread over the political spectrum, including as its most powerful propagator D. H. Lawrence, and consequently has been adopted by the strongest pressure group in modern criticism. In relation to such a 'tradition', Nadine Gordimer cannot avoid being something of an outsider; that she feels this, as a specific problem in her art, was evident from the whole tenor of *The Lying Days*. The main reason for the strategic choice of Toby the upper-class well-educated apolitical Englishman as narrator, here is the need to obtain at least the aura of self-confidence, of stability in relation to a tradition of values, that Helen Shaw so completely lacks.

This is not to say that the author wants to pass judgment with the assumed authority of the metropolis, in order to make her condemnation of provincial evils more convincing. In fact, what she is doing is subtly undermining Toby's position, and working towards the creation of a viable South African point of view – an enterprise of the greatest importance, both for herself and the South African novel. Toby's sub-Lawrentian rantings, his Birkinesque fustian, expose him helplessly to the discovery, sprung a very short time afterwards, during the same evening's entertainment, that Anna had been married to, but has been divorced from, an Indian. This is only the first in a series of shocks for Toby.

I had just picked up a snapshot of Anna, standing beside a smiling Indian woman, and herself wearing Indian dress, when she came back into the room.

'A sari suits you very well. Have you been in India?'

She shook her head. 'I was married to an Indian. He gave me this, too; isn't it beautiful?' She showed me the white Kashmir shawl she was wearing. I admired it and we talked about it for a few minutes, while she went round locking up the cottage.

In the car, she said, 'Were you surprised about my marriage?'

'Well, yes. I suppose I was.'

'But of course, it doesn't seem so very extraordinary to English people.'

'No.'

'Not the way it is here.' She added, in her matter-of-fact voice, the voice of the conscientious committee member drawing the attention of the meeting to something she does not want them to overlook: 'It was before the Mixed

Marriages Act, of course.'

I suddenly choked with the desire to laugh; I couldn't help it, it came spluttering out. 'I can't think of a marriage in terms of legislation. That's all I mean.' Did she think of anything in any other terms?

'Was it very difficult, being married like that in this country?' I asked, as I might have asked about the cultivation of some plant in her garden.

She hesitated a moment. 'A bit. Didn't seem so then; seems so now.'

She changed gear with a typical, neat, considerate movement. And I had a sudden sense of loneliness, her loneliness, that appeared unsummoned behind her flat, commonplace talk like a face at the window of a locked house. (pp. 124–125)

The passage works very intricately, though the rhetoric of the ending is suspect (even this may be sustained by arguing that its inclusion is necessary if the author is to explode Toby's assumed reliability of judgment). Toby's deflation is evinced in the flatness of his answers, his need to be evasive before he can admit that the news has surprised him, the almost churlish gaucherie of his laughter when Anna mentions the Mixed Marriages Act, and the clumsily apologetic tone of his explanation.

Thus the dominant stereotype of the metropolitan tradition fails; Anna's political commitment is not divided from her humanity, nor does it dominate her perceptions, or at least not in the unhealthy manner and to the extent Toby has been assuming. Toby's posturing is, of course, rendered convincingly enough, in terms of the artistic requirements, as an adolescently brutal reaction to his mother's and Faunce's political engagement. As the situation develops, and the polarity between Anna's position and that of Cecil develops, it is clear which is the healthier (in terms of the realities of day-to-day life) without being obsessive or neurotic.

It is an unsurprising confirmation of Anna's qualities of humanity, kindliness and patience that when she and Toby sleep together some weeks later, it is like an 'extension of conversation', because as Toby understands South Africa better, through Cecil as well as Steven, the High House as well as the House of Fame, he approaches a common political ground with Anna. They are both liberals in the distinct and peculiar South African sense of the word: each *has had to become* one, through a baptism of fire in a wilderness where liberalism either withered long before flowering, or has not yet been born.

The difference, or distance, between the 'South African' and the accepted English meaning of 'liberal' is, in a sense, the subject of the book. It is a study in the semantics of life, and a critique of the impact of the metropolitan culture, of its system of 'meanings' or values, on South African society. Liberalism in its English sense connotes breadth of experience, inclusiveness, universality, a 'broad-based tolerance'; the narrow and precarious bridge across the chasms of everyday insanity that the word as life-style suggests in its South African context is fully evoked at the end of the book, after Steven's death and Cecil's permanent defection from life. Toby is to go to Cape Town on business for a month; he has lent his car to Sam, who takes him to the railway station and stays to see him off. Anna Louw has just been arrested on a charge of treason (the reference is to the famous mass 'treason trial' of political dissidents in the late 'fifties, which failed in 1961). In the same issue of the newspaper announcing the arrests, on the 'social' page, Toby notices 'the face of Cecil, with Patterson, at a charity cabaret in a night-club'. At the station, with Sam, Toby notes:

> The two pieces of newspaper rested in my wallet in polarity. In a curious way, they set me at peace; the letter that lay with them was the long letter to Faunce, written at last, asking him if he was still serious about replacing Hollward, and if so, telling him that I would stay on indefinitely. (p. 265)

Thus, just before the end, with the resolution of the tension between the two women he has in some way loved in the world of strangers, Toby's commitment appears to have been made – for the time being, at least. But there is an element of profound doubt, which tends to negate the whole constellation of beliefs and attitudes which constitutes liberal humanism, and which Toby has in the end adopted as a basis, in default of a better, for his dealings with South Africa. This is introduced by Sam, and it is actually a restatement, a structural complement of an important thematic note struck once before. Sam's intelligence is penetrating; his steady adherence to the values of bourgeois liberal humanism is informed by a relentless and deep knowledge of the facts, of the truth of his situation. Twice, after Steven's death, he illuminates the reality of life in a way his dead friend could have done; after the funeral he and Toby walk together.

> . . . to the top of the ash-heap that made a promontory near

their house. Spring was coming; even up there, a stripling peach-tree that had found a hold of soil under the ash put out a few fragments of thin, brilliant leaf. Beneath us, the township smoked as if it had just been pillaged and destroyed. 'I've sold my car,' [Sam] said. 'That's where I was on Tuesday when you came. I'd promised to deliver it.'

I knew how proud he was of the little Morris, how to him it was part of the modest stake in civilized living it was so hard for Africans to acquire. 'But why? What was wrong with it?'

'My brother had to have some money. Ella's got two sisters who want to go on at school. Oh, a dozen different reasons, all boiling down to the same thing – cash.'

'That's a damned shame.'

He smiled, to put me at ease. 'Toby, man, the black skin's not the thing. If you know anybody who wants to know what it's like to be a black man, this is it. No matter how much you manage to do for yourself, it's not enough. If you've got a decent job with decent money it can't do you much good, because it's got to spread so far.

'Steven once said it wasn't worth the effort to live as you and Ella do, to try and keep up some sort of standard against the odds.'

'It's always worth it, for me,' said Sam, grinding the heel of his shoe into the ash. A group of children wandered up on to the ash heap; they seemed to belong there, as seals belong on rocks – the dusty skin, the bare backsides, the yellowed eyes, the animal shrillness of their wanderers' voices. As we passed them, they called out at us. 'They only know how to curse,' Sam said, and turning on me in sorrow, shame and anger, burst out, 'The way that he died! A man like him! Running away in a car with a bunch of gangsters! D'you think if he'd been a white man that's all there would have been for him?' (pp. 255–256)

It may be that Sam succeeds better as a character than Steven simply because the values he adopts, the behaviour he is known by, are closer to a familiar norm than Steven's, and thus he is less of an imaginative creation than Steven. He is a kind of polarity to Steven in the very moderation of his desires, as the passage just quoted shows. It demonstrates the futility of Steven's counter-ideology by an exposition of the black situation which is crushing in its finality. If one is black, one is committed – there can be no such thing as a private life until freedom is sufficiently achieved to enable the individual to choose it. Sam feels it better to acknowledge this because such an acknowledgment is a conscious step on the road to freedom. The symbol of the peach-tree on the ash-heap, surrounded as it is by an image of destruction which is the quality of daily life, and by corrupted, cursing children – a poignant image – and in the shadow of Steven's death, demonstrates how tenuous is the hope which the author sees in the situation. But hope, quite explicitly, she does see, and she reposes it mainly in Sam. It is fitting that Toby's last encounter in the book should be with Sam. Three levels of consciousness of the South African reality operate in the structure – all of which Toby comes into contact with and learns from: the existential plane shared by Steven and Cecil, that ends in despair; the level of political activism, which in practical terms may end in futility but is at least an honest and healthy response to a sick reality – this is the level of Anna Louw; and the deepest and most persistent awareness that human beings have a duty to live on a level of conscious self-acceptance, to try to create themselves whatever the hostility of the environment, in accordance with their instinctive needs for decency and dignity. This is Sam's endeavour, and it springs from a knowledge of his circumstances that amounts to wisdom of life.

This wisdom is epitomized in two encounters between Sam and Toby, one at the beginning of their acquaintance, the other the closing episode in the book. In the first, Toby telephones to Sam to get Steven's address:

'You can try him at this number, Mr Hood. He's not there all the time, but they'll take messages for him. It's a printer's: 31-6489- got it?' I thank him and said I hoped I'd see him again some time. He laughed embarrassedly and said, 'I wonder if we will,' as if it were not a simple matter that would be likely to be brought about without any particular effort on our part. (pp. 111–112)

Passed over at the time as less than ominous, and apparently denied by the course of events, this is taken up and developed at their parting, which concludes the book. At the railway station they say good-bye; Sam's wife is pregnant.

'I don't suppose we'll get down to writing, but I'll send you a telegram when the child's born. If it's a boy we're going to call it after Steven. I wish you could have been the godfather, Ella says she doesn't know anyone else she wants . . .' he was

panting under the weight of a heavy case, and we were being
buffeted together and apart by the press of people.

'Good God,' I said, twisting my head to him, 'you talk as if
I'm going for good. I'll be back in a month.The baby'll be just
about born. I'm not leaving the country.' . . .

'What's that? I do what?' shouted Sam, grimacing in the
effort to follow what I was saying . . . We stopped at the top of
a flight of steps; he would have to use the other, for black men,
further along . . . he was looking at me, a long look, oblivious
of the people pushing past, a look to take me in, and he was
smiling slowly, wryly, the pure, strange smile of one who is
accustomed to the impossible promise that will be broken, the
hand, so warm on the quay, that becomes a flutter across the
gulf and soon disappears.

He looked at me as if he had forgiven me, already, for
something I did not even know I would commit. 'Who
knows,' he shouted, hitching up his hold on the case, as people
pushed between us, 'Who knows with you people, Toby, man?
Maybe you won't come back at all. Something will keep you
away. Something will prevent you, and we won't –' the rest
was lost as we disappeared from each other down our separate
stairways. But at the bottom of the steps, where the train was
waiting, he was there before me, laughing and gasping, and we
held each other by the arms, too short of breath to speak, and
laughing too much to catch our breath, while a young
policeman with an innocent face, on which suspicion was like
the serious frown wrinkling the brow of a puppy, watched us.
(pp. 264–266)

The cadences of *The Dry Salvages* – 'the impossible promise
that will be broken, the hand that becomes a flutter across the gulf
. . .' – indicate the appropriate level on which optimism is declared
at the moment of parting. Sam is committed to history, to the
historic process of the advancement of his people; in terms of this
level of historic experience can the here and now of personal
redemption be found in his life? He knows the short-term
disappointments of the individual, personal dimension, but he
nonetheless seeks to operate on this level. He and Toby are subject
to 'the irritated eddy of the people whose way we were deflecting' –
the image conveys the isolation of liberals on the stream of South
African life – but Sam is better aware than Toby of the chances of
being swept apart by that eddy.

Thus the ending is nicely balanced between cautious optimism for a future where friends may celebrate a birth together, and an awareness of the peculiar and terrifying quality of innocence possessed by the evil that will prevent that celebration, if it can. Sam embodies a further stage of awareness: it concerns the nature of European – what I have loosely called 'metropolitan' – liberalism. Sam sees as the major component of white liberalism good, honest and sincere intentions – and he discounts them. A person in Sam's position cannot rely on good intent alone, and Nadine Gordimer is not yet ready to indicate how the white liberal is to approach the problem of operating on the same historic plane as the blacks in South Africa, though this is the subject of her next two novels.

3   Occasion for Loving

The links between Toby in *A World of Strangers* and Jessie, the
central character of *Occasion for Loving*, Nadine Gordimer's next
novel, are strong, and reinforced by one short story – the last one,
and the only one to embrace an explicitly political theme, in
Friday's Footprint,[1] the collection that comes between the two
novels. Called 'Something for the Time Being', it deals with a black
politician's attempts to find work. Released after three months in
prison awaiting trial – because he has refused bail – on charges that
are eventually quashed, he is dismissed from his skilled job as
foreman packer in a china factory by exasperated but not
unsympathetic employers; he has been in prison 'three or four
times since 1952'. A white liberal contact finds him unskilled
employment in the factory of a friend's husband; the latter is one of
those cautious 'civilized men' whose business success makes them
see the political and human anguish in South Africa in rather
academic terms, so he won't allow Daniel Mngoma to wear his
Congress button to work. The effect of his attitude is treated as two
separate but obviously linked and juxtaposed episodes in the two
marriages concerned: Chadders, the businessman, confronted by
his intuitive wife Madge, betrays the selfish caution of his real
nature to her; while Ella Mngoma turns on *her* husband's
principles, on the man himself, the arrogance of whose purity has
robbed her and her child of such security as their environment
might have otherwise afforded them – or so it seems. Two
apparently similar acts, each within a marriage, are being
compared; and the author does not flinch from judgment.

> She took her hand down swiftly and broke into trembling,
> like a sweat. She began to breathe hysterically. 'You couldn't
> put it [the badge] in your pocket, for the day,' she said wildly,
> grimacing at the bitterness of malice toward him.

[1] *Friday's Footprint*, (London, Gollancz, 1960), p. 236.

He jumped up from the table. 'Christ! I knew you'd say it! I've been waiting for you to say it. You've been wanting to say it for five years. Well, now it's out. Out with it. Spit it out!' She began to scream softly as if he were hitting her. The impulse to cruelty left him and he sat down before his dirty plate, where the battered spoon lay among bits of gristle and potato-eyes. Presently he spoke. 'You come out and you think there's everybody waiting for you. The truth is, there isn't anybody. You think straight in prison because you've got nothing to lose. Nobody thinks straight, outside. They don't want to hear you. What are you all going to do with me, Ella? Send me back to prison as quickly as possible? Perhaps I'll get a banishment order next time. That'd do. That's what you've got for me. I must keep myself busy with that kind of thing.'

He went over to her and said, in a kindly voice, kneading her shoulder with spread fingers. 'Don't cry. Don't cry. You're just like any other woman.'[1]

This passage, which is the finale of the story, contrasts with the last exchange between the liberal, intuitive Madge and her high-principled businessman husband, who has allowed her to persuade him to employ Mngoma and then insisted on various theoretical grounds that he may not wear his Congress badge, but actually because he is afraid of the opinion of his conservative business partner. This conversation takes place on the same night, almost at the same time, as the parallel exchange between Daniel and Ella Mngoma.

. . . presently she said, in exactly the flat tone of statement that she had used before, the flat tone that was the height of belligerence in her, 'He can say and do what he likes, he can call for strikes and boycotts and anything he likes, outside the factory, but he mustn't wear his Congress button to work.'

'. . . Yes, of course, anything he likes.'

'Anything except his self-respect,' she grumbled to herself. 'Pretend, pretend. Pretend he doesn't belong to a political organization. Pretend he doesn't want to be a man. Pretend he hasn't been to prison for what he believes.' Suddenly she spoke to her husband: 'You'll let him have anything except the one thing worth giving.'

They stood in uncomfortable proximity to each other, in

[1] *Friday's Footprint*, pp. 233–34.

the smallness of the bathroom. They were at once aware of each other as people who live in intimacy are only when hostility returns each to the confines of himself . . . She felt herself an intrusion and, in silence, went out.

Her hands were tingling as if she were coming round from a faint. She walked up and down the bedroom floor like someone waiting to be summoned, called to account. I'll forget about it, she kept thinking, very fast, I'll forget about it again. Take a sip of water. Read another chapter. Don't call a halt. Let things flow, cover up, go on.

But when he came into the room with his wet hair combed and his stranger's face, and he said, 'You're angry,' it came from her lips, a black bird in the room, before he could understand what she had released – 'I'm not angry. I'm beginning to get to know you.'[1]

The similarities and differences add up essentially to the same situation as was portrayed in *A World of Strangers* – of gaps permeating the texture of relationships in the society, preventing intimacy, and arising from one source only – the fact of colour, which is the foundation of social conventions, determining with finality all issues regarding personal relationships. Madge is closer to Dan than to her clever, 'principled' husband; but they, like Steven and Cecil, will never meet. Chadders' intellectual freedom is revealed in the vanity of its posturing; Dan's political gesture, in its practical futility, comes from his integrity as a human being. He, like Madge, judges situations and people intuitively, through the clarity of vision that comes from wholeness of purpose. The gap between him and Madge is the result of his familiarity with what, because of the colour of her skin, she will never be required to experience.

The linking factor between Steven in *A World of Strangers*, and Daniel Mngoma and Gideon Shibalo in *Occasion for Loving* is an aspect of the reality Nadine Gordimer was most interested in exploring during this phase of her development. Each is black, therefore oppressed, and concerned with the problem of making a conscious approach to freedom. Each defines his own response to the problem. Steven is a life-artist, and to some extent takes refuge in his art. Daniel Mngoma seeks in the political kingdom his individual destiny, and Gideon Shibalo is a painter, who is also a

[1] *Friday's Footprint*, pp. 233–34.

veteran of political activity. Each is distinguished by an integrity which is confirmed through the experience of suffering – the only kind that matters in the author's work. The final and insurmountable barrier to fulfilment as individuals for all the white characters – the best ones – in her novels and stories is that they are prevented by the vast irony of their limitless power and comfort from undergoing this confirming experience.

Thus Jessie, thus Ann, thus Boaz, thus Tom in *Occasion for Loving* have a tentative desire rather than hope for a change which will not come in time for the salvation of the present generation: hence perhaps Nadine Gordimer's interest in children in *Occasion for Loving* and its successor, *The Late Bourgeois World*.

If *The Lying Days* dealt with a world being created through a vision developing towards maturity, and *A World of Strangers* with growth and change in an adult perception of a new environment, *Occasion for Loving* is characterized by a feeling of fixedness – of a world in which all the possible deceptions have been located and the depressing nature of reality charted, resulting in a stasis or equilibrium in which growth towards fulfilment is the most marked impossibility. It is also a world fixed in the present, for it has no discovered past. The novel marks a crisis in the author's development.

The central character, Jessie Stilwell, personified an aspect of the liberal dilemma in South Africa. She is South African enough, in a necessarily ambiguous way: her background – the mine – resembles that of Helen Shaw, but with important differences.

> She was the daughter of a petty official on a goldmine; her father had been manager of the reduction works or something of that sort – she did not remember him. He died when she was eighteen months old and by the time she was three her mother had married again, this time a Swiss chemical engineer on the same mine, an intimate friend of the family, Bruno Fuecht. The Fuechts had no children and Jessica Tibbett remained a cherished only child. She was her mother's constant companion, and this intimacy between mother and daughter became even closer when the child developed some heart ailment at the age of ten or eleven and was kept out of school. She was taught at home by a friend of her mother's, and when she grew up, during the war, she left her mother's house only to marry. A son was born of the war-time marriage, and her young husband was killed. She lived on her

own – with the baby, of course – for the first time in her life, and worked and travelled for a few years before she met, and finally married, Tom Stilwell.[1]

When the story opens she has been married to Stilwell, a lecturer in history at the university in Johannesburg, for eight years, and they have three girls besides the son of her first marriage. They live in a large old house with a garden which 'did not have many flowers but . . . was dark and green'. (p. 9). The novel is set in the late 'fifties or early 'sixties, during the struggle against the introduction of apartheid in the universities. The Stilwells are expecting house guests, a researcher in African music and his young wife. The musicologist, a Jewish South African called Boaz Davis, has been in England for ten years, and his attractive wife, Ann, though born in Rhodesia, has lived most of her twenty-two years in Britain.

The Davises come to stay with the Stilwells: Boaz goes on frequent field trips; Ann discovers through Jessie the places where black and white society overlap, and has an affair with Gideon Shibalo, a gifted artist who has forfeited a scholarship for study in Europe because the government refused him a passport, on account of his political activities. The Davises' marriage flounders, then seems to be mending; but suddenly Gideon and Ann decamp, share a wild and dangerous odyssey in a small car in the South African countryside and turn up for shelter at a secluded beach cottage at the south coast where Jessie is on holiday with her daughters. The couple decide to escape from South Africa and make plans to do so; but suddenly and mysteriously Ann returns to her husband. She and Boaz leave immediately for Europe via the east coast and the Seychelles; Gideon is left behind.

Although, as this outline suggests, there is plenty of coming and going within the plot, in fact the significant action is located entirely within the personality of Jessie Stilwell. The novel is a sort of psychological mystery, an internal quest for identity that has to be undertaken by Jessie Stilwell; it belongs to the mystery genre because there are gaps, blanks, missing clues which must be sought, and jessie doesn't know in which direction to turn to find them. But at the same time she is a human being, housewife, mother, she works, and must live a 'normal' life. Thus she cannot be, like the detective in fiction, single minded in her search for a resolution of a particular puzzle, pursuing it to its end with only brief diversions for the satisfaction of physical needs.

[1] *Occasion for Loving* (London, Gollancz, 1963), pp. 24–25.

Thus her neurosis (for that is what she is trying to resolve) is an internal analogue for the day-to-day dilemma of the South African liberal, who must make so many daily compromises simply to carry on living, that he is often quite quickly reduced to a static position in relation to the moral problems of his surroundings.

One of the structural problems of the book is that one is not quite sure which of the two is the objective correlative of which. Jessie's neurosis is the liberal dilemma; the liberal dilemma causes Jessie's neurosis. There is thus an uncertainty of focus that runs throughout the action, blurring its continuity; but within the very area of this stricture lies the boldness of the author's project.

Tom Stilwell is an historian, and at the time of the action he is devoted to

> . . . collecting notes for a history he hoped to write – a history of the African subcontinent that would present the Africans as peoples invaded by the white West, rather than as another kind of fauna dealt with by the white man in his exploration of the world. (p. 14)

In the character of his wife Nadine Gordimer creates the objective correlative for that process: because what she lacks is her past, and much of her time and spiritual energy is spent on the task of finding it. She is not merely typical or symbolic as a South African; indeed, the former she is certainly not, and to insist on the latter would be to beg the question. She emerges as a kind of archetype; as though she doesn't realize that the past that she is searching for is in fact the history of the land. On this fact the structure of the book is built.

> Like many people, Jessie had known a number of different, clearly defined, immediate presents, and as each of these phases of her life had closed by being replaced with another, it had lost reality for her; she no longer had it with her. The ribbon of her identity was always that which was being played out between her fingers; there was no coil of it continuing from the past. I was; I am: these were not two different tenses, but two different people. (p. 23)

This sensation of being without a past or future, of living from moment to moment, is the immediate cause of her unhappiness, her suspicious unwillingness to have the Davises to stay, her almost brutal rejection of Morgan, the adolescent son of her first marriage, her uncreated past. The first weekend after Ann Davis's arrival, a party is arranged to take her to see the traditional tribal dancing presented by the goldmines on Sunday mornings near the mine compounds. Jessie, who had grown up on a mine, sits with her daughters and watches:

> Their feet echoed through Jessie's ribs; she felt the hollow beat inside her. The Chinese-sounding music of the Chopi pianos, wooden xylophones large and small, bass and treble, with resonators made of jam tins, ran up and down behind the incessant shrill racket of whistles. Now and then a man opened his mouth and a shout came out that is heard no more wherever there are cities; a voice bellowed across great rivers, a voice that bellies wordlessly through the air, like the trumpeting of an elephant or the panting that follows the lion's roar.
>
> And it was all fun. It all meant nothing. There was no death in it; no joy. No war, and no harvest. The excitement rose, like a breath drawn in, between dancers and watchers, and it had no meaning. The watchers had never danced, the dancers had forgotten why they danced. They mummed an ugly splendid savagery, a broken ethos, well lost; unspeakable sadness came to Jessie, her body trembled with pain. They sang and danced and trampled the past under their feet. Gone, and one must not wish it back. But gone . . . The crazed Lear of old Africa rushed to and fro on the tarred arena, and the people clapped.
>
> (p. 37)

The suggestion is that the source of Jessie's neurotic unhappiness, her sense of living outside the process of time, is very closely linked to certain aspects of the African experience in South Africa. The connection has to be unravelled, understood; the process of doing so is complex and dangerous. The fundamental stumbling block for white liberals in South Africa is the difficulty they must undergo in reversing the basic assumption of separateness with which they are brought up. This is much more subtle than mere political or educational indoctrination; it is the inevitable result of the pattern of living that every white South African child experiences in one way or another, to one degree or another. The evidence of the senses is overwhelming and it all seems to indicate the total separation of fates between black and white: the black man serves, the white is served, but all meaningful areas of behaviour are acted out in complete separation. Of course, this pattern in itself is a distortion of a relationship, a reality that is already badly distorted. Nadine Gordimer's argument in this book is that for the white liberal the first task is to correct this distortion, to appreciate the depth not only of the historic, but also the emotional inter-dependence of the two groups. This means literally undoing the experience of childhood; reliving its traumas in the searing light of mature judgment, and readjusting the conclusions by which one's life has been lived. This is analogous, on the individual level, to the task Tom Stilwell has set himself – the reinterpretation of South African reality using the tools of the professional academic historian. His wife's is the harder task; the author's suggestion is, however, that it is a prerequisite not only for personal fulfilment but also for political effectiveness.

Thus Jessie, in her search for a personal past relevant to the reality she recognizes around herself but in which she is unable to successfully participate, internalizes the relationship between Gideon and Ann. Her past takes on meaning and substance when she learns to locate it within this stream of events and relationships; she gradually becomes the book her husband is writing, and Tom Stilwell's enterprize coalesces with Nadine Gordimer's – it is a momentous project. Thus, in some important respects *Occasion for Loving* takes up where *The Lying Days* leaves off. Jessie and Helen share basically similar backgrounds: they possess a common ideology and move in a similar adult ambience, though Jessie's is the rendition of the reality of nearly a decade later. Jessie is an older woman, and her perceptions are correspondingly more mature than Helen's; but the greater clarity of her judgment precipitates rather than prevents her inner crisis.

Because, after all, if Jessie's discovered world is the mature end of Helen's `seekings, what does it amount to? The answer to this question is positively dusty. Jessie is a liberal (within the South African context): she knows the rights and wrongs of that particular situation and tries, as much as she can, to put her knowledge into practice. She is, however, cut off from the larger tradition through which her liberalism comes to her, and she is well aware of this limitation.

A significant aspect of her symbolic status as South African is the ambiguity of her background. Early in the action her elderly and slightly crazed stepfather, the Swiss chemical engineer, decamps dramatically, to enjoy a last flicker of life in Europe, leaving behind the wife he hates and the country that has made him what he is. He dies within a week of his return to the continent of his birth; but before that, in a bare hotel room in Johannesburg while waiting for his flight to depart, he tells Tom Stilwell:

'I didn't expect [Jessie] to come. She's never been much like a daughter. Well, that's an old story. Never mind.'

Tom smiled. 'Well, she's only a stepdaughter.'

'Yes, her mother kept that up. For the memory of poor Charles, she said. We both loved poor Charles. Only she couldn't have loved him so much, could she? Eh?'

Tom was bewildered by the old man's wry grin, the surly, sly self-contempt that sounded in his voice.

'Charles?'

'Charles!'

'Jessie's father?'

The old man nodded with exaggerated vociferousness, like someone satisfying a child with a careless lie. 'All right, Jessie's father. My friend Charles. Only I couldn't have been such a good friend, after all, eh? She makes a great fuss, she bursts in tears when I bring up the name of Charles. Because we both loved Charles, she says. What's the difference; the girl and I never had much to say to each other, anyway.' (pp. 80–81)

Thus the element of deceit in the South African heritage from Europe, the dubiousness of its provenance, is stressed; on the individual level it is just another source of difficulty in Jessie's struggle to construct an identity.

In this respect she is crucially different from her complement, the black South African, Gideon Shibalo. He is forced on her perceptions in an intimately human situation, when he and Ann, exhausted and insecure, impose themselves on Jessie and her daughters at the beach cottage that is part of the dead Fuecht's estate. In two long conversations vital areas of the South African psychic landscape are mapped out; a dimension is added to the history of the culture.

No other person came. Ann went into the village one day and brought back a pair of swimming trunks for Gideon and gradually he found himself doing what she did, lying for hours as if he, too, had been washed up on this shore, like the fish or the seagull. The abandonment to the natural world was something that seemed to come so easily to the two women; even while he succumbed to it he watched them with some kind of alienation and impatience – it belonged to a leisure and privilege long taken for granted. If he sat about doing nothing it was always a marking-time, an hiatus between two activities or desires. It was a matter of despair, exhaustion or frustration.

'How long'd you been here before we came? A couple of weeks?' he said to Jessie one afternoon.

'That's right.' . . .

'What'd you do? Same as now?'

She leaned back on the book and smiled. 'I was alone. It isn't the same.'

'What's it all about, this alone business?'

'What business?'

'I asked your kid Morgan one day why he hadn't gone away with you, and he told, my mother likes to be alone.' . . .

'I'd always thought painters liked to be alone,' she said, questioning his question to her. '– Had to be alone, were alone.'

'I'm not a real one, I suppose. I don't feel it. There's always a feeling of others around, even if I'm working.'

'Really?' She began to have that look of pursuing the other person that comes when interest is roused. 'But what about those empty landscapes of yours, with the dust?'

'Just fooling about. Seeing the sort of thing some painter had done and trying it out.' He often went in for the sophistication of deprecation; he hid behind it where no one could get at him.

'Even when you're actually there with the canvas in front of you –' She returned to it, disbelieving.

'Yes, man, there's always the business of a friend who's going to turn up in half an hour, or something on your mind.'

'You feel connected all the time.'

'Mmm. You've got the pull.'

'When you're alone, you're connected but there's no pull,' she said. 'Now that you are here, I feel lonely.' (pp. 220–221)

What may seem an almost technical aberration in the normally meticulously constructed narrative is in fact a clue to the significance of this conversation. The very unusual device in the author's longer fiction of a dual point of view, here existing in the compressed span of a single passage, suggests the existence of two parts of a single mental experience, trying to communicate and achieve an organic wholeness. From this conversation emerges the revelation of the extent to which Gideon is the cultural victim of assumptions that have no intrinsic meaning for him but are part of the dominant group's day-to-day equipment; thus his ability as a painter is distorted in meaning almost to the level of the antics of the mine-workers' Sunday-morning tribal dances.

Thus within the same culture and the same historic experience, exist perceptual modes that seem in certain quite basic respects to be mutually exclusive, and yet their possessors are capable of sharing particular goals – those of political change, for instance. Gideon, for example, finds it impossible to understand that Jessie's behaviour is something central to the European liberal tradition, with its emphasis on solitude and individualism, personal fulfilment as a life goal, and the idea that each man is able to aspire to Godliness through his very separateness from other beings.

But this is all part of a process of exploration; at this stage no judgment is being made in favour of one part of the organism at the expense of the other. The paragraph which precedes the lengthy quotation above dwells on natural imagery.

A dead seagull on the sand was busy as a factory with the activity of enormous flies, conveyor-belts of ants, and some sort of sand-flea that made a small storm in the air above and about the body. Butterflies fingered the rocks and drifted out to sea. Dead fish washed up among smashed shells were pulled apart and dragged away to their holes by crabs. There was not *nothing here*, but everything. (p. 220)

The first connection that follows is between Gideon and these images, but the link is much stronger with the women, Jessie and Ann, through whom he learns this 'abandonment to the natural world', 'lying for hours as if he, too, had been washed up on this shore, like the fish or the sea-gull.' What are they being associated with, in this way? They are being associated with after-images of violent destruction, images of wreckage and rather disgusting decay, a whole concert of carrion-eating: fleas, flies, ants and crabs devour the dead flesh of the gull and the fish, the conventional symbols of power, beauty, integrity, and above all the purposeful solitude of romantic freedom, which immediately becomes the subject of Gideon's discussion with Jessie.

The implications are disturbing, and they prefigure a conclusion for which neither Jessie nor her creator was ready at this stage, and which is nonetheless prophetically hinted at near the end. Certain areas of the 'past', the 'tradition' Jessie is in the process of discovering, are dead, at least in the place she finds her existence. The romantic myths, potent forebears of the liberal ideology she

85

professes, are so much carrion washed up on South African shores. Yet she thinks she can find a life of moral meaning only through them. She has to discover an area of her past in which they still live, or a way of resurrecting them.

She explains the dilemma as it presents itself in practical terms, to those who are responsible for its current manifestation, Gideon and Ann.

> 'A year ago, *then*, I didn't want Boaz and Ann to come to us. But I didn't do anything to stop it. It was the sort of thing Tom and I have always done. One must be open to one's friends. You've got to get away from the tight little bourgeois family unit. In a country like this, people like us must stick together – we live by the sanctions of our own kind. We haven't any anonymous, impersonal code because the South African 'way of life' isn't for us. But what happens to you, yourself ... I don't know. The original impulse towards decency hardens round you and you can't get out. It becomes another convention.' (p. 243)

The image of the dead seagull does not augur well for her attempts to realize the 'anonymous, impersonal code' Jessie and other South African liberals need so desperately; neither does the departure of Fuecht, her eviscerated European father. (There is a remarkable image of his departure, seen through the eyes of Tom Stilwell, who has been manoeuvred into taking him to the airport:

> ... Tom watched him walk down the brightly-lit ramp to the dark runway. He did not look back or wave. He walked slowly but the extreme lightness of his body, hardly there at all inside the tailor's shape, suddenly came to the young man watching. (pp. 81–82)

Fuecht, the immaculately-clad but empty walking corpse, and the dead seagull express the meaning of the visitation of Europe upon this tip of Africa: Feucht the technologist gives his technology, is robbed of his humanity even as he robs his friend of his bride's love, and escapes to die; the seagull, European symbol of the free spirit, is eaten by ants and flies on the South African shore.)

As a result of the impact of the specific situation created by the arrival at her refuge of the lovers, one of whom happens to be in a mysterious way her archetypal complement, Jessie is able to come to understand through her enforced day-to-day participation in the highly artificial reality of the cottage – artificial only because it takes place in the diseased environment of South Africa – that if her moral life is to live and be lived by her, she must accept the negative implications. She must accept that liberal commitment to personal freedom in South Africa will entail at least initially a loss of freedom, and necessitate the curbing of one's natural impulse to secure one's own inner liberty.

Almost immediately after this vital act of self-clarification, Jessie is able to respond to Gideon in a new way – even to take the initiative in challenging *him* to an attempt at self-definition. This is of the greatest importance to *her* because of their psychic and historic relationship. She comes upon him alone in the living-room, making sketches of Ann.

'She's beautiful,' Jessie said.

'She is.'

She watched him, amused by his attitude of repose, while his hand and eye worked on their own.

'Gideon, you've got a wife somewhere, I suppose?'

'In Bloemfontein, to be exact.'

When she had been in the living room a certain time, she was always drawn to the curtain that sagged and the bit of carpet that had frayed away. Sometimes, as now, she even wandered up to these things as if she were going to mend them. She slid out of her sandals and stood on the divan to take a look at the top of the curtain, where it hooked to a rail. 'I've got a child, too,' Gideon said. 'I don't know if I'd know him if I saw him somewhere.'

She was trying to work loose a runner that had rusted against the rail, and her voice was tight with effort. 'Oh why is it like that?'

'You change.'

She could not get the runner free and stopped, with the confusion of an obstinate task in her face. 'But it's like lopping off fingers. In the end your life is nothing but bits and pieces.'

He did not want to be reminded of the woman who had been his wife and did not know what had made him suddenly mention the child. 'What's gone is gone,' he said.

'Then what's going to be left in the end?' She stood there on the bed. 'In a year's time, in five years, *this*'ll be gone perhaps. You'll see yourself here as if it happened in someone else's life.'

He saw that this frightened her in some way, but there was

no room in him for curiosity about others, there was no part of his apprehension that was not cut off by the concentration of forces that had brought him there; by what he shared with the girl, and what he could not share with her. He could not answer the woman, either, with the rush of affirmation for the present that suddenly came to him – but *this* is my life! Yet she spoke as if he had: 'You can't pick and choose,' she said. 'You have either to accept everything you've been and done, or nothing. If the past if going to be past, finished, this will be as lost as the things you want to lose.'

'There are things that are over and done with,' he said. 'You must know how it is.'

'I know how it is. You shed yourself every now and then, like a snake.'

'Got to live,' he said with a shrug.

'What's one going to be, finally? The last skin before one dies?'

He laughed. '– Ah but it's different. You have a nice settled life that goes on, a home and so on. If things get too hot here, you'll take your husband and your children and go and live the same way you've always done, only somewhere else, isn't that so, Jessie? – You've got the man you want, haven't you?' he added.

'Yes, but I lived before I loved him, and maybe I'll go on living after. I had another husband. I have another child. Sometimes I don't know him when I see him . . .' She seemed to expect something, and he looked up for a moment. 'But I am what I was then as well as what I am now; or I'm nothing.' (pp. 244–245)

This is the climax of the book: the final sentence of the passage states Jessie's case, explains her behaviour, defines her situation. The technique of presentation mirrors that of the previous long conversation between Jessie and Gideon, in the device of the dual or joint narration; again, it is as if one organism is undertaking an internal dialogue between two constituent elements, and again they complement one another, though this time the encounter ends on a note of tension which is unresolved – a sign of mutual recognition, of acceptance by each of the other's distinctness, a necessary step to whatever resolution is to be possible in the future.

Structurally, the presentation is not dissimilar from the

corresponding moment in *A World of Strangers*; the framework is identical, in that the exchange leading up to it takes place between a white and a black character, each in a way representative in terms of experience of a particular segment of South African life, each in pursuit of meaning. At these points the situations of Toby and Steven correspond with those of Jessie and Gideon, except that what Toby knows about the reality around him he knows from the outside, from the perspective of normality; whereas what Jessie experiences is a part of her being. Jessie, like Helen Shaw, has to construct and correct her perceptual equipment while living in, and with, the pressures that tend to its distortion; she may look outside for help, but it is at least possible that she will not understand what she sees.

This suggests the extent of the *difference* between Jessie and Toby, and the necessity for the rather tortuous method of construction used by the author in establishing the former. To some extent her technical approach may be said to fall between two stools, in that the inner explorations and probings that Jessie undertakes scarcely dovetail, one feels, with the fine net of detail with which the smallest jerks and collisions of personal relationships are recorded. It is as if a Lawrentian Gordimer does the introspective Jessie while a Jamesian one executes the exterior, as it were, with a fine brush. With Toby there is no such problem because the purpose of his existence is to take for granted, in a non-ideological, half-unconscious way, the very values, or moral position, which Jessie (and Helen Shaw) have to struggle so hard to achieve.

The climactic distinction between *Occasion for Loving* and *A World of Strangers* is an interesting one in terms of the development of Nadine Gordimer's view of the reality she chose to write about. The central assertion of the climax of *A World of Strangers* was one of identity, of common values and shared aspirations in a situation designed to keep people apart from one another, to prevent the normal possibilities of fulfilment arising out of personal relations; in *Occasion for Loving* it is a demarcation, a point of difference that cannot be ignored or overlooked, between Jessie and Gideon, between white and black, an unresolved tension between two complementary parts of the same historic reality.

So Jessie recognizes and announces Gideon's response to the terms of her historic separateness from him:

His attention covered the restive, furtive look in his eyes. She knew this withdrawal that came sometimes in the closest conversation, when you were made aware that you had lost yourself in the white man's preoccupations, when you were relegated to a half-world of doubts and nigglings that only whites afforded and deserved.

'I don't see much sense in digging up the past.'

She smiled, looking at him from a distance. 'We're not talking about the same thing. It's a question of freedom.'

'Freedom?' He was astonished, derisive.

'There's more than one kind, you know.'

'Well, one kind would do for me.'

'Yes, perhaps it would, because you haven't got it. Perhaps you'll never have to ask yourself why you live. – A political struggle like yours makes everything very simple.'

'You think so?'

'Of course it does. You're completely taken up with the practical means of changing the circumstances of your life . . . It's all done from outside, and from necessity.'

'I don't think it's quite as passive as all that,' he said ironically.

'Passive! That's the whole point. It's *all* action, agony, decision – oh my God, it's wonderful' – she made a mock blissful face, to break the mood between them. (pp. 245–246)

Although Jessie may seem to carry this passage on the back of her breathless spoken introspections, the presence of Gideon, subtly conveyed, is a formidable counterweight to her rather strained apologia. 'I don't see much sense in digging up the past' is the pivotal point of contrast; for the rest Jessie's personal discovery conveyed as self-revelation, seems to fail to reach its mark. Paradoxically, the expression of the discovery of areas of mutual isolation seems to reinforce the isolation itself.

Within the historical framework that contains them both, Gideon possesses certain advantages over Jessie of a somewhat less obvious and more convincing kind than those she advances in her passionate establishment of self we have just looked at. This is partly because they have an organic existence, whereas Jessie has been using the terminology of an ideological system that has no roots in the local soil; the duality of action and suffering only includes Gideon's situation in relation to Jessie's if their relationship (the word is used at full stretch) is resolutely stuffed into the ontological framework of Western humanism. The indications are almost extreme enough to suggest that Jessie is using what is in the South African situation a form of cant; clearly Gideon appears to think so at times.

Gideon's involvement with history and time is mainly seen through Jessie's eyes, though there are one or two daring occasions when Gideon alone becomes centre of consciousness. These are faintly uneasy township episodes, one general and the other more specific, put there to try to present a representative idea of South African reality, and to establish Gideon's personality more fully by giving him an environment, a world, of his own, where his operation is inevitably and infinitely easier than that of any white man. In this they do not altogether succeed, though the passage in which he talks to his brother-in-law at the latter's general store, is drawn with a fine eye for naturalistic detail and a successful idea of dialogue (no easy matter, it should be remembered, in the particular situation). It is also an opportunity for flashbacks, as Gideon remembers his married life: this gives him the dimension of depth in time.

While Gideon put the cup of coffee to his mouth, Sandile said, 'Clara was here. She was up here last week and she was talking to me a long time, and, well, she wants to come back to Jo'burg. It seems so, yes.' . . .

Gideon had just filled his mouth with the warm liquid and for the moment the impact of its taste, flooding his body, produced by far the stronger reaction. What is the word for nostalgia without the sentiment and the pleasure nostalgia implies? The flavour set in motion exactly that old level of consciousness where, in the house of the old aunt with whom he had been farmed out as a schoolboy, matriculation was drawn like the line of the horizon round the ball of existence; where, later, in the two neat rooms in Orlando, he had paid off a kitchen dresser and drawn 'native studies' on cheap scarves for a city curio shop. Threshing, sinking, sickening – the sensation produced by the taste became comprehension of what Sandile was saying . . .

Gideon felt himself drawing further away every second; the cosy store-room with its high barred window, the deal table and the primus, the smell of paraffin and strong soap, the familiar face of Sandile and the taste of coffee – a hundred doors were closing in him against these things.

'Right out, I can tell you.' (pp. 172–173)

Thus he rejects his wife's desire to rejoin him, because it stands for a negative continuity. His relationship with Ann, his access to his white friends' flat, his having won the scholarship, seem to combine to constitute a break with the past that is, in his case, final. On the face of it, there is nothing desirable or attractive in his experience of that past. Of course to a large extent the book is concerned with the general level of past existence: Tom Stilwell is engaged precisely, though theoretically, in the construction of a concept of it that will embrace Gideon's experience and place it in the context of its own continuity, while Jessie is involved with the same quest in practical, personal terms. The suggestion seems to be that the gap between reality in time and the experience of that reality cannot be resolved, in the South African situation, until Gideon becomes aware of the problem of continuity as it affects himself and others in the society. Because, as Jessie perceives, he forms part of an effortless historic continuity into which she herself may have to find some way of integrating her own experience.

Of course, she is only equipped to make this kind of discovery after the prolonged encounter at the coast between Gideon, herself and Ann. As they drive back to Johannesburg her inner voyage is paced by what she sees in the passing landscape.

> She drove ahead of them, parting an empty countryside where a tiny herd-boy, flapping like a scare-crow in the single garment of a man's shirt, waved to the car. Little groups of huts were made out of mud and the refuse of the towns – rusty corrugated iron, old tins beaten flat, once even the head of an iron bedstead put to use as a gate. The women slapped at washing and men squatted talking and gesticulating in an endless and unimaginable conversation that, as she passed, even at intervals of several miles, from one kraal to another, linked up in her mind as one. In this continuity she had no part, in this hold that lay so lightly, not with the weight of cement and tarmac and steel, but sinew of the earth's sinew, authority of a legendary past, she had no share. Gideon had it; what an extraordinary quality it imparted to people like him, so that others were drawn to them as if by some magic. It was, in fact, a new kind of magic; the old magic lay in a personality believed to have access to the supernatural, this new one belonged to those who held in themselves for this one generation the dignity of the poor about to inherit their earth

and the worldliness of those who had been the masters. Who
else could stretch out within himself and put finger-tips on
both touchstones at once? No wonder the girl had turned her
back on them all, on Boaz with his drums and flutes, on Tom
with his historical causes, on herself with her 'useful' jobs, and
chosen him. (p. 269)

While the imagery in the first part of this passage is certainly
successful, and one knows what the author means when she
contrasts sinew with steel, the second section fails to achieve the
significance it clearly aims at. The long and clumsy sentence that
distinguishes between two kinds of magic is dismally vague where
the need for the concrete texture of a specific presence is glaring;
and it is doubtful whether the author has established the necessary
degree of objectivity for either of the 'touchstones' she goes on to
talk about. It is all too assertive, too little related to fictively realized
experience on the part of Gideon; and too subjective, in that one
would expect something more definitive from Jessie at this stage.

Jessie goes on to complete her insight a few days later, when she

> . . . happened to have to drive through the township where
> Gideon lived, the continuity of the little communities of mud
> and tin on the road was picked up again. Mean shops and
> houses lurched by as she bounced along the rutted street . . .
> She sat among shiny furniture behind coloured venetian
> blinds; then in an office converted from an old house, where a
> money-lender and book-keeper, with a manner of business
> irritability and suspicion, hovered over the scratchings of a
> girl clerk who went about in slippers between black exercise
> books and a filing cabinet like a weary woman in her own
> kitchen. The verandah outside the place was littered with the
> torn-off sheaths of mealiecobs, and the children with mouths
> and noses joined by snot watched from the gutter. A mule was
> being beaten and a huge woman, strident-voiced, oblivious of
> her grotesque body and dirty clothes, bared her broken teeth
> at a man. Gideon had someone he loved here; parents,
> perhaps; friends. Taking Gideon, Ann was claimed by this,
> too, this place where people were born and lived and died
> before they could come to life . . . That was the reality of the
> day, the time being. Oh, it would take courage to choose this,
> to accept it, to plunge into it, to belong with it; for that was
> what one would do, with Gideon, even if one were to be living
> in another country. (pp. 269–270)

Again the rhetoric intrudes, too much is taken for granted or generalized from a trivial incident or image; the writing is too close to an evocation of local colour. Thus the total insight is flawed, though the controlling idea is valid, indeed, on two connected levels: Gideon is perceived as living in time, with past, present and future inter-relating a unified individual existence; and Jessie is capable of this perception because of the progress she has made in seeing herself in the same way, in resolving her antagonisms with the past and integrating herself into her historic reality. It would be too much to say that the author succeeds in conveying the impression that Jessie now sees Gideon as he really is. She is, however, insisting on the need to improve the texture of the liberal apprehension of reality, to make the liberal vision fuller by incorporating a much greater awareness of the complexity of existence – in a situation which her own prose shows to be deplorably susceptible to the elicitation of simplism. In other words, while it is necessary as a first conscious step for the liberal in the essential process of self-creation to realize for himself that 'all men are men', it does not follow that the *South African* liberal's *next* step should be 'all black men are white men'. Abolishing the difference at a stroke leads to the danger of living in a fantasy world. What Nadine Gordimer wants Jessie to aim at is an historic understanding, which expresses the magnitude of the task she has set herself.

Thus there is a contradiction between Gideon's stated rejection of the African past (made most explicitly at one of the author's set-piece dinner-parties – at the Stilwells', a most civilized affair, with both Gideon and Boaz present and making polite, not to say profound, abstract conversation – pp. 151–152), and the insights into and about him that Jessie gains as the result of her own quest. In fact, neither he nor Jessie reflects the historic past so much as a period in their own lives. In the end Jessie can come to terms with the failure of the historic tradition she is connected with, and vivify in the present those aspects of it that are relevant to her situation. But by the end of the book Gideon remains confused, because Ann rejects him, because he is unable to reveal the historic past in all its meaning to himself; and thus cannot locate himself in the present.

Of course Gideon (like Steven Sitole) is in an impossible situation in this respect: born in cities in a new culture, which is the deformed offspring of a collision between its parents that amounted to rape, the past is for him as intolerable as the nightmare of their present reality. For him the rural past is truly dead, and truly forbidding; that it extends into the present can only be ignored, as Gideon's remarks about his landscape painting poignantly illustrate:

'But what about those empty landscapes of yours, with the dust?'

'Just fooling about. Seeing the sort of thing some painter had done and trying it out.' (p. 221)

This renders with force and precision the image of Gideon as one who is perpetually excluded from the culture to which he (somewhat automatically) aspires to belong. (Compare the passage in Peter Abrahams' *Tell Freedom* in which he decides the matter – and certainly spares no effort to justify his decision – of which culture, in the South African context, is preferable to Africans.) For people like Gideon and Steven Sitole the need is to uncover the past in its full significance for the individual consciousness, by an effort of that consciousness; but the small matter of the political kingdom, the author acknowledges, has first to be sought and attained. She also suggests that the absence of an historic consciousness makes the immediate political aim so much more difficult to achieve. So Gideon is part of a vicious historic cycle.

This is illustrated by the way the book ends. Ann departs, suddenly and unexpectedly, with Boaz, back to Europe via the Seychelles; Gideon turns to drink, as he had done before, when he was refused a passport to take up his art scholarship abroad.

... None of his African friends took his drinking very seriously; he would 'come out of it', or perhaps would simply become one of those who always remained one of themselves, carried along, however broken, by their unchanging re-cognition of what he really was aside from the brawling and buckling legs and slurred tongue with which he was trying to destroy it ...

They came again and again to the stony silence of facts they had set their lives against. They believed in the integrity of personal relations against the distortion of laws and society. What stronger and more proudly personal bond was there than love? Yet even between lovers they had seen blackness count, the personal return inevitably to the social, the private to the political. ...

The Stilwell's code of behaviour was definitive, like their marriage; they could not change it. But they saw that it was a failure, in danger of humbug. Tom began to think there would be more sense in blowing up a power station; but it would be Jessie who would help someone to do it, perhaps, in time. (pp. 278–279)

This is not, of course, the finale; for a novelist like Nadine Gordimer it could never be. The personal level remains, elusive but eternal, surrounding all the temporary attempts of ideologies and codes of behaviour to come to terms with, impose form upon or grasp it. In the end, Jessie has come to terms with her past, which is illustrated by the return of her son Morgan from his school holiday and her much easier acceptance of him; but Gideon is a different matter. She next sees him at a party to which she goes alone, because Tom is busy completing his book, the new model history whose penultimate scene is about to be enacted by his wife, and which still, as it were, lacks its climax.

... Jessie left the room where the tape-recorder was for the room where Simon played the piano, and, slumped on a sofa with his head against the shoulder of a women as if against a doorpost, there was Gideon. He was drunk; he must have come very drunk. They had put him down there, out of the way, but apparently he wanted, every now and then, to get up and make a nuisance of himself, because the woman had the air of sitting there kindly to restrain him ... Jessie had come into the room to get away from the noise, and although the room was not much less loud than the one she had left, she felt the blare displaced at once by a deep, uncomplicated affection for this man. It flowed in in peace, one of the simplest things she had ever felt in her whole life ... She went up to him, putting aside her old superficial feeling that he would want to avoid the Stilwell household. But he was drunk, and did not answer her. She spoke to him again, and his gaze recognised something, though perhaps it was not her. He mumbled, 'White bitch – get away.'

Somebody said, 'Get him out before he spews over everything, for God's sake.'

'Even the pigment in his lips has changed – from drinking, you know how horrible it goes. What's going to happen to him?'

Jessie stood drawn up before Tom as before a tribunal.

Tom turned away. 'He'll be all right. He'll go back and fight; there's nothing else.'

When Jessie saw Gideon again, he clearly had no memory

of what he had said to her. They continued to meet in a friendly fashion, sometimes in the Lucky Star, occasionally at the houses of friends, but the sense of his place in the Stilwells' life and theirs in his that she felt that night never came again. So long as Gideon did not remember, Jessie could not forget. (pp. 287–288)

So in the end Gideon is left – or revealed – as holding all the power, the key to the resolution of an historic as well as a personal situation; but he is not yet free to use it, though of course the final irony is that Jessie, the heroine, is more than ready, she is prepared for its use. The final sentence in the book returns to, insists upon, the historic dimension as theme, tying it in irreversibly with the personal level.

For Tom and Jessie, as for Helen Shaw and even Toby Hood, there is no present time, and by the end of her third novel Nadine Gordimer's inability to endow her central character with a sense of living in a real present has come to constitute a weakness. Her heroines in *The Lying Days* and *Occasion for Loving* have both been preoccupied with the effort of establishing themselves in the present: their energies are constantly engaged in a conflict between the present and past or present and future or both; and the first three novels end with a sense of expectancy, of a new reality which will perhaps be reality itself, that may be about to dawn. Toby will return from Cape Town, Helen from Europe, and reality will be there: Jessie may one day help to blow something up, and then she will be participating in it.

In *The Late Bourgeois World*[1] the author attempts a fusion, and the attempt reveals the process of her development, and also makes *The Late Bourgeois World* a very different kind of novel from any of her previous ones.

The shift to the present – and future – is signalled in *Not for Publication*[2], the collection of short stories which appeared almost simultaneously with *The Late Bourgeois World*. The title story is about the childhood of a future black Prime Minister. The first paragraph turns the body of the story into flashback, and naturally a gap is left at the end, between the disappearance of Praise Basetse

[1] *The Late Bourgeois World* (London, Gollancz, 1966).
[2] *Not for Publication* (London, Gollancz, 1965).

from mission school on the eve of writing his university entrance examination, and his (presumed) reappearance as political leader. But the beginning sets the context for the action in what becomes the author's established territory, which might be called South Africa's historic present. It is, I think, important to understand precisely what is meant by this term, and the first paragraph of *Not for Publication* is a good starting point for a definition.

> It is not generally known – and it is never mentioned in the official biographies – that the Prime Minister spent the first eleven years of his life, as soon as he could be trusted not to get under a car, leading his uncle about the streets. The uncle was not really blind, but nearly, and he was certainly mad. He walked with his right hand on the boy's left shoulder; they kept moving part of the day, but they also had a pitch on the cold side of the street, between the legless man near the post office who sold bootlaces and copper bracelets, and the one with the doll's hand growing out of one elbow, whose pitch was outside the YWCA. That was where Adelaide Graham-Grigg found the boy, and later he explained to her, 'If you sit in the sun they don't give you anything.'[1]

This is a contemporary scene; the events within it could have taken place at any time within the last fifty years, remain current today, and show no signs of becoming less likely in the immediate future. From now on we find again and again Nadine Gordimer using such a situation as a starting point, from which she can interpret past and present simultaneously as a historically continuous process, denying the disjunction that plagued her heroine in *The Lying Days* and *Occasion for Loving*. The connections and relationships are all there, simultaneously present, cause and effect acting and reacting within the same fictive time-slice without the illusion of historicity, and offering a basis for at least a shrewd guess at, if not a commitment to, the future, the form and nature of the continuation of this phenomenon. This story terminates with the disappearance of Praise, the genius, perhaps to return to a version of his previous life. As one of his distant relatives in the township expresses it casually to the desperately searching Anglican priest who was Praise's headmaster:

> 'Maybe he's with those boys who sleep in the old empty cars there in town – you know? – there by the beerhall?' (p. 21)

[1] *Not for Publication*, (p. 7).

The final story in the collection, 'Some Monday for Sure' (pp. 193–208), possesses an identical structure, though its scope in time is a little less elastic. The opening paragraph links present and future, and places the action (again an extended flashback) in this continuous historic present.

> My sister's husband, Josias, used to work on the railways but then he got this job where they make dynamite for the mines. He was the one who sits out on that little iron seat clamped to the back of the big red truck, with a red flag in his hand. The idea is that if you drive up too near the truck or look as if you're going to crash into it, he waves the flag to warn you off. You've seen those trucks often on the Main Reef Road between Johannesburg and the mining towns – they carry the stuff and have DANGER–EXPLOSIVES painted on them. The man sits there, with an iron chain looped across his little seat to keep him from being thrown into the road, and he clutches his flag like a kid with a balloon. That's how Josias was, too. Of course, if you didn't take any notice of the warning and went on and crashed into the truck, he would be the first to be blown to high heaven and hell, but he always just sits there, this chap, as if he has no idea when he was born or that he might not die on a bed, an old man of eighty. As if the dust in his eyes and the racket of the truck are going to last forever. (p. 193)

The figure clamped to the back of the truck full of the sum of centuries of intellectual endeavour is, of course, symbolic, in his blackness as much as his apparent unawareness of time. One of the points emerging most strongly about South African reality in *The Late Bourgeois World*, and which appears for the first time towards the end of *Occasion for Loving*, is the idea of the experience of that reality having been frozen in time, almost like an extended repetition of itself. Everything moves, and goes on, along a timescale, and at the same time remains unchanged. This obviously suggests a crisis in values. The truck containing explosives thus may symbolize (or even represent allegorically) the author's vision at this stage (and it is a sort of temporary culmination) in her work, of the South African present. The truck may make trip after trip over the same route – and it does – always carrying the horrible potential of more than its own destruction within it. This suggests the historic significance of the underground movement's attempt to hijack it; it is an endeavour to change the present, to shift the current of history. And they do succeed, in a limited way: the man clamped to the back becomes conscious, or at least acts upon his consciousness against his fate.

When the narrator and his sister hear the plan to hijack the truck, their responses differ: the woman has a vision of her husband's death, which places her firmly in the repetitive cycle of the historic present; but her brother's perceptions are sharpened, the future beckons him.

> I knew it must be a Monday. I notice that women quite often don't remember ordinary things like this, I don't know what they think about – for instance, Emma didn't catch on that it must be Monday, next Monday or the one after, some Monday for sure, because Monday was the day that we knew Josias went with the truck to the Free State Mines. (p. 197)

The phrase 'some Monday for sure' introduces the same note of historic inevitability as is carried in the first sentence of the title story. Monday is the beginning of the working week and stands for the start of a new phase of the historic present – the future. The end of the story sees the beginning of this: the 'job' half-successful, Josias gone on from Dar-es-Salaam to Algeria or Ethiopia for guerrilla training, and the narrator and his sister installed in a flat in Dar (he waiting his turn to follow his brother-in-law, she working as a nurse in a local hospital) he with his face turned welcomingly towards change, she in a state of neurotic depression.

> I suppose she wants to be back there now. But still she wouldn't be the same. I don't often get the feeling she knows what I'm thinking about, any more, or that I know what she's thinking, but she said, 'You and he go off, you come back or perhaps you don't come back, you know what you must do. But for a woman? What shall I do there in my life? What shall I do here? What time is this for a woman?' (p. 207)

There have been signs before this that Nadine Gordimer has been trying to elevate the differences between masculine and feminine sensibility into matters, or at least a matter, of principle in relation to time. In both *The Lying Days* and *Occasion for Loving*, the men live for the present; the women in the future, while spending all their emotional energy scrabbling for a firm foothold in the present. One of the weaknesses shared by these two novels is that the author attempts to cover too much territory. The present is insufficiently known, the ground uncharted; so the search for stability must be accompanied by a description (which is often at the same time a discovery) of the topography. Thus the major advance in *The Late Bourgeois World* is the completeness of the degree of knowledge of the ground of action, the environment, the external reality of white South African experience. The historic present is at last fully created. It brings about the fusion, in the character of the heroine, of past, present and future, and thus (for the first time) depicts the emergence of a free spirit.

In order to understand the development of this process in the author's work until she produces *The Late Bourgeois World*, it is necessary to go back to the beginning, to two short stories in her first collection, *Face to Face* (1949). These are 'The Train from Rhodesia' (pp. 94–100, and pp. 48–55 in *The Soft Voice of the Serpent*) and 'Is There Nowhere Else where we can Meet?' (pp. 115–119, and pp. 92–96 in *The Soft Voice of the Serpent*). Time and place are sufficiently emphasized in these stories to suggest a powerful symbolic action in each; and in both, this action can be elicited from the imagery. In the first, 'The Train from Rhodesia', the opening sentence constitutes a section on its own:

> The train came out of the red horizon and bore down toward them over the single straight track.[1]

It is followed by a page of scene-setting, 'atmospherics' designed to evoke the placid ugliness of the tiny country station, with its 'squatting native vendors waiting in the dust', through whom 'a stir of preparedness rippled'. The writing is rather uneasy and rough at the edges, the imagery forced and even, at times, fanciful:

> The flushed and perspiring west cast a reflection, faint, without heat, upon the station, upon the tin shed marked 'Goods', upon the walled kraal, upon the grey tin house of the station-master and upon the sand, that lapped all around, from sky to sky, cast little rhythmical cups of shadow, so that the sand became the sea, and closed over the children's black feet softly and without imprint. (p. 94)

The metaphor is overwrought, but it is the kind of attempt at 'fine writing' that is excusable in a young writer. And perhaps the most gauche-seeming sentence in this section turns out in the end to possess definitive structural significance:

[1] *Face to Face* (Johannesburg, Silver Leaf Books, 1949), p. 94.

> The train called out, along the sky; but there was no answer;
> and the cry hung on: I'm coming . . . I'm coming . . . (p. 95)

The first sentence sets the symbolic frame of reference: it carries suggestions of power, destructive potential, control, and above all inevitability, a sense of determinism – '. . . bore down toward them over the single straight track.' There would appear to be no alternative to some kind of encounter between the train and 'them', the people at the station.

The symbolic connotations are realized in the specific encounter of a young (possibly honeymoon) couple on the train with one of 'them', the native curio vendors who line the platform. The event takes place amid the standard images associated with the halt of a mainline train at a country station in South Africa: dust, barefoot piccanins begging for pennies, passengers throwing them oranges and chocolate ('It wasn't very nice . . .') from the train windows. It centres around an artefact:

> It was a lion, carved out of soft dry wood that looked like sponge-cake; heraldic, black and white, with impressionistic detail burnt in. The old man held it up to her still smiling, not from the heart, but at the customer. Between its vandyke teeth, in the mouth opened in an endless roar too terrible to be heard, it had a black tongue. Look, said the young husband, if you don't mind! And round the neck of the thing, a piece of fur (rat? rabbit? meerkat?); a real mane, majestic, telling you somehow that the artist had delight in the lion. (p. 95)

The lion, symbolic artifice of Africa, is meant in some respects to confront the train, the symbol of the alien invader's inventiveness and power; it possesses individuality and life, participating in the idea of its creator; it is unique. It is also soft (but organic), wood against hard metal, a soundless roar against the hissing scream, the 'creaking, jerking, jostling, gasping' of the train, the symbol of change, 'civilization', and that movement in time called progress. The reaction of the 'young husband', and the nature of the artist's smile 'not from the heart, but at the customer', indicate that the two cultures have immediately taken up their accustomed positions for contact on the neutral ground of commerce. There is to be no real communication, and the ground is not really neutral, for the artist must submit his work to the necessity imposed on him by the alien values by which he has to live – or starve. He asks three-and-six for his lion, which the young woman wants to buy.

Too expensive, too much, she shook her head and raised her voice to the old boy, giving up the lion. He held it up where she had handed it to him. No, she said, shaking her head. Three-and-six? insisted her husband loudly. Yes baas! laughed the boy. Three-and-six? – the young man was incredulous. Oh leave it – she said. The young man stopped. (p. 97)

The young man waits at the window until the train begins to move out, and then:

Here, one-and-six baas! – As one automatically opens a hand to catch a thrown ball, a man fumbled wildly down his pocket, brought up the shilling and sixpence and threw them out; the old native, gasping, his skinny toes splaying the sand, flung the lion . . . The old native stood, breath blowing out the skin between his ribs, feet tense, balanced in the sand, smiling and shaking his head. In his opened palm held in the attitude of receiving, was the retrieved shilling and sixpence. (pp. 98–99)

By simply recording the normal actions and gestures that characterize casual contact between white and black in South Africa, the author renders the attitudes that underlie them, or did at that time, twenty harsh years ago. Arrogance, suspicion, patronage on the part of the young white man, a scarcely-hidden assumption that he is the arbiter of the value and nature of reality itself, and a helpless submissiveness on the part of the black, whose resignation is not untinged with ironic awareness. In their respective ages the purchaser and vendor stand in symbolic relation to one another: the old 'boy' accepts the young man's judgment about the value of his soul.

The young man, the male white South African, is thus, symbolically, dedicated to the present: his consciousness is the common consciousness of day-to-day reality, and he sees nothing wrong or unusual about what has passed. He feels no uncertainty over the validity of the present. He is thus surprised by his wife's reaction when he enters the compartment from the corridor, bearing his gift.

He was shaking his head with laughter and triumph; Here! he said. And waggled the lion on her. One-and-six! . . .

But how could you, she said. He was shocked by the dismay of her face.

Good Lord, he said, what's the matter?

If you wanted the thing, she said, her voice rising and breaking with the shrill impotence of anger, why didn't you buy it in the first place? If you wanted it, why didn't you pay for it? Why didn't you take it decently, when he offered it? Why did you have to wait for him to run after the train with it, and give him one-and-six? One-and-six! . . .

She sat down again in the corner and, her face slumped in her hand, stared out of the window. Everything was turning round inside her. One-and-six. One-and-six. One-and-six for the wood and the carving and the sinews of the legs and the switch of the tail. The mouth open like that and the teeth. The black tongue, rolling, like a wave. The mane round the neck. To give one-and-six for that. The heat of shame mounted through her legs and body and sounded in her ears like the sound of sand pouring. Pouring, pouring. She sat there, sick. A weariness, a tastelessness, the discovery of a void made her hands slacken their grip, atrophy emptily, as if the hour was not worth their grasp . . .

She sat there not wanting to move or speak, or to look at anything, even; so that the mood should be associated with nothing, no object, word or sight that might recur and so recall the feeling again . . .

The train had cast the station like a skin. It called out to the sky, I'm coming, I'm coming; and again, there was no answer. (pp. 99–100)

The rendition of the young woman's inner state is handled without much art, but the underlying point is not lost. The key image is the slackening of her hands 'as if the hour was not worth their grasp'. The malady is in the present and of it; the relaxation of grip reverberates beyond the young woman as far as those who made the train, whose hands and brains constructed the artefact of *her* civilization, that is conveying her in an irreversible direction to an unknown destination. Twice in the story, the beginning and the end, western civilization called out to the African sky 'I'm coming, I'm coming'; and twice there is no answer from the unknowable goal that lies in the future. Meanwhile the present is swiftly traversed, ungraspable, never satisfactory and never resolving into meaning. For the maker of the lion, perhaps, it has a meaning; but if that is so, then he may also be master of the future.

The general thematic resemblance to the concerns of two of the author's first three novels is clear: the agonized consciousness of the female main character circling round the central reality of things, debarred by historic customs from understanding it and prevented from fulfilment within it unless she does.

The other story, 'Is There Nowhere Else where We can Meet?' is perhaps less symbolic, in some ways more immediate; but it is also an expression of a well-known South African archetype. A girl walks across the veld on a winter morning, carrying a parcel and a handbag. She passes a black man dressed in tatters, smelling of old sweat. He follows her and confronts her, then attacks her, and the sense of the ultimate taboo being broken is captured:

> She wanted to throw the handbag and the parcel at him, and as she fumbled crazily for them she heard him draw a deep, hoarse breath and he grabbed out at her and – ah! It came. His hand clutched her shoulder. (p. 117)

But she is mistaken: the present is not about to be transformed into reality. Instead, one of the current myths about it is to receive its dubious, customary corroboration.

> . . . but he snatched at the skirt of her coat and jerked her back. Her face swung up and she saw the waves of a grey sky and a crane breasting them, beautiful as the figurehead of a ship. She staggered for balance and the handbag and parcel fell. At once he was upon them, and she wheeled about; but as she was about to fall on her knees to get there first, a sudden relief, like a rush of tears, came to her and instead, she ran. She ran and ran, stumbling wildly off through the stalks of dead grass, turning over her heels against hard winter tussocks, blundering through trees and bushes. The young mimosas closed in, lowering a thicket of twigs right to the ground, but she tore herself through, feeling the dust in her eyes and the scaly twigs hooking at her hair. There was a ditch, knee-high in black-jacks; like pins responding to a magnet they fastened along her legs, but on the other side there was a fence and then the road . . . She clawed at the fence – her hands were capable of nothing – and tried to drag herself between the wires, but her coat got caught on a barb, and she was imprisoned there, bent in half, whilst waves of terror swept over her in heat and trembling. At last the wire tore through its hold on the cloth; wobbling, frantic, she climbed over the fence. (p. 118)

Nadine Gordimer transforms the surroundings from the conventionally romanticized wintry scene of the opening paragraphs of the story ('It was a cool grey morning and the air was like smoke . . . Overhead a dove purred. She went on over the flat straw grass, following the trees . . . Away ahead, over the scribble of twigs, the sloping lines of black and platinum grass – all merging, tones but no colour, like an etching – was the horizon, the shore at which cloud lapped.') to a truly hostile spiritual winter, in which trees, grass, and everything together hinder, obtrude, impede the woman's progress, preventing her easy escape. The effect of this is twofold: it transforms the character's perception of her environment, her *present*, and it abruptly introduces the reader to the real nature of present reality. The battering she receives from the natural environment begins the suggestion of what it feels like to be a black man in tatters, skin cracked by cold, in South Africa; and her momentary imprisonment in the fence and the tearing of her coat complete the experience. For a moment the real nature of the present is revealed to her, and she must, of course, reject the revelation, but the author allows it a vestigial though important effect:

There was the gate of the first house, before her.

She thought of the woman coming to the door, of the explanations, of the woman's face, and the police. Why did I fight, she thought suddenly. What did I fight for? Why didn't I give him the money and let him go? His red eyes, and the smell and those cracks in his feet, fissures, erosion. She shuddered. The cold of the morning flowed into her.

She turned away from the gate and went down the road slowly, like an invalid, beginning to pick the black-jacks from her stockings. (p. 119)

In questioning her actions she is questioning the entire version of the present on which her world, the world of white South Africa, rests. For a moment she has been confronted by the real present and such is its power that she is forced to recognize how unsatisfactory her version is, how like a pale and anaemic water-colour her idea of the wintry veld, compared with the reality of the grass-tufts tripping her, the mimosa-branches lashing, and the black-jacks pricking into her skin. Like the heroine of 'The Train from Rhodesia', she is brought face to face with the unsatisfactory nature of her interpretation of the present, the limited relevance to it of an assumed tradition (in the first case the superior technological civilization of the conqueror, in the second the sentimentalized poetasting of a decayed European romanticism); and for both of them, the future is, in an as yet indeterminate way, altered. The title of the second story clinches its symbolic meaning, confirming the importance of place as well as time.

These two stories are early encounters between black and white in the author's work. Each operates on a symbolic level, marking up the psychological and economic factors that complicate, and even determine the form of, such events. But in both of them, the key idea is to be found in the handling of time: the movement of the railway train constitutes an imposed version of the value of time, and its hour is not, in the end, worth grasping; and even the winter suffers the same kind of imposition, until its real presence is released. These encounters remain far from a true, human meeting-point between black and white, but they point the direction of Nadine Gordimer's development, and establish the very important connection in this respect between the white South African version of reality in general and the deep confusion about the significance of historic time that it entails.

In her first three novels, it can be argued, she explores the implications of the statements in these two early stories very thoroughly, but without arriving at a resolution of the prevailing historic confusion – though she has clearly a path in mind. It is significant that the novel which eventually breaks this time-barrier and presents a clear view of the true present, was dictated by events similar in meaning to those described in 'Is There Nowhere Else where we can Meet?' but historic in scale. And the outcome, the resolution of the plot, is not dissimilar, though different.

4 The Late Bourgeois World

And so we come to the point of fusion, hinted at but not reached by the end of *Occasion for Loving*, which ended, like its predecessors, in dissolution, tempered with a note of hope. *The Late Bourgeois World* starts with final dissolution, with a past doubly distanced by news of the suicide of the heroine's former husband. Elizabeth van den Sandt's activity may be compared to that of an archaeologist excavating and reconstructing the fragmented ruins of a past age, and arriving at a clearer idea of its meaning than its original inhabitants possessed. Somewhere among the ruins lie the shattered bits of the liberal's code. Whether they can be remade into a meaningful structure is the main problem posed in the book.

Nadine Gordimer's attitude to liberalism at this time had been made clear in *Occasion for Loving*, where she acknowledges the failure of the Stilwells' code, but leaves them with no alternative but to go on practising it. That her aesthetic world is largely a political one is borne out by her own account of the events that influenced this attitude between the completion of *Occasion for Loving* and the composition of *The Late Bourgeois World*.

> In 1962 a novel of mine was banned in the Penguin edition. There was no black-white sex relation in the novel . . . But there was close friendship across the colour-line, in fact the central relationship of the novel was that of a white Englishman and a Johannesburg African, neither in the least politically committed, who were drawn together out of temperamental affinity and a love of life. Far from exacerbating racial tensions, they and their circle showed – if anything – how easy it is for people of different races to get to know and respect each other simply as human beings.
>
> I then wrote a novel in which the central situation was a love-affair between a white girl and a black man, with all its social and personal implications. The book was not banned.

Last year I wrote a book on a very different theme. In the interim, many terrible events had taken place in the society from which I, like every other writer, take the substance of the life around me; political trials, detentions, repeated acts of sabotage, an attempted assassination of a Prime Minister. Poems, novels and paintings come not out of events themselves, but out of the echoes that arise from events. It is the creative writer's task to take soundings, to listen with the inner ear, to ask why; not to put things behind him, but to seek them out and examine them in depth. My short novel *The Late Bourgeois World* was an attempt to look into the specific character of the social climate that produced the wave of young white saboteurs in 1963–64. I tried to follow the threads of observation and intuition back, through individual lives, to examine how this tragedy might have come about. As an artist, I am not concerned with propaganda and my characters were shown in all their human weaknesses. What interested me was not to 'prove' anything, but to explore the interaction of character and situation in private and personal lives. What emerged from the book was the guilt of white society toward its own sons, who are, by its own definition, its failures: those sons who, if they won't act as white men for white men, are not allowed to act at all.

This book was banned. It moved in the area of doubt about the traditional way of life and thought in South Africa, it moved into the most heavily mined area of censorship. And – here is the crucial point – *it came up with conclusions that did not fit in with the official view of events.*[1]

The Late Bourgeois World is constructed to bring within one orbit the areas of certainty and the area of doubt, their common history and the common outlook underlying them. Max van den Sandt, Elizabeth's former husband, is the son of a prominent industrialist who was a United Party member of parliament – until his son was arrested for sabotage, and he resigned his seat. His party represents what may loosely be defined as the 'English' tradition in the white South African polity; one of Nadine Gordimer's longest-standing preoccupations has been the attempt to elucidate the meaning of this tradition in the day-to-day life of the present. She acknow-

[1]"South Africa: towards a desk-drawer literature', a talk to the students of the University of the Witwatersrand, published in 'The Classic', Johannesburg, vol. 2, no. 4, 1968, pp. 66–74 (extract quoted from pp. 70–71).

ledges the complexity of the problem and her own past failures, however partial, by the device of making Max's father into a (literally) representative figure, and then allowing the meaning of the tradition he represents to work itself out existentially in Max himself. Thus the tradition is seen in its function as heritage.

The heritage is in pretty bad shape. It is examined from several angles, turned upside-down and shaken, as it were, and what is revealed is mainly the weakness of its fabric. Max is neglected as a child, and turns viciously against what his parents offer him when he comes to maturity. He seeks, instead of their gimcrack substitutes – the cocktail party and the country club – the real thing: personal relationships, love, brotherhood, tolerance and compassion. In other words he seeks the Western Christian heritage, of which his father is the self-appointed preserver in the political realm. But when van den Sandt M.P. and his friends discuss politics, they talk about other things.

> . . . when Mrs van den Sandt spoke of 'we South Africans' she meant the Afrikaans- and English-speaking white people, and when Theo van den Sandt called for 'a united South Africa, going forward to an era of progress and prosperity for all' he meant the unity of the same two white groups, and higher wages and bigger cars for them. For the rest – the ten or eleven million 'natives' – their labour was directed in various Acts of no interest outside Parliament, and their lives were incidental to their labour, since until the white man came they knew nothing better than a mud hut in the veld.[1]

This is part of a flashback, related to similar hints and glances found in *The Lying Days*. Of course, Helen Shaw's parents are representative in a different kind of way from Max van den Sandt's, but they stand for the same historical phenomenon – indeed they themselves would no doubt consider that they 'stood for' the same 'things'. Meanwhile, Max is at university, operating somewhere basically in the same field as Helen Shaw and her friends, though in an area of it where the going is faster.

> When Max was a student they didn't take him very seriously, of course, and regarded what they knew of his activities in student politics, along with his pointed non-appearance at dinner parties and his shabby clothes, as youthful Bohemianism. I don't know whether they ever knew that he was a

[1] *The Late Bourgeois World* (Victor Gollancz, London, 1966), p. 40.

member of a Communist cell; probably not . . . They had no idea that he was spending his time with African and Indian students who took him home where he had never been before, to the locations and ghettoes, and introduced him to men who, while they worked as white men's drivers and cleaners and factory hands, had formulated their own views of their destiny and had their own ideas of setting about to achieve it. For the van den Sandts none of this existed . . . (pp. 39–40)

This reminiscence develops out of another one, of Max's trial, which in its turn is evoked by a passing snatch of conversation that takes place in the fictive present. It is a good moment to indicate the main lines of Nadine Gordimer's structural strategy in her first extensive attempt to deal with the historic present. The book is split into three levels: past, present and future time. The central and most immediate level is the fictive present, and the action within it is limited in its duration to one day. But all the events, subjective or objective, of this day, have their references in the past or future, and attain fulness of meaning, where they do, as a result of these references. The major event of the day is the suicide of Max, who has driven himself and a car full of documents into the sea at Cape Town harbour. The action opens with the heroine, at breakfast with her lover, receiving this news in a telegram. Obviously, this event has its point of departure in the past; but its relationship to the future (and its influence on the heroine's activity in the present) are demonstrated at once by her realization that she must spend the morning in driving out to the boarding school to the south of Johannesburg to tell her son (and Max's) what has happened, so that he does not hear of his father's death from another source.

Max's death thus sets up the long train of reminiscence and flashback which takes up much of the early stages of the book. But the author succeeds in the balancing feat of keeping the past in the background, as a source of information and meaning to the present, even though the duration of the fictive present is much shorter. This balance is achieved partly through the dramatic nature of the events that take place within the historic present: the heroine telling her son of his father's death, visiting her senile grandmother in a home for the aged, entertaining an activist underground politican, who is wanted by the police, to dinner.

However the relationship between time-levels is not one-sided. The past derives depth and meaning from the present almost as much as it supplies. Moreover a further, transcendental dimension, underlines the author's message: the day on which these events take place is also the day of the first American spacewalk. The incorporation of this spectacular event adds substance to the most difficult time-level to render with conviction – the future. It is not, however, an arbitrary structural device, but has its place in the story of Max, Elizabeth, their son Bobo, and Luke, the resistance fighter, and in the significance of this particular day to the life of the late bourgeois world.

In more immediate terms, if Max represents a stretch of the past made meaningful, and Elizabeth embodies that meaning – and others – in the present, it is Bobo first who continues the line and is identified with the future. Elizabeth's first excursion into memory, occurs as she drives through the highveld to Bobo's school:

> It was all exactly as it had been. When I was a child. When Max was a child. It was the morning I had woken up to, gone out into again and again; the very morning. I felt the sun on my eyelids as I drove. How was it possible that it could be still there, just the same, the sun, the pale grass, the bright air, the feeling of it as it was when we had no inkling of what already existed within it. After all that had happened to us, how could this morning, in which nothing had yet happened, still exist? Time is change; we measure its passing by how much things alter. Within this particular latitude of space, which is timeless, one meridian of the sun identical with another, we changed our evil innocence for what was coming to us; if I had gone to live somewhere else in the world I should never have known that this particular morning – phenomenon of geographical position, yearly rainfall, atmospheric pressures – continues, will always continue, to exist. (pp. 11–12)

With this first flashback the process of working through Max's life as a guide to the meaning of the present is begun. But the breadth of its frame of reference should not be allowed to obscure its intensity, which works well on two levels: that of the perceptual experience itself, rendered in the emphatic repetition 'again and again' and the variation 'the very morning', as well as the kinetic 'I felt the sun on my eyelids'; and the intense quality of the thought generated by the experience, rendered again through repetition, this time of concepts rather than words – '. . . which is timeless, one meridian of the sun identical with another', or 'this particular morning – phenomenon of geographical position, yearly rainfall, atmospheric pressures – continues, will always continue, to exist' –

the last example amounting to mirror-imagery. All these structures revolve around the central, striking statement: '– we changed our evil innocence for what was coming to us.' In the midst of the essential impersonality, the cyclical repetitiveness of everyday events, something *did* happen which was outside as well as within this scheme, and this something, contrasted with the apparent stability in time of the surroundings, is characterized as change. Although the change is unspecific at this stage, it is nonetheless defined to determine (in a remarkably compressed manner) the framework of judgment for the particularization that ensues. The certainty that emerges is that what is left behind as the change takes place is the main evil: unconsciousness, unawareness, insensitivity. And the nature of 'what was coming to us', no doubt depends upon the manner of the emergence from 'evil innocence', and unconsciousness to awareness. Its substance forms the heart of Elizabeth's exploration of her past with Max, but carries over into the fictive present, Elizabeth's 'real' world, as well. The wording 'what was coming to us' conveys a suggestion of inevitability, of nemesis; prefiguring, perhaps, the personal unease evoked by a historic description such as 'the late bourgeois world'. There is also an interesting hint that the act of change is itself conscious, *not* the inevitable result of a process: 'we changed . . .' – the verb is active. The idea behind this may be that many members of the same group do not make this choice, but remain in the state of 'evil innocence' which is associated in the passage with the South African landscape through which Elizabeth van den Sandt is driving.

Thus this memory, overflowing from the fulness of a particular experience (of course, this experience does not stand alone; its intensity comes partly out of the past, out of the news of Max's suicide) begins Elizabeth's voyage into the past, her rounding out of the meaning of both past and present through memories of Max.

This level of the action, involving the past through and with Max, is rendered as a movement in time running parallel and simultaneously with the fictive present. Beginning with the chain of memories sparked off by Elizabeth's perceptual flash during her drive through the countryside, the continuity of the 'simultaneous past' is sustained through a series of carefully-operated technical devices. For example, when Elizabeth returns from her son's school, she stops in a 'suburban shopping centre . . . to pick up cigarettes and something from the delicatessen.'

I had a cup of coffee in a place that had tables out on the

113

pavement among tubs of frost-bitten tropical shrubs. It was almost closing time for the shops and the place was crowded with young women in expensive trousers and boots, older women in elegant suits and furs newly taken out of storage, men in the rugged weekend outfit of company directors, and demanding children shaping icecream with their tongues. A woman at the table I was sharing was saying, '. . . I've made a little list . . . he hasn't got a silver cigarette case, you know, for one thing . . . I mean, when he goes out in the evening, to parties, he really needs one.'

And when he goes down to the bottom of the sea? Will he need a silver cigarette case there? (p. 32)

Thus the link is forged, between past and present, between two qualities of life that actually exist together in space and time but have a different historic significance, the difference being as absolute – but as subject to qualification – as that between past and present. The woman who speaks at the restaurant speaks from the world of the 'past', of 'evil innocence'. The extract continues:

She was exactly like Max's mother, pink-and-white as good diet and cosmetics could make her, the fine lines of her capacity to be amused crinkling her pretty blue eyes, her rose finger-nails moving confidently. (p. 32)

It is the world of *Max*'s past, Max's parents, the world of the white bourgeoisie – whose arrogation to itself of the right to total power, and the right to judge all in the terms reserved for itself, has not even been a conscious act, but has proceeded out of the quality of evil innocence that the author selects as the basic condition of the situation she is describing.

From this point the narration flows easily backwards in time, sweeping through a description of the good life of cocktail parties and braaivleis at the van den Sandts' country estate, the tolerant acceptance of 'little' Elizabeth, the country shopkeeper's daughter made pregnant by the spoiled son, and, swinging forward again, comes to rest at a moment during Max's trial.

I say of the van den Sandts that they 'were' this or that; but of course, they *are*. Somewhere in the city while I was drinking my coffee, Mrs van den Sandt, with her handbag filled, like the open one of the woman sitting beside me, with grown-up toys – the mascot key-ring, the tiny gilt pencil, the petit-point address book, the jewelled pill-box – was learning that Max was dead – again. (p. 36)

Each movement into the past is carefully linked with a perceptual event in the present; the gadget-stuffed handbag leads back to Mrs van den Sandt, whose world continues in its state of evil innocence, not merely to exist but to dominate. Once again the importance of time is stressed; the persistence of the late bourgeois world in the present is the starting point for this segment of the past.

> Their son was dead for them the day he was arrested on a charge of sabotage. Theo van den Sandt resigned his seat in Parliament, and he never came to court, though he made money available for Max's defence. She came several times. We sat there on the white side of the public gallery, but not together. One day, when her hair was freshly done, she wore a fancy lace mantilla instead of a hat that would disturb the coiffure. Her shoes and gloves were perfectly matched and I saw with fascination that some part of her mind would attend to these things as long as she lived, *no matter what happened.* (p. 36)

Nadine Gordimer is concerned to illustrate various inadequacies in the dominant world view. Thus she begins by describing its various techniques of defence – the fortification by gadgetry, the fanatical but automatic emphasis on external appearances – then she casually lets slip a suggestion of fearsome vulnerability. In a world view that doesn't regard time, there can be no understanding of death; so a man can die twice. The horrifying implications are confirmed almost immediately.

> At the recess as we all clattered into the echoing corridors of the courts, I smelt her perfume. People talking as they went, forming groups that obstructed each other, had squeezed us together. The jar of coming face to face opened her mouth after years of silence between us. She spoke. 'What have we done to deserve this!' Under each eye and from lips to chin were deep scores, the lashes of a beauty's battle with age. I came back at her – I don't know where it came from – 'You remember when he burned his father's clothes.' (p. 37)

The unconsciousness, the almost conscious ingenuousness that is the basis of Nadine Gordimer's 'evil innocence', persists into age, a continuing defeat running parallel in time with the superficial battle

115

of the beauty with age – the only level on which time is appreciated and understood. Elizabeth's rejoinder is pointless; she is talking to a sphinx.

> 'What? All children get up to things. That was nothing.'
> 'He did it because he was in trouble at school, and he'd tried to talk about it to his father for days, but his father was too busy. Every time he tried to lead round to what he wanted to say he was told, run away now, your father's busy.'
> Her painted mouth shaped an incredulous laugh. 'What are you talking about.'
> 'Yes, you don't remember. But you'll remember it was the time when your husband was angling to get into the Cabinet. The time when he was Chief Whip, and was so busy.' (pp. 37–38)

Mrs van den Sandt's confidence in the values she has inherited precludes her from the experience of understanding, which would lead to suffering, but which in turn might hold out hope of growth. She is immobile, fixated in a moral childhood. The realization of this does Elizabeth no good.

> I was excited with hatred of her self-pity, the very smell of her stank in my nostrils. Oh we bathed and perfumed and depilated white ladies, in whose wombs the sanctity of the white race is entombed! What concoction of musk and boiled petals can disguise the dirt done in the name of that sanctity? Max took that dirt upon himself, tarred and feathered himself with it, and she complained of her martyred respectability. I wanted to wound her; could nothing wound her? She turned her back as one does on someone of whom it is useless to expect anything. (p. 38)

Mrs van den Sandt's superficial invulnerability is all too symbolic of the white establishment which her son with his inefficient little bomb has tried to attack. The implication, a little buried under the somewhat muddled and exaggerated rhetoric of Elizabeth's denunciation, again relates to the group's unconsciousness of time – the suggestion that such a life is in fact a living death, since it admits of no change or growth. This suggestion is supported by the images of smell and decay with which the passage begins its metaphor of the preparation of a corpse for embalming. A picture begins to emerge of a group of people with no awareness of time, unaffected by change, a world of all-powerful grown-up children playing their selfish games to deadly purpose, but unable to learn from the blows they encounter, the cuts and bruises they inflict upon themselves as well as others.

The contrast between the narrator and the people whose colouring is their camouflage is achieved through the use of a device in the narrative technique. Elizabeth understands that she is subject to time, and even has her theory about it: 'Time is change; we measure its passing by how much things alter.' (p. 12). This knowledge enables her to adapt to the medium of time and intellectually to move about freely within it. But the author never allows this movement to become entirely 'free', that is wholly cerebral and unrelated to the real world. Thus the next, and last, specific recollection in this series is characteristically prefaced by a swift glance at her surroundings.

They were gathering together their weekend purchases all round me, the good citizens who never had any doubt about where their allegiance lay. The steady winter sun, so bonewarming, so reassuringly benign (perhaps we can't help feeling that if we have the best climate in the world we must deserve it?) shone on the shapes of bottles of wine and whisky, the prawns and cakes and bunches of flowers, plain evidence of the superior living standards of white civilization, that they were taking home . . . Home-made bombs have not shaken the ground under their feet, nor have the riots, the marches, the shootings of a few years back . . .

I too have my package of pork fillets and my chair in the sun; you would not know me from the others. We are all still alive and the cars are crawling impatiently one behind the other. Whereas Max is in the sea, in the soup, at the bottom of the sea . . . (pp. 42–43)

In their own terms (those of external appearances and the timelessness of experience) Elizabeth is indistinguishable to those 'good citizens', her fellow-whites, whom she happens to be judging; but the transition to Max raises the question of whether they would pay any attention to her, even bother to separate themselves from her, if they knew her thoughts. Max is at last irrevocably distinct, after all, only in death. What follows, organically related to the glance at the world outside that introduces it, is a reminiscence of the absurd, ineffectual, hopelessly gauche verbal attempt at establishing this sort of distinction in terms of present reality between himself and these very same 'good citizens' Max once made, years before, in a speech at his highly conventional sister's equally conventional wedding. Elizabeth squirms at the memory of his priggishness; but perhaps her shame comes from her own inability at the time – or since – to make that particular type of gesture, within the enemy stronghold which is at the same time one's own and only home.

Max's mistake in this instance (as in others) is also connected with time. He is prepared to take at face value what operates within his parents' group as a strictly limited and formal gesture to a dead past. As Elizabeth remembers the terms of his equally formal castigation, she finds the tellingly appropriate analogy:

> Poor Max – *moral sclerosis*! The way he fell in love with that prig's phrase and kept repeating it: *moral sclerosis*. Where on earth had he got it from? And all the analogies he kept raking up to go with it. Like our old Sunday school lessons – the world is God's garden and we are all His flowers, etc. (The Blight of Dishonesty, Aphids or Doubt.) And could there have been a more unsuitable time and place for such an attempt? What sort of show could his awkward honesty make against the sheer rudeness of him? *They* were all in the right, again, and he was wrong; and I could have kicked him for it. (pp. 50–51)

At this point they are both captives of a particular situation; in Max's case, however, the trouble goes deeper. He is still enmeshed in the moral confusion that typifies his parents' community, and although he has recognized the confusion, he is not destined to be free of it, however much he struggles. He is breaking rules that he still recognizes in his attempt to get other people to abide by them; for these others they have long been empty of active meaning. And so Max falls into the inevitable traps that await the privileged revolutionary. He can be, and is, got at in a number of ways from both sides. His ostensibly principled rejection of the values of white society as they are embodied in his parents simply make him a victim of those very values. He is thus unused to poverty and cramped conditions; he cannot function adequately as a husband, father or political activist, and his disordered life is the outward sign of a desperate search for order.

> Max shunned the van den Sandts' standard of success but in a way they triumphed in him passing on, like a family nose

or chin, the rage to succeed. He did not weigh in on their scale, but he retained the revengeful need *to be acknowledged*. It came from them: the desire to show somebody. What? The objects of his purpose were not demonstrable in the way that money and social prestige are. Why is it that these people always win, even if only by destruction? (p. 88)

Long before this point is reached, Elizabeth's reminiscence has ceased. She is driving home, brought down to earth by the ready response of a traffic policeman to her embarrassed smile as she remembers the phrase 'moral sclerosis'. The major flashback which will include almost all of her married life with Max requires a freer framework, in the (technical) interest of narrative continuity. It also demands facts, a number of points of reference fixed firmly in the present, from which to move back into the past. These are provided in a way which emphasizes the idea of the link, the process by which present grows out of past while at the same time defining it. But the relevant passage is constructed to relate backwards and forwards within the microcosmic time-scale of the single day of the book's action. Thus when Elizabeth arrives home, she finds the telephone ringing, but it stops before she gets to it. She also discovers flowers – Graham, her lover, whom she has asked to buy flowers for her grandmother at the old peoples' home, has thoughtfully had a bouquet sent her.

> They were pressed like faces against glass; I ripped them free of the squeaky transparency and read the card: With love, G. Graham and I have no private names, references or love-words. We use the standard vocabulary when necessary. A cold bruised smell came up from the flowers; it was the snowdrops, with their onion-like stems and leaves, their chilly greenness. He knows how crazy I am about them. And about the *muguet-du-bois* that we bought when we met for a week in the Black Forest in Europe last year. There is nothing wrong with a plain statement: with love. (p. 53)

This is a prelude to a lengthy reminiscence which covers the whole of the heroine's relationship with Max – a relationship in which there is no elegance, little simplicity and an absence of plain statements. The contrast between the present and past relationship is being set up, and the stability and security of a present informed by love is emphasized in order to establish an objective viewpoint on an emotionally muddled but deeply involving past reality. The

119

wider dimension of the current relationship with Graham is also
hinted at: the dimension of Europe, which later assumes its full
significance. When Graham rings a few minutes later, the process
outlined above is maintained on all levels.

> Graham told me there was something about Max in the early
> edition of the evening paper. 'Do you want me to read it?'
> 'No, just tell me.'
> But he cleared his throat as he does before he reads
> something aloud, or begins his plea in court. Unlike most
> lawyers he has a good voice. 'It's not much. There's no
> mention of you, only his parents. The case is exhumed, of
> course . . . and it says he was a named Communist – I don't
> somehow remember . . . ?'
> 'Which he wasn't. He was never named. However.'
> 'A diving team managed to bring up the car. There was a
> suitcase full of documents and papers in the back, all so
> damaged by water that it will not be possible to determine
> their nature.'
> 'That's good.'
> 'Nothing else. – His father's career in Parliament.'
> 'Oh yes. No mention of Bobo at all?'
> 'Fortunately not.'
> We might have been cool criminals discussing a successful
> getaway. (pp. 55–56)

Another dimension of contrast between past and present is being
put forward. This dimension is between what might be called the
subjective and the objective view of the past from the vantage of the
present, or perhaps more exactly the contrast between private and
public knowledge and interpretation of the past, which of course
depends upon, and illustrates, the contrast between the individual
and the publicly accepted interpretation of the present. Graham
and Elizabeth are detached from the newspaper's version: they feel
somehow outside the pale of its knowledge, understanding its
language but not responding to it. Nevertheless they are subject to
it, for they are vulnerable to the type of sanction it can impose –
'cool criminals discussing a successful getaway.'

But the accepted version is wrong both in fact, and in its
interpretation of the past. The sheer inadequacy of its information
about the past is steadily revealed in the subsequent pages; and it
makes the particular blunder (which *is* almost a matter of
interpretation) of asserting that Max 'was a named Communist'.

This assumption illustrates something of the ground rules of its interpretation of reality, and of the scale of values by which public judgment is guided. The nature of public judgment is strikingly confirmed by what is excluded from the report as much as by what is given. The only important things about Max now, the author argues, are Elizabeth and Bobo – the present and the future. The important things about his personal existence in the past he has taken with him, perhaps in the form of the indecipherable documents. The irrelevant things, embedded in a past that has always been in a sense dead, are his father's career, his trial, his parents. They belong to the white world which has lost the ability to perceive the passage of time, or to understand its significance – the world in which one can die twice without changing into a corpse. They are the 'facts' of the newspaper version of Max's life.

But when Elizabeth supplies the missing information it is carefully prised free of any institutionalized wrapping. She starts the process by stressing her independence.

> The call-box bleeped at his end and I said something again about the flowers, before we hung up. Once alone, I didn't feel the slightest inclination to go out, after all; I felt, on the contrary, a relief. . . Many of the demands one makes on other people are nothing but nervous habit, like reaching for a cigarette. That's something for me to remember, if I were ever to think of marrying again. I don't think I'll marry again. But I catch myself speaking of Max as my 'first husband', which sounds as if I expect to have another. Well, at thirty, one can't be too sure of what one may still do. (pp. 57–58)

She goes on immediately to contrast this independence, acquired partly through sacrifice and loss, with her past, which works double-edgedly by reminding the reader that the past in the intellectual structure of this book stands for and embodies everything that is not free, that opposes even the desire to be free. 'At eighteen I was quite sure, of course. I would be married and have a baby.' (p. 58). Her present is, however, very different, self-created. She defines her relationship with Graham in the same, cautious terms.

> In Europe last year, we enjoyed ourselves very much, and lived in the same room, the same bed, in easy intimacy. We each went our own way some of the time, but we'd planned the holiday together and we stayed together for the greater part.

I don't think we once felt irritated with each other. Yet since
we've been back we've lived again just as we used to,
sometimes not sleeping together for two weeks, each taking up
large tracts of life where the other has no claim. I didn't need
him, sitting in the sun on my balcony.

A sexual connection. But there is more to it than that. A
love affair? Less than that. I'm not suggesting it's a new form of
relationship, of course, but rather that it's made up of the bits
of old ones that didn't work. It's decent enough; harms
nobody, not even ourselves. I suppose Graham would marry
me, if I wanted it. Perhaps he wants it; and then it would all
change. (pp. 60–61).

'These fragments . . .' – but the fragments may be more meaningful
than complete structures that have become derelict. In any event,
the kind of freedom that is being defined is essentially a freedom in
time, a freedom from the past. The present comes into focus, in a
moment of apparent reconciliation, as Elizabeth sits drowsily in the
afternoon sun on the balcony of her flat.

. . . two children I couldn't see, but could hear shooting
water-pistols at each other, below my feet, and the men on the
bit of grass above the pavement opposite. They were black
men with their delivery bicycles, in working overals. They lay
flung down upon the grass, the legends of firms across their
backs. They were drinking beer out of the big red cartons, in
the sun. We were all in the sun. There is a way of being with
people that comes only by not knowing names. If you have no
particular need of anyone, you find yourself belonging to a
company you hadn't been admitted to before; I didn't need
anybody because I had these people who, like myself, would
get up and go away in a little while. Without any reason, I felt
very much at home.

In spite of everything.

. . . It was the hour when all the flat-dwellers were at lunch
and only they had time to lie on the grass, time that had no
label attached to it. (pp. 62–63)

The particular quality of freedom which is established suggests that
the subject is aware of its temporary nature, and of the impossibility
of maintaining the state continuously. Not all time is no-time, but
there are moments during which the individual is neither lonely nor
involved with people, dwelling neither in past nor future, engaged

in no activity which ties him to an awareness of the present moment.

It has been suggested that this quality of freedom is connected with the existence of public patterns of ritual, communally accessible and charged with symbolic meaning according to the defining ethical values possessed by the group. In *Four Quartets*, for example, Eliot works through ritual to vision (but only does so after having achieved the difficult task, for the modern sensibility, of rediscovering a meaningful ritual – an achievement that is necessarily less than satisfactory, because of the absence of collective acceptance that underlies the validity of ritual practice). An analogous process appears in Will Brangwen's experience in Lincoln Cathedral in *The Rainbow*; although Lawrence's conclusion is precisely opposed to Eliot's – for him, meaningful ritual is dead.

In the present case, the author is relying upon the shared rituals of white society in South Africa, which are both very potent and extremely confused. In this, of course, they mirror the state of the value structure of the group. Elizabeth has achieved this freedom from time by an existential experience of these rituals – and an understanding of the experience; Max underwent the same process, but fell short of understanding and was destroyed by it.

Such, then, is the quality of freedom to Elizabeth, as she goes to lie down on her son's bed to sleep; the stage is set for the long excursion into the past that will account for this present state, and make it meaningful for the future as well.

The importance of establishing Elizabeth's position in relation to time does not rest solely in the necessity of providing an explanation of present self, or her actions performed in the present. The past reaches out, over the present's head, and fertilizes the ground of the future. Thus the extended reminiscence of Elizabeth's marriage to Max and their life together has to do with the problem of freedom. In other words, Elizabeth's present state emerges from her experience of the past. In itself it may be exceedingly vulnerable, because although the rituals and values it has shed are very negative, the general historic state of the present precludes any substitute. Thus the resistance of freedom to future time – to whatever challenges the future may hold – is precarious; it is Elizabeth's awareness of this precariousness that is important, and is her major gain in wisdom derived from her experience of reality in the past.

The memory of the past begins at the most recent end, with a half-waking vision of the physical circumstances of Max's suicide:

A vision of seaweed swaying up from deep underwater.
. . . He had succeeded in dying.

I was lying still in the room and my eyes were filled with
tears. I wept not for Max's death but for the pain and terror of
the physical facts of it. The flowers had stirred and opened
while I slept and the warm room was full of scent. I lay quite
still and felt myself alive, there in the room as their scent was.
(pp. 63–65)

Again, the contrast between past and present is asserted, even at the
expense of suggesting a degree of discontinuity; this is the
necessary dramatic illusion, however, for what follows. It is
incidentally a device used frequently by T. S. Eliot in *Four
Quartets*, a work which in content and even in structure bears
sufficient similarity to *The Late Bourgeois World* to indicate
conscious recognitions, if not influence. No matter what great gaps
there are in ideological conviction, the nature of their preoccupation with time bears a close resemblance. In both cases their
approach is essentially modern and equally essentially involved
with the problem of the individual's position in relation to time in
an intellectual situation where the traditional significance of time is
greatly eroded. The basic difference in their conclusions is that
Nadine Gordimer's final commitment to the life of this world is, as
we shall see, secular, while Eliot's idea of individual redemption is a
theological one. Another area of near identity is the shared
conclusion that certain central aspects of the European moral
tradition are dead, and are wrongly (and damagingly) regarded by
many as continuing to possess significance.

The extract begins with a compressed evocation of the political
and social mood among members of 'the left' at the time of Max and
Elizabeth's marriage. This is epitomized in a devastatingly
perceptive closing sentence, which immediately precedes the
elaboration of detail.

The future was already there; it was a matter of having the
courage to announce it. How much courage? – I don't think
we had any idea. (p. 65)

With a dash, perhaps, of the wisdom of hindsight – not that this
vitiates the power of insight – Nadine Gordimer arrives at the
climax of the long argument about the moral significance of
history in the South African experience that she has been exploring
in all her novels up to now. How can people who do not understand

the past that made them, bring to life a future that has coherence in the moral terms they assume for their own? She goes on to trace in detail the thread of Max and Elizabeth's marriage: poverty-stricken Bohemianism extending through most of the phases of disillusion, with Max emerging as the dominant figure, very much the product of the background from which he imagines himself completely to have broken away. He is volatile, subject to moods, periods of depression; is preoccupied with the need for recognition, for admiration, for love; yet is himself unable to recognize the independent existence of any other person within his ambit. He is easily bored, disorganized, displays little persistency, and has no consideration for the immediate needs of others. He is sexually inconstant and emotionally fickle. Yet overriding all these faults is the single factor of his political involvement. This is continuous, and all his acts are at least coloured by it. After the dissolution of the Communist Party he becomes a member first of the Liberal Party, then of the Congress of Democrats, a white branch of the African National Congress and to an extent a Communist Party 'front'. His family life is incidental to his political work.

> Max was unable to be aware of anyone's needs but his own. My mother once called this inability 'horrible selfishness'; whereas it was the irreversible training of his background that she had admired so much, and that she saw him as a crazy deviate from. (p. 70)

In other words, he is a prisoner of his past without being aware of it, and with this point made, Max suddenly, almost dizzyingly, scales symbolic heights. The real nature of his behaviour is now revealed without the artificial colouring of the particular political convictions he has espoused. In personal relations Max is guilty of the irresponsible use of considerable gifts, even a certain power, in a way which mirrors precisely the political behaviour of the ruling class in the white community into which he was born. So that in terms of practical day-to-day morality Max can be said to betray the heritage of European liberal humanism (not that he has any alternative, since his creator sees it as dead at the time and place he receives it), while the white community betrays in daily life the political aspect of their European heritage.

Thus in some ways Max is a microcosmic version of the white community. On a larger time-scale, his progression from romantic rebel, espouser of the cause of the oppressed, to dupe of violence, to political prisoner, to betrayer of his friends can be seen as a parallel to the historic role of the 'English' South African: and his suicide with documents as representing the final self-destruction of the political and moral tradition that the 'English' South Africans may be taken to possess. All this is implied in the judgment:

> Max wasn't anybody's hero; and yet, who knows? When he made his poor little bomb it was to help blow the blacks free; and when he turned State witness the whites, I suppose, might have taken it as justification for claiming him their own man. He may have been just the sort of hero we should expect. (p. 28)

Max is being used as a symbolic confirmation of Nadine Gordimer's conclusion, which has to do with liberalism. I use the term here because it best denotes the values generated by English traditions of culture, government and history when they are in action, specifically in an alien environment. We come back yet again to that queer paradox that accompanied the author as she started out on her path as a novelist: everything positive about the world she is born into and knows best is called 'English'; to some, England is still 'home'; her language is English and the value system that is handed on to her is called English and clothed in that language. But there are jarring notes, which, as her perceptions develop, grow into a cacophony. The English in South Africa are not really English (Max's father is Flemish by descent), and their value system is a pretence, a dressed-up corpse. The best things about the heritage they claim are dead and rotten. This is the hardest thing to accept, and must be subjected most severely to the test of experience. Max's career, or rather Elizabeth's account of it, works on two levels in this respect. On one it is an extended critique of the orthodox left in South African politics – the Liberal Party, the COD, the Communist Party, the ANC and so forth – a critique of the 'past' in the special sense of people living and acting without an awareness of the real time-framework in which their actions are taking place. But on the other, it is also an indication of the grounds for action of the white participants in this dramatic episode: an acute need for identity, couples with an equally acute absence of any feeling of it. Elizabeth says:

> [Max] hovered irresistibly towards what could never be got down, what Spears didn't need to get down because it was his – an identity with millions like him, an abundance chartered by the deprivation of all that Max had had heaped upon himself. (p. 80)

But why should Max hanker after this particular kind of identification? It is because all his life his heritage has been split into two mutually contradictory parts: the language of liberalism and the deeds of selfish repression that characterize the white man's way of life in South Africa. It is the lifelong attempt to reconcile the two that breaks him. He discovered that the language was dead, so to try to change the way of life was in those terms, irrelevant. To try to implant European social and political ideas and ideals in South African soil leads to public tragedy and personal disaster.

This is not a new idea in the South African novel. What differentiates Nadine Gordimer's conclusion from Jacobson's bald, symbolic statement in *A Dance in The Sun*[1] or Plomer's prophetic derision in *Turbott Wolfe*,[2] is that she alone has refused to treat it as foregone and inevitable. She has subjected the evidence to searching enquiry throughout her fiction; her first heroine had to discover what the European values were for herself; Toby Hood imported them 'pre-packaged'; Jessie and Tom Stilwell perfected them in personal relations; Elizabeth and Max lived them out in political action. The first two novels end ambiguously, and hope is not absent from the possibilities they engender. Jessie and Tom realize they have failed, but the political conclusions are left open and some kind of regeneration is not ruled out. But in *The Late Bourgeois World* the final and most conclusive evidence is marshalled. Max, in betraying his friends and political associates, is in a perverse way being true to a version of the European tradition that he has believed in:

> In one of those twists of an ancient code degenerating far from its source that is characteristic of a civilization brought over the sea and kept in mothballs, the van den Sandts interpret honour as something that exists in the eyes of others; you can do each other to death, in private: shame or pain come only from what leaks out. (p. 44)

Max betrayed this degenerate version by refusing to live white, by refusing to place the necessary emphasis on appearances; and his subsequent betrayal can be seen as an act of loyalty to this decayed grotesque. On another level there is an echo of an idea that floats freely and rather dangerously in *A Passage to India*, with its roots in a different kind of literary expression: the idea that the individual

[1] *A Dance in The Sun* (London, Weidenfeld and Nicolson, 1956).
[2] *Turbott Wolfe* (London, Hogarth Press, 1925).

asserts his identity against such a code at his peril, because the code itself possesses inherent, if mysterious, powers of redress. In this way the assumptions of white society may be said to take their revenge on Max, the deviant, by bringing him publicly (and ritualistically) into line. In terms of the time dialectic in the book this is an assertion of the past and a negation of the present and what is to come; the implications of this are depressing because they suggest the unimportance of what happens at the level of the individual. As the plot develops the inexorable movement of an historic process is unfolded. At the end one cannot be sure, for all the care that Elizabeth, having struggled to become free, takes to remain so, whether the notion of freedom in relation to the individual human life is not merely an illusion generated by the need to alleviate the bitterness of man's foredoomed contention with time.

Thus it is a measure of the attraction of the past, the force of tension still remaining within the dialectical opposition, when later in the book Elizabeth gives her reasons for entertaining to dinner someone who has not appeared in the novel up to that time:

> I don't know why I asked him again. I rather wish he'd leave me off his visiting list, leave me alone. But I miss their black faces. I forget about the shambles of the backyard house, the disappointments and the misunderstandings, and there are only the good times, when William Xaba and the others sat around all Sunday under the apricot tree, and Spears came and talked to me while I cooked for us all. It comes back to me like a taste I haven't come across since, and everything in my present life is momentarily automatous, as if I've woken up in a strange place. And yet I know that it was all no good, like every other luxury, friendship for its own sake is something only whites can afford. (pp. 118–119)

The passage illustrates the complexity of Elizabeth's situation. The past exerts a pull on her which is dangerous to her freedom, for she knows that though it is dead, some of its values may stretch out and paralyse the individual in time; and she grimly makes the necessary though devastatingly negative statement, as though to free herself from a spell: '. . . friendship for its own sake is something only whites can afford.' This is the final denial of the basis of action – or even of self-justification – in terms of the European code, of liberal humanism. If not even friendship on the individual level can survive, the situation is beyond redemption.

But on the other hand, the limitations of freedom that appear in this passage (though Elizabeth is not fully aware of their presence, let alone of all their implications), indicate a pull on her that is operating from the other end of the dialectic – the future. The future may be black, it is unlikely to be exclusively white, it is unknowable anyway – but it clearly exerts an attraction on Elizabeth, perhaps even disguised as an aspect of the past.

What, then, is the nature of Elizabeth's present reality, if she is as free of the errors and illusions and false values of the past as anyone may be expected to be? This is, of course, a crucial question, since the answer to it may indicate the reality of South Africa's historic present. Elizabeth's present reality is defined through her relationship with her lover, Graham. Graham is a barrister, who accepts unpopular briefs to defend political prisoners. Elizabeth is a laboratory technician,

> analysing stools for tapeworm and urine for bilharzia and blood for cholesterol (at the Institute for Medical Research). And so we keep our hands clean. So far as work is concerned, at least. Neither of us makes money out of cheap labour or performs a service confined to people of a particular colour. For myself, thank God, shit and blood are all the same, no matter whom they come from ... I'm not suggesting it's a new form of relationship, of course, but rather that it's made up of the bits of old ones that don't work ... If I wanted a man, here, at this time, in this country, could I find a better one? He doesn't act, that's true; but he doesn't give way, and that's not bad, in a deadlock. He lives white, but what's the point of the gesture of living any other way? (pp. 60–61)

Graham also has his share in the irrelevant past.

> Graham and I have known each other since the trial. I was already divorced from Max, but there was no one else to do anything; that's how I met Graham. I was told he was the right man for the case. As it happened he couldn't take the brief, ... but he remained interested and afterwards, when Max was in prison, he helped me make various applications on Max's behalf ... He had a wife once; she was a girl he'd gone about with since they were school-children, and she died of meningitis when she was younger than I am now. There are still traycloths in the house on which she embroidered her initials. (p. 59)

129

Elizabeth, as we have seen, is unwilling to marry Graham, because marriage, both the bourgeois theory and her own practical experience of it, belongs to the past, and was a confining, unfree experience. 'Most of what there was to learn [about marriage] from my family and background has turned out to be hopelessly obsolete, for me.' (p. 59). The most interesting aspect of their relationship is connected with both time and place:

> In Europe last year, we enjoyed ourselves very much, and lived in the same room, the same bed, in easy intimacy. We each went our own way some of the time, but we'd planned the holiday together and we stayed together for the greater part. I don't think we once felt irritated with each other. Yet since we've been back we've lived again just as we used to, sometimes not sleeping together for two weeks, each taking up large tracts of life where the other has no claim. (p. 60)

What flourishes in Europe, and has, almost, to be rationed in South Africa, is love. As we saw in Elizabeth's reception of Graham's gift of flowers, she had to remind herself:

> There is nothing wrong with a plain statement: with love. (p. 53)

Love that flourished amid flowers, those romantic tokens, in Europe, is a European emotion, or at least between them takes a European shape; put in another way, their love takes shape in Europe because there at least are the living remnants of the tradition which gives it meaning. That is why Elizabeth sees the flowers as a reminder, even a memorial of what was possible in a different place, where a different time-scale operates. There may be 'nothing wrong with a plain statement: with love', but for one other character, who has lived out his life trying to learn how to make that statement mean something, it was an impossibility – because of the circumstances of time and place in which he was caught. 'In his attempts to love he lost even his self-respect, in betrayal.' (p. 39)

There is no point in arguing that Max's love was a different sort from Graham's, because one of the reasons for beginning the section which describes most of Max's life with all the necessary information about Graham, is to present the one not only as a contrast to the other, but as sharing at least a common intellectual background. Not for nothing is Graham's surname Mill; it is not coincidence that Max spent his childhood and youth alone educating himself on the European masters: Dostoevsky, and Flaubert, Ibsen and Wells. Graham gains something in his loving, because he recognizes the limits of its possibilities. Such hedged bets were not for Max, whose romanticism is pure and not disillusioned. In a sense, in the European tradition, romanticism is the youthful forerunner of mature liberalism. Elizabeth participates with Max in the beginning in this illusion (see p. 103 – 'Truth and beauty . . .'). Unfortunately, mature liberalism of all ideologies can least afford – or is least able – to live in a vacuum: it needs the nourishment of an established romantic tradition, in art and in life. So Graham's (and to an extent Elizabeth's) life is reduced in stature by the necessity of having to learn to 'sit still' in South Africa.

So Elizabeth's life with Graham – her experience of the present – is only satisfactory within certain recognized and precise limits. The historic nature of these limits, or perhaps limitations, is expounded in the longest encounter between the two, when unexpectedly Graham turns up in the evening at Elizabeth's flat for a drink, and catches her out in a petty deceit. She has told him previously that she would be going out to dinner, while in fact when Graham arrives she is preparing a meal for the friend she is later to entertain.

The deceit is in its very pettiness the clearest demarcation of the limits of fulfilment in her life – and in Graham's – or in any relationship based on love in that time and place. Because her dinner-guest is to be a black man, involved in underground politics, connected with sensitive areas in her past – Graham must be completely excluded. The conversation between Graham and Elizabeth is admirably handled by the author: its very self-consciousness, provides a context for accepting the inevitability of betrayal. It is very much related to time and place: sunset, winter, Johannesburg. The sunset is spectacular, either because of a volcanic explosion half the world away or because of fall-out from nuclear test explosions. Graham admires it.

> 'Suppose it is fall-out,' I said.
> 'Well?' He is sometimes a little patronizing toward me, though not offensively.
> 'Then it's not beautiful, is it.'
> 'There's nothing moral about beauty.' He smiled; we were having what he calls an "undergraduate chat".
> 'Truth is *not* beauty.'
> 'Apparently not.' (pp. 109–110)

This straight rejection – refutation even – of the Romantic apotheosis and goal is preceded by a viciously ironic meditation on Elizabeth's part, inspired by sunsets:

> It comes from a volcanic eruption on the other side of the world, from particles of dust that have risen to the upper atmosphere. Some people think it's from atomic tests; but it's said that, in Africa, we are safe from atomic fall-out from the Northern Hemisphere because of the doldrums, an area where the elements lie becalmed and can carry no pollution. (p. 106)

Other northern things besides radioactive fallout remain excluded by the doldrums, with their illusion of eternal stillness, from the dominant white sensibility in South Africa – a true awareness of time as change, for instance.

The suitability of the sunset as symbol, both because of its position within the Romantic bestiary and because of its sense of an ending, is apparent from the outset, as is its relationship with the central event of the book – Max's death. It is made explicit in the conversation between Elizabeth and Graham, particularly at a later point where a significant breakdown in communication between the two takes place:

> ... Graham said, 'How would you say things are with us?'
>
> For a second I took it as going straight to all that we competently avoided, a question about him and me, the lie he had caught me out with on my hands – and I could feel this given away, in my face.
>
> I did not know what to say.
>
> But it was a quiet, impersonal demand, the tone of the judge exercising the prerogative of judicial ignorance, not the partisan one of the advocate cross-examining. There was what I can only describe as a power failure between us; the voices went on but the real performance had stopped in darkness ...
>
> ... 'Today, for instance.' He was serious, tentative, sympathetic ...
>
> ... I said, 'Graham, what on earth do you think they'll call it in history?' and he said, 'I've just read a book that refers to ours as the Late Bourgeois World. How does that appeal to you?'
>
> I laughed. It went over my skin like wind over water; that

feeling you get from a certain combination of words, sometimes. 'It's got a nice dying fall . . .' (pp. 112–114)

The sunset is extravagant and lush in the manner of decadent art; it hints at the undisciplined materialism characterizing the civilization it symbolizes. The sense of an ending is linked by a subtle emphasis on certain qualities typical of such an historic period – qualities connected specifically to the individual and his (or her) relationships with others. Communication is difficult, understanding a matter of chance, betrayal inadvertent and inevitable, guilt always present. Elizabeth's awareness of betrayal and guilt leads to the momentary confusion and noncommunication between herself and her lover. Significantly, at that moment, each is operating, intellectually, on a different time-scale, and the emotional result is a sense of intense spiritual isolation.

This is a situation that crops up repeatedly, in varying forms, though none is so acutely felt as the occurrence that takes place between Elizabeth and Graham. The situation itself is made into an institution, as it were, of the book's world in the afternoon of the plot's action, when Elizabeth goes to visit her senile grandmother in the home for the aged. The grandmother is descended from pioneering European stock ('her father was an engineer associated with Rhodes and Beit' – p. 100); in other words, from the point of view of cultural tradition, she has generated nothing of her own but has lived on what the past – the European past – has managed to transmit in usable form to the present.

> . . . but – my mother says – she won't leave any behind her, the expenses of her senility are eating up the last of her capital. (p. 100)

The most obvious form her senility takes is loss of memory, and her position in the span of generations as the bridge between Europe and Africa, between European heritage and its potential white inheritors in South Africa, is annulled by her inability to remember. Her family association with the Europeans who did most to create a version of Europe in South Africa is thrown into symbolic relief by the question she asks towards the end of the visit:

> The old lady's face drained of meaning. I chatted on but she gave me only a slow blinking glance, half-puzzled, half-indulgent. I was talking but there was a dignity, final, bedrock, in her ignoring me; it was true that I was saying nothing.

She said suddenly, 'What happened?'

There is nothing to say.

She asks now only the questions that are never answered. I can't tell her, you are going to die, that's all. She's had all the things that have been devised to soften life but there doesn't seem to have been anything done to make death more bearable. (pp. 104–105)

The Europe-in-Africa she represents, the dynamism and self-sufficiency of the protestant ethic (always suspect, because always dependent upon black labour for the execution of its plans), no longer exists in any real, historic sense. What is missing, significantly enough, is the individual consciousness of time. There are two phenomena present in the situation: the feebleness of the relevance of a generation that has passed or is passing, whose values have no relation to a changed present reality; and the foolishness of a generation (represented by the coarse and insensitive nurse, Sister Grobler, who attends to the needs of Elizabeth's grandmother) that never grew up, never became aware of the meaning of time, and therefore cannot be said to have an existence in the present.

Confronted with the past, Elizabeth has adjusted herself to an impoverishment, a sense of loss. Her grandmother's signed photographs of the people she has met, of Heifetz and Noel Coward, never become meaningful for the granddaughter; they possess no cultural potency nor present the possibility of a common cultural experience. The only worthwhile bequest the old woman will have to make to the future (and it, significantly, will go to Bobo) is an object that symbolizes the most important gift that Europe brought to Africa – and lost there –

When my grandmother dies, Bobo will get her father's gold hunter and chain, that Beit gave him. (p. 103).

Elizabeth's faith in Bobo and hope in the future is reflected in this statement. She has faith in the possibility of renewal by a generation which will live once again in harmony with the normal processes of time and change. This possibility is absent from her present existence, even in her relationship with Graham, where their attempt to understand intellectually the nature of that present is accompanied by a breakdown in living emotional communication as complete as that which is occasioned by her grandmother's senile withdrawal.

The dinner party, which is the climax, is a set piece, one of Nadine Gordimer's most successful pieces of writing. It begins with an old challenge, one that has not been hinted at in the course of the book up to the moment when, after sunset, Elizabeth has taken Graham home and returned to her flat to complete the preparations for her guest.

> I'd said about half-past seven, but I could safely count on eight o'clock, so there was plenty of time. I was expecting Luke Fokase. (p. 118)

The approach to the challenge of rendering a black character is entirely different from any of the author's previous attempts, and is in pretty direct contrast to the method used in her preceding novel, *Occasion for Loving*, in which the portrayal of Gideon received a more extended treatment than any black character in her work, and yet fell short of success.

The emphasis throughout *The Late Bourgeois World* is on the difficulty of making contact, on the pitfalls that beset all attempts at communication between human beings. While in *Occasion for Loving* liberal values could still be said to be on trial, by the end of that book their failure has been announced and a certain level of intimacy between black and white (not sexual – the relationship between Jessie and Gideon, or Boaz and Gideon, rather than Ann and Gideon) declared impossible under the prevailing historic circumstances. *The Late Bourgeois World*, however, begins with a full acceptance of this limitation – Elizabeth knows from her own experience what is possible and what is not. This acceptance develops naturally into a full statement of the difficulties mentioned above.

Thus it is not an arbitrary choice of technique that leads Nadine Gordimer to present Luke Fokase entirely from the outside, through the eyes of Elizabeth, a narrator who is especially sensitive to the likelihood of communicative failures, and who has no illusions about relationships in depth.

The technique is very successful. Luke is a politician, a member of the Pan-African Congress, living in Basutoland but operating underground in South Africa. This emphasizes his strangeness – barriers against knowing him are raised. The method here is to make him distinct from similar characters in Elizabeth's past. He is P.A.C. and not A.N.C. – in other words, he belongs to the organization which rejects rather than welcomes white support and co-operation. He is younger than her African friends from the time of her marriage, and a different breed altogether: non-ideological, non-intellectual, a man of action and detailed practicality; he is the child of the new time, when:

> Decades, eras, centuries – they don't have much meaning, now, when the imposition of an emergency law or the fall of a bomb changes life more profoundly in a day than one might reasonably expect to experience in a lifetime. (p. 89)

Physically he is a very solid object, presented with force and precision:

> ... a plump young man with a really black, smooth face – almost West African – and enormous almond eyes that were set in their wide-spaced openings in the black skin like the painted eyes of smiling Etruscan figures. (p. 120)

In this first description of him one encounters a clever balance of the vivid with the mysterious. The very quality of his blackness is pronounced – the image is both visual and kinetic, but it is essentially a surface image – the word 'smooth' used in its primary sense, referring to surfaces: the familiarity of the black skin emphasized at the same time as its remoteness – 'really black . . . almost West African'. The mystery is made strikingly visual, endowed with reverberations in time so far back into the past (but to a very intense moment, conveying an unfathomable but intensely human gut-meaning to the senses) as to be timeless. But 'painted' again suggests of the surface, artificial. For all his presence, Luke is quintessential mystery. His actual presence is rendered again in terms of concentrated physical immediacy:

> When he – Luke – stood in the doorway I realized that he is not present to me in any way when I don't see or hear him. He exists only when his voice is on the other end of the telephone or when he stands there like this, a large, grinning young man, filling his clothes . . . He is immediately *there* – one of those people whose clothes move audibly, cloth on cloth, with the movement of muscle, whose breathing is something one is as comfortably aware of as a cat's purr in the room, and whose body-warmth leaves fingerprints on his glass. (p. 126)

The imagery borders on the sensual, and the reader is aware that Luke cannot be ignored. Indeed, the description takes off, supercharged with physical immediacy, on to the symbolic plane. And like all symbols he is at least in part enigmatic: 'What a face,

those extraordinary cloisonné eyes, you could put your finger on the
eyeball to try the smooth surface.' (p. 138)

The narrative strategy operates on two levels here. In the
accumulation of physical detail (an accumulation peculiarly rich in
metaphor) the author is insisting upon those things the eye denies in
the world of the book, in white South Africa: the absolute
distinctness and individuality of every black person, each
possessing a particularity of features that could not be shared by
anyone else. In other words, she is revealing a world both rich and
strange where too many of her predecessors have faithfully
mirrored what their community has betrayed itself into seeing – a
sea of stereotypes, a blank and faceless mass. From Elizabeth's
point of view a new form of perception, a fresh and deeper level of
awareness, like someone wideawake, alert amidst totally new
surroundings, a different element, is being explored. Freed from
the restrictive dimension of the past, she can now proceed from
substantial self-knowledge to get to know the world afresh, from the
outside, beginning without preconceptions and illusions about
herself or others.

The interaction between these two levels creates a third, which is
really a corollary to the first: the 'normal' attitude to black faces and
the people possessing them is a contemptuous supposition that they
are easily known – 'I know the kaffir,' the singular being
representative, metonymous. It is clear that Elizabeth is well aware
that she *does not* 'know' Luke, that no matter how distinct his
physical delineations become to her, even if they make love, he will
remain ultimately unknown to her. But there *is* a level on which
they can meet – and the early story of that name reverberates
throughout their dinner, where it is mirrored and magnified into a
subtlety of design with manifold implications. In the story each
character *did* want something of the other; what was decisive was
the physical repulsion felt by the white woman, for which she is
paid out, as it were, by the sudden hostility – or reality – of the
environment which she had perceived in so irrelevant, 'European' a
manner. Elizabeth's has progressed in the truth she has learnt not so
much about her surroundings as about the value of the myth from
which her predecessor in Nadine Gordimer's fiction had drawn her
vision of reality. Romantic Europe's dead and gone – a truth
realized by Olive Schreiner in relation to South African reality in
her very first novel.

Elizabeth is helped by this tragic realization: the limitations on her 'knowledge' of Luke lead her to play the game according to its right rules. She has no reason to expect more from her relationship with Luke than from any other relationship, and its limitations become the shortcomings peculiar to the age, to the era in which they live. Thus the tension between Luke and Graham is that between two men with different outlooks and different goals – but it is in many ways less than a contrast, so little is there in it of black and white beneath the surface. The most fundamental difference between them is that of location in time. Graham, with his roots in a European tradition, is morally immobile in South Africa. He knows enough not to pit the past against the present, as Max did. But Luke doesn't know the same past. For him the present has only one tendency, towards an inevitable future state. The past may be tailing him, but it is doubtful whether it will ever catch up.

> If he hasn't someone on his tail, he would never admit it, and if he has, well, the fact has long since been accepted by both trailed and trailer, they will run their course together. (p. 144)

At this point, a crucial one in Nadine Gordimer's work, her own development through time and the current state of her fiction become analogous. Luke and Elizabeth are 'present' versions of the two characters in the early short story, 'Is There Nowhere Else Where We can Meet?' Significantly, there is a hint of consummation in the air; that it does not come about suggests the unfinished quality of the work, its intentionally open-ended structure. The contrast between Luke and the African in that early story is rendered in straightforward visual and olfactory terms, though of course in 'Is There Nowhere Else where We can Meet?' the reader is confronted with the impression received by an immature and dreamladen sensibility, still subject to the quality of 'evil innocence', of the young black man whom she encounters; it is not as straightforward a description as the one of Luke I have quoted above. The contrast, on both levels, is most instructive:

> His one trouser leg was torn off above the knee, and the back of the naked leg and half-turned heel showed the peculiarly dead, powdery black of cold . . .
> The eyes were red, as if he had not slept for a long time, and the strong smell of old sweat burned at her nostrils. Once past, she wanted to cough, but a pang of guilt at the red-weary eyes stopped her. And he had only a filthy rag – part of an old shirt?

– without sleeves and frayed away into a great gap from underarm to waist.[1]

Thus Luke and Elizabeth may be seen as transmutations into the present of the man and woman of this early story. Each has greatly changed; yet in many ways the structure of their encounter is parallel. Luke has his demand to make of Elizabeth; like his precursor, he delays making it until he can surprise her with it. Elizabeth, like the girl in 'Is There Nowhere Else where We can Meet?' is conscious of the potential existence of the demand, and not wholly surprised when it does come. Something of the story of the author's own development, as well as that of the historic changes in the white South African consciousness (of which she is, of course, the most sensitive chronicler), is told in the contrasting facts that while what the heroine of 'Is There Nowhere Else where we can Meet?' most dreads is a sexual demand, and surrenders with happiness, almost, to the theft of her possessions instead, it is clear that Elizabeth's response would be the opposite: for her, the ugly truth is that she has nothing special to offer in terms of human relationships, and she is reluctant to accept the reduction of the situation between herself and Luke to a merely economic level.

I was afraid Luke would somehow divine – not the actual fact, but that there was a *possibility*; that there really was something for me to conceal. His hand, his young, clumsy presence (there at my pleasure, I could ask him to leave whenever I wanted) hung over it. And at the same time I had the feeling that he had somehow known all along, all evening, that there was a possibility, some hidden factor, that he would get me to admit to myself. Probably just the black's sense that whites, who have held the power so long, always retain somewhere, even if they have been disinherited, some forgotten resource – a family trinket coming down from generations of piled-up possessions.[2]

... Luke knows what he wants, and he knows who it is he must get it from. Of course he's right. A sympathetic white woman hasn't got anything to offer him – except the footing she keeps in the good old white Reserve of banks and privileges. And in return he comes with the smell of smoke of

[1] 'Is There Nowhere Else where we can Meet?' from *Face to Face*, 1949, p. 116.
[2] *The Late Bourgeois World* (Victor Gollancz, London, 1966), p. 147.

braziers in his clothes. Oh yes, and it's quite possible he'll make love to me, next time or some time. That's part of the bargain. It's honest, too, like his vanity, his lies, the loans he doesn't pay back: it's all he's got to offer me. It would be better if I accepted gratefully, because then we shan't owe each other anything, each will have given what he has, and neither is to blame if one has more to give than the other. And in any case, perhaps I want it. Perhaps it would be better than what I've had – or got. Suit me better, now. Who's to say it shouldn't be called love? You can't do more than give what you have. (pp. 159–160)

It is Luke who emerges from this most strikingly; and one would claim a distinct first here for Nadine Gordimer. Consider Luke's fictive ancestry, then Plomer's attractively pompous or feckless clowns, or Abrahams' mouthing 'intellectuals' or raw mine boys, or the flashing-eyed nigger of the diamond fields in Schreiner's *Undine* (or Schreiner's actual experience of the 'educated native' in the person of the portly imitation country squire, D. D. T. Jabavu) – in a way, all these South African possibilities and more have been assayed by the author and she has almost always fallen short of success, insofar as her own vision was clouded by the legitimate novelists' light of liberal humanism, of a world whose values didn't hold for her time and place.

But in Luke she has created out of all her own past efforts and experience a man of the present and a herald of the future, an individual who is of the moment, confident and self-aware, adopting the convenient white man's conventions of garb and gesture in order, in a way, to protect his white associates (particularly Elizabeth) from his own terrible invisibility. Luke is neither the old-time church-bred schoolteacher sitting on the edge of his chair at tea parties in genteel white liberal parlours; nor is he the drink-sodden political drenched in ideology but floundering before the necessities of action. He fits none of the expected moulds, and the key to the author's success in him (and it constitutes an important moment for the South African novel) is that she is proclaiming that she *doesn't* 'know the kaffir', only individual men and women insofar as they are knowable.

And so he's gone, my Orpheus in his too-fashionable jacket, back to the crowded company that awaits him somewhere in the town-outside-the-town. In a way it must be a relief to leave behind pale Eurydice and her musty secrets, her life-

insured Shades (Graham has made me take out an all-risk
policy) . . .

    . . . Perhaps he's talking now in the language I don't
understand, full of exclamations and pauses for emphasis,
telling them he's found a white woman who'll do it. (pp.
150–152)

By an impudent, scarcely-noticed inversion, the underworld is
the white woman's domain, and the real world the black man's
'township' or 'location'; an echo of the old strategy of massive
deceit which operated in the early works. What is totally unreal to
the white perception, and cannot be grasped by it, is the real world
of life in the present. This is the reason why no real tension exists
between Graham and Luke. Graham has chosen the illusory
present to live his life in, though the foundation of his choice is firm
and probably timeless, both in values and because it is made
consciously. Luke has no alternative but to be of the real present,
and therefore no possibility of accepting or rejecting, or assessing
with justice, Graham's choice.

When Luke has gone, having requested her to allow funds for the
underground movements to be channelled from abroad through
whatever facilities she may (and he presumes she does) possess,
Elizabeth goes to bed, thinks, sleeps and wakes at an unknown time
to a vision of the day's meaning which is parallel to her earlier
afternoon awakening to a similar state of heightened perception,
(pp. 62, 153). This time the day is complete, all that needs to be
known has at least been presented to the senses, and the possibility
of resolution exists.

However, the problem of meaning has been transformed by
Luke's request: to paraphrase one of the book's epigraphs, the one
from Kafka, Elizabeth has found the stone under which her
possibilities lie. Her senile grandmother's bank account is
administered by her, and sums from abroad are from time to time
paid into it. Thus it would meet Luke's basic requirements. Of
course, this would involve a complete acceptance of Luke's terms,
even as far as personal relations went. In order to live rather than
merely think in terms of living in the present, Elizabeth has to
decide to lift the stone and reveal the dangers lurking beneath.

The injection of practical danger into her life that this would
entail (a missionary colonel has just been sent to jail, 'protesting
quite truthfully that he didn't know that the money in the charitable
fund he was administering was being used to send people out of the

country for military training' – p. 143) is balanced, in Elizabeth's meditation, by the fact of the American cosmonauts, walking in space during that day, the day that Max was drowned and Luke made his request.

> You can go down after love or up after the moon.
>
> But if you master something *outside* our physical environment, isn't it reasonable to believe you are reaching out beyond the fact of death? If you master that beyond, as those men up there have done, isn't that the closest we've ever got to mastering death? Won't it seem the prefiguration, the symbol of that mastery?
>
> They are alive, up there.
>
> . . . there's no reason Luke shouldn't come back here . . .
>
> Why on earth should I do such a thing?
>
> It seems to me that the answer is simply the bank account. I can't explain; but there is the bank account. That's good enough; as when Bobo used to answer a question about his behaviour with the single word: 'Because.' Am I going into politics again, then? And if so, what kind? But I can't be bothered with this sort of thing, it's irrelevant. The bank account is there. It can probably be used for this purpose. What happened, the old lady asked me: well, that's what's happened . . .
>
> It's so quiet I could almost believe I can hear the stars in their courses – a vibrant, infinitely high-pitched hum, what used to be referred to as 'the music of the spheres'. Probably it's the passage of the Americans, up there, making their own search, going round in the biggest circle of them all.
>
> I've been lying awake a long time, now. There is no clock in the room since the red travelling clock that Bobo gave me went out of order, but the slow, even beats of my heart repeat to me, like a clock; afraid, alive, afraid, alive, afraid, alive . . .
> (pp. 154–155; 157;159;160)

The clearest thing about Elizabeth's 'decision' is that it transcends the rational. The return to a response of Bobo's, the child who represents the future and in whom she has faith, to clinch her commitment suggests that she is aware of moving forward, by this act, towards the future; becoming a part of the enterprise also shared by the spacewalkers; transcending the rational limits and acceptances of her day-to-day life imposed by common-sense and Graham. She is taking herself out of the safe stasis, the suspended animation of her life stabilized in the 'present', and connecting that present to an unsure but living future. In this vision the adventures of Max and the spacewalkers, which begin, so to speak, at the opposite ends of the dialectic, become complementary, their goals, at least, identical. The image of cosmic harmony in the penultimate paragraph suggests an individual, at last, who is for the moment, in a state of congruence with time. It may follow that her decision is in some sense correct, but clearly the moral scheme which she has lived by (and shared with the author's heroines who have preceded her) is a casualty of this shift in her life to a new level of being; she sees it as a dedication to life. The possibility of illusion is not excluded, but the old basis for testing such matters is negated, as the image of the broken clock confirms. It is as if the whole European heritage coalesces in this moment: Elizabeth's grandmother, with her cheque-book and memories of Beit and Heifetz; the Van Den Sandts (especially Max, the romantic born a century too late); Graham in his uncompromising liberal immobility; and Bobo, who accepts that he and his mother are not 'like other people', but who 'will be all right'. Elizabeth, in the end, is the historic locus of convergence of all these generations: she rises to the historic responsibility thus arbitrarily conferred.

The Late Bourgeois World is an impressionistic work, dealing in symbols, the vocabulary of the dead land and the painful stirrings of rebirth. There are verbal echoes of Elliot, from the images of urban dreariness in 'Preludes' and passages in 'Gerontion' – compare

> And now a gusty shower wraps
> The grimy scraps
> Of withered leaves about your feet
> And newspapers from vacant lots: . . .

(T.S. Eliot: Preludes I)

with

> The empty red beer cartons were thick on every open space. If I were dumped back in it from eternity I should know at once that it was Saturday afternoon. (*The Late Bourgeois World*, p. 94)

Or with the third-last stanza of 'Gerontion', the one that begins 'After such knowledge, what forgiveness?' which more or less defines the ground of the metaphysical dialectic which governs the structure of the book. And the final section, with its reach towards transcendence, carries echoes of the *Quartets*, in particular

'Little Gidding':

> Who then devised the torment? Love.
> Love is the unfamiliar Name
> Behind the hands that wove
> The intolerable shirt of flame
> Which human power cannot remove . . .
>
> ('Little Gidding', iv)

And in any case, perhaps I want it. I don't know. Perhaps it would be better than what I've had – or got. Suit me better, now. Who's to say it shouldn't be called love? You can't do more than give what you have. (*The Late Bourgeois World*, p. 160)

In fact, in this bringing together of past, present and future, and finding at their meeting point the possibility of redemption through the acceptance and transcending of time, Nadine Gordimer's novel may be said to parallel the *Four Quartets* in its rhetorical structure.

The point has been made that the author's development resembles that of other major South African writers in terms of subject matter and approach, except that her order of coming to things can be said to be more logical, in that it mirrors the chronology of personal experience. Thus Jacobson's *The Beginners*, his last novel to date on a South African theme, is parallel to *The Lying Days*, the author's first; and *The Late Bourgeois World*, in its impressionistic treatment of its subject and pervasive use of symbols, resembles Jacobson's earliest works, *The Trap* and *A Dance in the Sun*. Both writers found themselves in much the same situation at about the same time. For each, the possibilities of the South African situation, both subjective and objective, had been exhausted; and from each a relatively long period of silence ensued, before the appearance of two works each suggesting a difficult search for a new direction had taken place. In each case, in Jacobson's *The Rape of Tamar* (1970) as well as Nadine Gordimer's *A Guest of Honour* (1971), the author is striving towards a much larger degree of universality, and the physical and psychological restrictions of the South African situation are left behind.

5   A Guest of Honour

A Guest of Honour is her longest and most ambitious novel: it is about politics and personal relationships; its broad outlines are bold and make a recognizable shape, but in detail its design is close and intricate. Caution over making uninhibited judgments at such relatively close quarters in time need not prevent one from stating two obvious parallels: if the book is the African novel's *Nostromo*, it is also Nadine Gordimer's personal *Middlemarch*. In it she triumphantly routs the problems characteristic of South African novelists, problems with which she has always had to grapple, such as the unselfconscious rendition of black characters; and she allows herself a much more confident and explicit statement of the values she regards as permanent against a background of bewilderment and instability.

Although almost all the action of this book takes place in a fictitious African country whose resemblance to Zambia is much more than accidental, the book is as much about Europe as it is about Africa. It is about that weird historic experience of Europe-in-Africa, the casual transplantation of ideas and values into a foreign organism, and the forcible suppression of any of the signs of natural rejection that occurred. It examines the relationship between Europe and Africa, what Europe did, and the results for both. Its 'message' is aimed uncompromisingly at the Western world, the world of European and especially liberal values. The book may be said to embody some African lessons in the history of Europe.

The hero (and for once Nadine Gordimer is unequivocal about this; his proportions, physical and intellectual, *are* heroic) is Colonel Evelyn James Bray, retired colonial civil servant. Bray had been deported from the country in which he was serving ten years before the action of the book begins, at the demand of the local white settlers, when as District Commissioner he had sided with and encouraged the leaders of the embryonic African nationalist movement as the struggle for independence from Britain was initiated. When the book opens, independence is about to be granted, and Bray, who has been living in semi-retirement with his wife Olivia in a house they have renovated – and in a sense revived – in a dead village in Wiltshire, is invited back to Africa by the man who is to be the country's first president, Adamson Mweta. Bray has helped and guided him both in Africa and England, through the stages of nationalist agitation and, later, negotiations at Lancaster House. Mweta sees Bray as returning to fulfil a task at which he had been interrupted by his deportation ten years before. Bray himself is sceptical about this, but accepts the invitation to be present as an official guest at the country's independence celebrations.

Once there, he finds it difficult to extricate himself: although he has booked himself onto a flight home, he significantly fails to include this information in a letter to his wife, and when Mweta finds him a task to perform, he accepts it.

> For some reason he had not given Olivia an exact date for his return, though his seat on the plane was booked; he was thinking he perhaps might stop off in Spain for a week, on the way. He had never really had a proper look at the Prado.
>
> Three days before he was to leave a letter came, delivered by hand. Mweta asked him to accept an immediate appointment as special education adviser – a newly created post – to investigate the organization of schools, technical schools, and adult education projects in the provinces, beginning with the largest, the northern province, Gala. He stopped himself from reading it through again.
>
> . . . Bray was moved and excited in a way that couldn't be acknowledged. Shut away there behind a Great Wall of responsibilities, echoed by sycophants, surrounded by the jailers of office, Mweta had torn out of the convention: Mweta hadn't believed any of it for a minute.[1]

Gala is the province where Bray had served as district commissioner, and whose local white settler community had successfully agitated to have him deported. Thus his return is a more nearly complete cycle of fortune than he had anticipated.

One of the most striking indications of Nadine Gordimer's maturity as a novelist is the enormously skilful creation of a secondary network of relationships which serves as an entirely

---

[1] *A Guest of Honour* (Jonathan Cape, London 1971), p. 70.

convincing backdrop to the main action of the plot. The tone of daily life in both the capital and Gala is precisely and unfalteringly rendered. The expatriate and indigenous intelligentsia of the capital – administrators, junior ministers, university personnel – mostly young, all at least superficially committed, for the time being, to their shared objective situation, generate a feeling of tension. Not unnaturally, this feeling current flows mainly in the form of gossip. The individual characters (especially the whites) constitute a marvellously characteristic cross-section of those who stayed on or came to do their bit with the advent of independence in any of the former British territories of Central Africa in the 'sixties. Neil and Vivien Bayley are young, attractive, upper-class, radical: he is the registrar of the new university; she, coincidentally, niece to the out-going Governor's wife. Bray, in the capital, stays with Roly Dando, illusion-free Welsh lawyer who had supported the nationalists from the outset and has 'stayed on' to become attorney-general in Mweta's government. Hjalmar and Margot Wentz are exiles first from Nazi Germany, and then, a generation later, from South Africa, this time with two almost grown children and the corresponding necessity to make a living (they are trying their hand at running a hotel).

These people constitute a kind of entity, an objective correlative called Europe-in-Africa: and they variously embody aspects of the recent and contemporary European experience. Some scarcely touch Africa, and are in turn unmarked by it; others have deeper emotional investments than they suspect. What emerges from them as a group is again a contradiction of their confident, elitist appearance: the clear impression is that they know neither where they are nor what time it is. They take sensible precautions of various kinds; Margot Wentz has her daughter Emmanuelle 'fitted up' with a birth-control device, while Vivien Bayley keeps her 'riot bag' packed. This sense of dislocation is borne out fairly conclusively by what Rebecca Edwards, who is one of them and yet essentially different in one crucial respect, says to Bray of the men of this circle when, later in the book, she and Bray are living – and having an affair – in the remote provincial town of Gala:

'. . . I got into a bad way down there. They didn't trust Gordon [her husband], any of them . . . I knew they were sorry for me. They persisted in being sorry for me. It made me behave funnily; I can't explain, but when they made passes at me – Neil, the others – I saw that they felt they could do it

147

Rebecca
blows out
my theas

because *to me* they could risk showing that things weren't so good for them, either. I felt sorry for them. I felt what did it matter . . .' (pp. 462–463)

The weakness in the European men is a matter of some significance in terms of what the book expresses about the relationship between Europe and Africa: it suggests the crisis of doubt that permeates an entire culture, from within.

Bray is at the centre of this. He is created to satisfy the historic requirements of Western culture: a courageous man intellectually and physically (a colonel in the Second World War, decorated for bravery), upper-class, liberal in politics, firmly wedded to the code of behaviour in personal relations that most clearly characterizes English liberalism. The basis of his decision to return to Africa at Mweta's request is rendered in terms of this code.

> 'He naturally assumes you'll come out of exile.' They laughed. But they were talking of Mweta; the strange shyness of twenty-two years of marriage made it impossible for her to say: Do you want to go? The passionate beginning, the long openness and understanding between them should have meant that she would know what he wanted. And in a way she did know: because it was for them a code so deeply accepted that it had never been discussed – one was available wherever one was of use. What else was there to live by? (p. 6).

His wife Olivia's conflict lies in her Englishness, in the feeling that she has become one with her rightful heritage, that:

> . . . this life in Wiltshire, this life – at last – seemed . . . the definitive one, in the end . . . She was, after all (in the true sense of after all that had gone before) an Englishwoman. (p. 7).

She nonetheless, or because of this, recognizes the code as possessing the kind of fundamental validity that might threaten the security of her patrimony.

The similarity of this starting-point to the position of the Stilwells in *Occasion for Loving* is clear and meaningful – and even more so are the differences.

> The Stilwells' code of behaviour towards people was definitive, like their marriage; they could not change it. But they saw that it was a failure, in danger of humbug.[1]

[1] *Occasion for Loving*, p. 279.

'. . . One must be open to one's friends. You've got to get away from the tight little bourgeois family unit. In a country like this, people like us must stick together – we live by the sanctions of our own kind. We haven't any anonymous, impersonal code because the South African "way of life" isn't for us. But what happens to you, yourself . . . I don't know. The original impulse towards decency hardens round you and you can't get out. It becomes another convention.'[1]

Jessie makes explicit the dilemma of Europe for the South African liberal, which is linked, of course, to the form the same dilemma takes for the South African novelist: the creative impulse, like the original impulse towards decency, needs precisely what it lacks – space among the rabbit-warrens of tradition to develop its individual shape and style, to take refuge or simply to rest without necessarily atrophying from exposure to a shrivelling climate that demands its continuous exercise. Bray inherits such a tradition, and in him the 'original impulse towards decency', though its statement is modified to an almost perilous simplicity ('one was available where one was of use'), is elaborated and sharpened into a finely-wrought but robust instrument of life. Another way of putting it would be that Bray's uncertainties begin at a much more complex level of experience than the Stilwells'. On the other hand, this very quality of almost inborn confidence of sensibility carries its own dangers, especially in the situation the author creates for her hero. The character-structure of the book is such that Bray, as hero, as quintessential European (the word is doing heavy duty here) is surrounded by a spider's web of alternative possibilities; and from time to time the filaments make contact with a fully-elaborated version of one of these potential Brays. On some levels Bray's lecherous old friend Roly Dando is one such; on other levels, more significantly, it is the defeated Hjalmar Wentz who fulfils an image of what Bray might have been. But there are chance encounters too, like the momentary aberration of the perceptions when one mistakes a stranger for a friend – and the experience possesses disturbing qualities. At an early stage in the plot, during the independence celebrations, Bray and Dando are in the bar of the capital's largest hotel, and Bray is confronted by one of these might-have-beens, an aborted doppelganger of himself:

. . . a tall, blond young man from out of town to whom they all

[1] Ibid., p. 243.

listened with the bright show of attention accorded to wits or experts. He was what is recognized as a Guards officer type, perhaps a little too typical ever to have been one. Not so young as all that, either; his small, handsome, straight-backed head on broad shoulders had longish, silky hair thinning on the pate, and when he smiled his teeth were bony-looking. He had a way of bearing down with his nostrils and drawing air audibly through them, to express exasperation or raise a laugh. Certainly his friends found this irresistible. His diction was something no longer heard, in England, anyway. Most likely explanation was that he must have taken part in amateur theatricals under the direction of someone old enough to have modelled himself on Noel Coward . . .

'. . . Oh Lord yes. Her father's getting right out too. *Right* out. The place at Kabendi Hills has gone. Carol's heart-broken over the horses . . . to Jersey, I think . . . Chief Aborowa said to me last week, there's going to be trouble over the culling – some of these chaps've had that bloody great government stud bull the department's spent a fortune on – and I said, my dear chap, that's *your* worry, I hope there'll be a couple of billion gallons of sea between me and your cows and your wives and the whole damned caboodle . . . "I don't want Pezele near my stool." I said don't be a damned fool, Aborowa – as soon as I see him alone there's no nonsense, I talk to him like a Dutch uncle, we were drinking brandy together –'

'– Priceless!' One of the women was so overcome she had to put down her glass.

'– Heavens, that's nothing – Carol buys old Aborowa's wife's corsets for her.'

More laughter . . .

'. . . your odd Portugoose wandering in from over the border . . . wily fellows, your Portugooses, but my boys always managed . . . now get this straight, Pezele, when I'm gone you can stew in your own *uhuru*, but while I'm doing my job . . . political officer, is he? – then tell him when he can read English well enough to understand other people's confidential reports that'll be time enough to get his sticky fingers –' The blue eyes, dilated fishily with vehemence, caught Dando and Bray on their way out of the bar with a half-smile of acknowledgement of the empathy counted upon in every white face. (pp. 44–46)

There can be no doubt that this aspect of Europe is also part of Bray's being; and its failure to develop in his case, by whatever countertropistic combination of historic light and shadow, is obviously in one sense fortuitous: the fatuous colonial civil servant belongs to his class, follows the same occupation as he himself once chose. Nor is the difference easily accounted for by the passage of time, because this analogue of Bray mouths the accepted wisdom of Bray's own earlier contemporaries.

Thus the possession of a tradition is one of those pleasant-seeming things that is in itself quite neutral, in the sense that the manner of its influence on a given individual, cannot be predicted. It cannot be simply asserted that Bray is in this respect more fortunate than Tom Stilwell or Elizabeth van den Sandt. Also, he operates in a different world from them.

Since this fact is of some importance in understanding the combination of choices the author has made at a crucial stage in her development, it may be as well to examine its implications without delay, as these will in any event bear on our conclusions about Bray. The movement from South Africa as locale to this fictive version of Zambia, or at any rate a newly-independent African state which was formerly a British colony in Central Africa, is as much a movement in time as it is in place. As a novelist Nadine Gordimer (as we have seen) is much preoccupied by time, by the interaction of historic process and human experience. Having taken for her material the matter of Southern Africa, and having reached a stage in her account of reality where to go forward would be objectively impossible without resorting to the techniques of science fiction or the extravagance of fantasy (in other words, because *The Late Bourgeois World* is the last stop before revolution in South Africa, and as that hasn't yet come) Nadine Gordimer finds a new state of being to explore; and this state of being represents, according to one kind of view of history, a 'step forward', 'progress' from the pre-revolutionary stage which she sees South Africa as having reached. 'Independence' is not really the same thing as 'freedom', even political freedom; nonetheless, a black majority enjoying political rights and ruling over a white minority is a potential extension of the South African experience – and it also constitutes the kind of base in reality from which Nadine Gordimer, as novelist, likes to write.

In terms of time, then, Bray's return, matched by the independence celebrations and the departure of types like the colonial civil servant in the bar, seems like a rebirth. The literary

rebirth

151

triteness of this idea is belied by the thoroughness, which deserves to be called unsparing, with which it is worked out in the novel. Indeed, a whole cluster of verbal and concrete images accumulate around it: a new state is born, Bray's oldest daughter gives birth to her first child, Rebecca initiates Bray into a new experience of love; Edward Shinza (Mweta's one-time mentor and present opponent, and Bray's contemporary in years) fathers a child. As the plot develops and Bray is forced to shed illusions and make basic choices, he chides himself for behaving like a virgin in terms of the moral decisions that are forced on him by political events (pp. 128–129, 197, 214, etc.), and through all this Bray is changing, as it were, into himself. The process is one whereby his code is jerked into use by a series of unexpected, random blows, and suddenly the finely-balanced mechanism, so apparently robust in overall design, has to perform against the bursting-forth of a new kind of reality – which may resemble the turmoil that surrounded the beginnings of the code itself. On this historic scale, the geographic provenance of the code is of little importance; what is called in question is the possibility of permanent validity.

> The house in Wiltshire with all its comfortable beauty and order, its incenses of fresh flowers and good cooking, its libations of carefully discussed and chosen wine came to Bray in all the calm detail of an interesting death cult; to wake up there again would be to find oneself acquiescently buried alive. At the same time, he felt a stony sense of betrayal. (p. 130)

This emotional process takes place as he drives back towards Gala after his first reunion with Edward Shinza in the remote Bashi area. There he has discovered that Shinza, his contemporary, has fathered a child, but he has made other discoveries as well: the uncommunicative young man to whom he had given a lift part of the way turns out to be a trade unionist who has been detained without trial for two months and seventeen days at the prison in Gala itself, and interrogated and beaten because the authorities have viewed him as a troublemaker. Shinza displays the boy's weals to Bray, as a symbol of the estrangement between himself and Mweta.

> On the calf-muscle of one strong, rachitically bowed leg another pale slash showed through the sparse hairs. Bray described it in the air an inch or two away from the flesh, looking at Shinza: and that?

152

'Somebody missed,' Shinza said . . .

> It might have been an old scar from some innocent injury – a fall, an accident – unconnected with the prison at Gala, but Shinza had no time for such niceties of distinction. Bray saw that to him all wounds were one; and that his own. (p. 125)

In a sense Shinza is a centre of life from whose immediacy of feeling Bray derives an enhancement of his own sensibility; the completeness of Shinza's experience at this point is contrasted with the plain fact of Bray's innocence, or ignorance. Working at the boma, on intimate terms with Aleke, the provincial officer of Gala, Bray has had no idea of the possibility of occurrences like the detention and torture of Shinza's young man.

The construction of the book takes the form of a pattern of polarities radiating outward from Bray. The polarities operate on the levels of both character and experience: thus, when Bray first meets Shinza, the former stands for the contribution age makes to youth, wisdom of experience to the energy of innocence, while Shinza is a man in his prime, who has just fathered a child and entered a new phase of political life, a man who is beginning again both physically and intellectually, planning for the future. Bray sees his contribution to the future as coming from the accumulation of past experience – his own and that of others; Shinza reckons himself a potent force, alive in the present with ideas about his own participation in a future he himself intends to help to create. This is a polarity that at least begins to operate on the level of character.

> Rough, dark-flanked mountains enclosed the road and himself. Shinza had another kind of confidence, one that Bray was provoked by, not just in the mind, but in the body, in the senses; Shinza moved in his immediate consciousness, in images so vivid that he felt a queer alarm. A restlessness stirred resentfully in the tamped-down ground of his being, put out a touch on some nerve that (of course) had atrophied long ago, as the vagus nerve is made obsolete by maturity and the pituitary gland ceases to function when growth is complete. Shinza's bare strong feet, misshapen by shoes, tramped the mud floor – the flourish of a stage Othello before Cyprus. He was smoking cigarettes smuggled from over the border; friends across the border: those who had cigarettes probably had money and arms as well. And the baby; why did the baby keep cropping up? – Shinza held it out in his hand as casually as he had fathered it on that girl. He did not

even boast of having a new young wife, it was nothing to him, nothing was put behind him . . . (p. 129)

The images make it clear that Bray is reached, physically, by Shinza's physical being. The phrase 'misshapen by shoes' carries connotations similar to Achebe's use of the Ibo characterization of the first white men in that area as 'men without toes'; it is also reminiscent of a conversation in *Occasion for Loving*, where the campaign of a Rhodesian nationalist party to get its members to discard their shoes as a particular instance of political protest is discussed. The shoes suggest the limitations on life and the human spirit imposed by the forms of European culture or 'civilization'. Shinza's vigour, opposing these restrictions, is expressed in 'bare strong feet'. The peculiar masculinity of this vigour is stressed in the conventionally male connotations of smuggled cigarettes, 'money and arms'; and at the end of the passage the implied contrast with Bray emerges significantly, on the dimension of time ('. . . nothing was put behind him . . .').

> Shinza might as well have been thirty as fifty-four. No, it wasn't that he was an ageing man who was like a young man – something quite different – that he was driven, quite naturally, acceptedly, to go on living so long as he was alive. You would have to have him drop dead, to stop him.
>
> The house in Wiltshire with all its comfortable beauty and order, its incenses of fresh flowers and good cooking, its libations of carefully discussed and chosen wine came to Bray in all the calm detail of an interesting death cult; to wake up there again would be to find oneself acquiescently buried alive. (pp. 129–130)

The personal polarity radiates various other levels of contrast: between Europe and Africa, between two notions of time, between the rigid separation of flesh and spirit and their natural coalition, and between two versions of the present political realities. As the moving parts in the structure begin to roll, the polarity between Bray and Shinza tends towards self-abolition. In a sense, in the end, in death Bray *becomes* Shinza; and in the process he undergoes a remarkable reversal of roles.

One of the major ways of identifying the relationship between Africa and Europe – a conventional identification, within whose frame of reference Bray was arguably working even at the time of his recall from the colony – is to see Europe as mentor, Africa as pupil. Of course, such a definition begs a great many questions, historically and economically speaking, and yet in the beginning Bray seems prepared to accept its validity – in fact, its stifling inevitability. After Bray discovers the illegal detentions and beatings, at his first reunion with Shinza, he feels that he must confront Mweta with his knowledge; but he is – partly – aware of the complexities such a decision must involve.

> He ought not, he was perhaps wrong to question Mweta about anything. He had made it clear from the beginning that he would not presume on any bond of authority arising out of their association because he saw from the beginning that there was always the danger – to his personal relationship with Mweta – that this bond might become confused with some lingering assumption of authority from the colonial past. I mustn't forget that I'm a white man. A white man in Africa doesn't know what to see himself as, but mentor. He looks in the mirror, and there is the fatal fascination of the old reflection, doesn't matter much, now, whether it's the civil servant under a topi or the white liberal who turned his back on the settlers and went along with the Africans to Lancaster House. If I don't like what Mweta does, I'd better get out and go home to Wiltshire. Write an article for the *New Statesman*, from there. (p. 130)

Full self-awareness is clearly ruled out, as Bray acknowledges. When he sees Mweta, he has a further realization:

> I have hurt him, I hurt him by so much as acknowledging the other one's existence. They couldn't change the relationship in which they had stood to each other, he – Bray – and Mweta; he must have endorsement from me, that is my old role. (pp. 164–165)

The mentor-pupil bond obviously constitutes a polarity, but just as obviously it is not of a kind which lasts forever. Pupils learn, and cease to be pupils. Bray appreciates the objective changes that have taken place, destroying the colonial structure within which the relationship had operated – and whose abolition was the symbolic ending of whatever was held automatically, by definition, in the relationship between white and black; but if he is to live up to his private contention that he has returned to Africa as an individual rather than a 'European' he has also to understand the implications of this change on the personal level. Nadine Gordimer is interested in illustrating the difficulty of this, and how Bray's position is all the more delicate because he is among the few Europeans who have, in the past, *understood* that the nature of their official relationship with Africa possessed within it the seeds of its own decay, as he later explains to Rebecca in an attempt to sort out his own reactions to his discovery that Shinza is associating across the border with Somshetsi, a militant exiled guerrilla leader expelled by Mweta from the country for endangering relationships with the leader of Somshetsi's homeland:

> 'I understood perfectly what I was doing . . . when Shinza and Mweta started PIP it was something I believed in. The apparent contradiction between my position as a colonial civil servant and this belief wasn't really a contradiction at all, because to me it was the contradiction inherent in the colonial system – the contradiction that was the live thing in it, dialectically speaking, its transcendent element, that would split it open by opposing it, and let the future out – the future of colonialism *was* its own overthrow and the emergence of Africans into their own responsibility. I simply anticipated the end of my job. I . . . sort of spilled my energies over into what was needed after it, since – leaving aside how good or bad it had been – it was already an institution outgrown. Stagnant. *Boma* messengers, tax-collecting tours – we were a lot of ants milling around *rigor mortis* with the Union Jack flying over it . . . But now I think I ought to leave them alone.' (pp. 246–247)

This awkwardly abstract apologia reflects his personal conflict, which amounts to a crisis, at finding himself caught, in a sense, on the Mweta-Shinza polarity, one on which the opposing forces are moving very quickly in opposite directions. But it also indicates the basis of his difficulties, since clearly his position on this continuum is personal as much as political in its nature. In this respect Bray's apologia is, to say the least, incomplete. There is a momentous level which he has left out, or ignored, on which he transgressed the official structure of his role, apart from the historic level to which he turns his attention; and the embarrassingly lifeless text-book phraseology of his self-justification is enough to indicate where the omission lies. In colonial times, for obvious reasons, broad though the interpretation of the instructive relationship may have been, one element of conduct was strictly excluded from it – the crucial element as far as English liberal morality was concerned – that of personal relations. Bray's transgression in this respect may have been unconscious, unintentional, inevitable; but its consequences were more complete, more final, than he perceives. At this stage the weakness in his position is largely that he is persistently unable to come to terms with this. On a previous occasion, not much before the one already quoted, he tries to express to Rebecca his unease at the way in which his relationship with Mweta is, he thinks, being misinterpreted. Lebaliso, Gala's chief of police, has been transferred, obviously as a result of Bray's having confronted Mweta with the fact of the illegal detention of Shinza's young protégé.

'I can't go explaining to everybody – but how difficult it is when people impose an idea of what one does or is . . . And others take it up, so it spreads and goes ahead . . . Coming back's a kind of dream, a joke – we used to talk about my part after Independence like living happily ever after. Mweta was in and out of jail, I was the white man who'd become victim, along with him, of the very power I'd served. I was a sort of symbol of something that never happened in Africa: a voluntary relinquishment in friendship and light all round, of white intransigence that can only be met with black intransigence. I represented something that all Africans yearned for – even while they were talking about driving white people into the sea – a situation where they wouldn't have had to base the dynamic of *their* power on bitterness. People like me stood for that historically unattainable state – that's all.' He thought, am I making this up as I go along? Did I always think it? – I did *work* with Mweta, in London, on practical things: the line delegations took, proposals and memoranda and all the rest of the tug-of-war with the Colonial Office. 'But the idea persists . . . Aleke thinks, now, Lebaliso's been removed at my pleasure. I can see that. He tells me this morning about Lebaliso being given the boot as if remarking on something I already know.' (pp. 220–221)

It is not really surprising that Bray's relationship with Mweta, his entire position, in fact, is seen by others solely in terms of power and influence, when Bray himself is sufficiently a victim of his code to be unable to admit the personal level as a factor. He fears to be seen as a mentor, knows (and tries to exploit the knowledge) that Mweta seeks his approval; but never subjects to the same kind of analysis the presence of the entirely different demands of personal friendship that in fact constitute the basic fabric of his situation. In this respect both of the above attempts at self-clarification and analysis of his situation fall short of being adequate. The simple fact of having once admitted Mweta and Shinza within the magic network of liberal values that apotheosizes personal relations puts him outside the framework which, according to his rationalization, he was simply working within at a pace relevant to the historic situation. When he corrects himself, mentally, during the second passage quoted above (his first self-justification), he leaves himself a wasteland to manoeuvre in. He falls short of recognizing his relationship with Mweta for what it is, and thus miscalculates his own situation. He is aware only of the dangers and complexities of being 'the European in Africa'; he has yet to learn those of being Mweta's friend but Shinza's ally.

Such a position is untenable in terms of the framework of English liberalism within which Bray's actions are located, and Nadine Gordimer takes the reader through a sequence of events that gradually makes this plain to Bray, producing the interesting structural effect of the integration of the Shinza–Mweta polarity into Bray's own psychic economy. The events include the annual party congress – an episode which evokes unrestricted admiration for the technical skill with which the author presents it – during which Bray uses the credit he had accumulated in his colonial past to persuade an old chief to get 'his' delegates to support the Shinza line. As a result of this 'service rendered', he is accepted, not without reluctance, by Shinza's lieutenants into their policy-making group. But Bray also has his customary tête-à-tête dinner with Mweta straight after the Congress, after Mweta's symbolic (and charisma-based) defeat of Shinza (the ostensible issue is whether the Secretary-General of the trade union movement should continue to be elected by the unions or become a presidential appointee).

The build-up of stress within Bray is illustrated at the Party rally at the end of the Congress.

Shinza had gone straight back to the Bashi – had left the capital, anyway: '– I'll see you at home, then,' presumably meaning Gala. Without him, it was almost as if nothing had happened. All these people before Mweta, old men in leopard skins with seed-bracelets rattling on their ankles as they mimed an old battle-stride in flat-footed leaps that made the young people giggle, church choirs with folded hands, marching cadets, pennants, bands, dancers, ululating women, babies sucking breasts or chewing roasted corn cobs, men parading under home-made Party banners – the white-hot sun, dust, smell of maize-beer, boiling pluck and high dried fish: the headiness of life, Bray felt it drench him with his own sweat. If he could have spoken to Mweta then (a gleaming, beaming face, refusing the respite of the palanquin, taking the full glory of sun and roaring crowd) he would have wanted to tell him this is theirs always, it's an affirmation of life. They would give it to another if, like a flag, you were hauled down tomorrow and another put up in your place. It's not what should matter to you now. And he wondered if he would ever tell him anything again, anything that he believed himself. The other night was so easy; how was it possible that such things could be so easy. Suddenly, in the blotch of substituted images, dark and light, that came with the slight dizziness of heat and noise, there was Olivia, an image of a split second. It was easy with her, too. She did not ask; he did not broach. It made him uneasy, though, that she and Mweta should be linked at some level in his mind . . .

He felt, with the friendly Hjalmar at his side and the amiable crowd around him, absolutely alone. He did not know how long it lasted; momentary, perhaps, but so intense it was timeless. Everything retreated from him; the crowd was deep water. A breeze dried the sweat in a stiff varnish on his neck. (pp. 377–378)

This frozen moment is the first symptom of what is going to lead to Bray's brief but fatal period of disintegration, and it is significant that Hjalmar, who in a sense, is to be his inheritor, is his only companion. The pendulum of their relationship in drawing towards the edge of its swing, and its return journey is swifter and more comprehensively catastrophic than could have been expected. There are, after all, two sides to Bray's background, and in a way their existence – the tension and continuity between them – constitutes the basis of the wider series of polarities that characterize the structure of the book. At this stage the side that tends to dominate may also be the form in which Bray's character is cast: it is part of a tradition, a European (or at least English) aristocratic cultural tradition which goes back historically to the age of chivalry. Bray feels guilty because he has betrayed love and friendship, his wife and his man friend, thus going against this very basic element in his make-up. He is 'uneasy' that Olivia and Mweta

159

– or rather, his behaviour towards each of them – 'should be linked
. . . in his mind.' This uneasc is a manifestation of what he has
distastefully called in himself 'the v⁻ ˸ːai drawing away of skirts
from the dirt.' (p. 214). It functions as a physical premonition of
death, and is associated, structurally, with what Bray himself has
seen as an 'interesting death cult' – the house in Wiltshire, which is
the end product of this tradition, this process of historic evolution,
from feudal chivalry through imperial 'justice' to modern
liberalism. The house in Wiltshire is a pole of contrast with the
house at Gala; at this moment, this polarity seems to work as an
allegory of life and death. The whole of the European experience is
summed up and ended by the house in Wiltshire; the house at Gala
sees the new beginning, the obstinacy of the will to live and change,
the desire to be involved in life. By a paradox that is only apparent,
Bray associates his 'betrayals' not with change but with continuity,
an internal consistency. Thus he has no control over his lost desire
for Olivia because one can never control the direction of desire –
which is the direction that life takes. 'The things I believe in were
there in me,' he says, 'before I knew Mweta and remain alive in me
if he turns away from them.'

It may be suggested that here Nadine Gordimer has abandoned
one of her fundamental positions in relation to the treatment of time
in her novels. Fulfilment – the word rings a bell – evokes a pretty
well-established conditioned reflex in Western novelists of the last
seventy years. This reflex is frozen for inspection, in the poetry of
T. S. Eliot, especially in *Four Quartets* (Nadine Gordimer's
susceptibility to Eliot's influence, particularly evident in *The Late
Bourgeois World*, has been indicated); but it is also present in the
novels of Lawrence, or Virginia Woolf, or Forster, or George Eliot
for that matter. In its 'modern' (that is, post-romantic)
form the individual experience of 'fulfilment' in the cant literary
sense takes place 'out of time'; in other words, its duration is not
immediately recognizable as such, subject to the normal processes
of experience in time. One need think only of the moment of Miss
Quested's misadventure, or Will Brangwen in Lincoln Cathedral,
or Clarissa Dalloway catching the old lady's eye across the
courtyard. In Nadine Gordimer's work we are reminded of many
incidents of this kind, such as Toby's first visit to a shebeen with
Steven in *A World of Strangers*, or Joel's revelation of his love to
Helen in *The Lying Days*, or Gideon's drunken insult to Jessie at the
end of *Occasion for Loving*. It will be realized from this last example
that by 'fulfilment' I sometimes mean the bringing to a sort of

historic climax certain tendencies or forces that have been at work in or on one or more characters in a novel. It is true that throughout Nadine Gordimer's own work she has given hints that the influences at work on her have been inducing another kind of issue or fulfilment: her preoccupation with the meaning of history. This preoccupation present from the start, has gradually developed into a powerful need to understand the *nature* of history, and in *The Late Bourgeois World* she begins throwing out tentative conclusions.

Such ideas, however, within the framework of a novel, are difficult to convey in an ordinary discursive manner; if the endeavour is to be artistically successful it must be embedded in the structure. To accomplish this, Nadine Gordimer carves the shape of Bray's life to correspond to her idea about the nature of history.

The orthodox presentation of the interplay of time and human character in the English novel is carried, it seems to me, on the same wave of radical optimism that bore the novel genre to the commanding heights of literary expression in English. That is, whatever tragic individual events may occur, the main tendency of development in human relations is ameliorative. Thus the possibility of fulfilment, on the individual or social level, is always present as a result of the pervasive if unrecognized underlying belief that people are capable of learning the lessons of experience. Examples immediately spring to mind; one may go as far back as the generally accepted eighteenth century beginnings or as far forward as the Second World War. Certainly Fielding, Jane Austen, Dickens, George Eliot, Lawrence and Forster all participate in this metaphysic of optimism. Of course, its manifestations vary, and certainly change with the erosion of time and the disillusion of experience. Hardy and Conrad contended with, but did not succumb to, Decadence, in a period when foundations of belief were shaken. Their scepticism about English liberal meliorism prefigures Nadine Gordimer's. Significantly, it is in Conrad's work, with its outsider's view on English ideology, that the most telling rejection of the melioristic myth occurs; and it is in his masterpiece, *Nostromo*, that we find the appropriate analogue for Nadine Gordimer's purpose in *A Guest of Honour*.

It is in the massive surface confusion of chronology, of the 'linear' approach, that the essential clue to what I hope we are getting, appears. Plenty has been written about the Tolstoyan scale of that work. It treats politics and human beings as the subjects of history, and history as the subject of Eternity; and it aims at totality. The result, as far as human cognition of time goes, is on one level,

161

an intentional, controlled jumble. Through this maze no individual character is able to find openings into possibilities of greater freedom, let alone any kind of fulfilment. The aims of *A Guest of Honour* are in many ways parallel to those of *Nostromo*. The topography of Nadine Gordimer's African state is disjoined in a rather similar manner to that of Costaguana. The heroes of both books are liberals faced with the problem, on the personal level as well as the political, of action, in order to secure the possibility of amelioration, of fulfilment. There is a remote, but recognizable connection between the relationships of Charles Gould and Nostromo in the one book, and Mweta and Shinza in the other, particularly in the manner in which good and pure intentions are affected in both cases by the necessity of action. Even the massively disjunctive endings of the two works have parallel structural functions.

For Conrad, then, a rejection of the common, optimistic metaphysic of the English novel is related through a confusion of the way in which human beings perceive and deal with time. Nadine Gordimer rejects the view of history that underlies conventional, linear time-perception as narrative method, and comes up with a resultant rejection of the connected melioristic metaphysic, though she sees it as irrelevant rather than fundamentally erroneous, and thus her irony is of a different and less tragically portentous kind than Conrad's.

What is the notion of history that she proposes, then? The clue to its nature springs from two sources: two meditations on death on pages 385 and 465 of *A Guest of Honour*, in which it is seen both as continuation and as 'interruption'; and the circumstantial parallel between Bray's death and that of Steven Sitole in *A World of Strangers*. In Nadine Gordimer's developed work it emerges clearly that the only experience that really transcends time is death, and either it is arbitrary and without significance or its significance is a barren enigma. History has no individual human consolation in *A Guest of Honour*.

Its direction, however, is informed by a larger purposefulness. The dialectic seems to be the governing force, though for individual characters confusion arises out of the persistent semblance of a cyclical shape to experience. As Mweta's 'pragmatism' becomes more pronounced – by allowing, for instance, the big mining company to arm its own private army to put down strikes – and Shinza's ideological commitment more fervent, and closer to expression in action, Bray finds that decision has ineluctably taken place within him, rather than been made by him. If it is political freedom he is interested in, circumstances rather than an act of free will commit him to action on behalf of his interest. His last meeting with Shinza, in a servant's room in riot-torn Gala, expresses the dilemma in terms of the shape of Bray's participation in history.

'. . . look, James, I want you to go for us. Now.'
'To Switzerland.'
'Anywhere. Everywhere.'
Bray looked at him.
'Oh that ILO thing – well, it's too late. There's a chance now that may never come again. You know what I'm talking about. This mine strike wasn't my doing, I don't have to tell you that – but now that it's going this way, I'll have to move if I'm ever going to move at all. We must make use of it, you understand . . . If Mweta can't hold this country together and we hang back, what're you going to get? You're going to get Tola Tola [a right-wing former cabinet minister arrested on charges of attempting a coup]. You see that. Tola Tola or somebody like him. That's what you'll get. And the bribes'll be bigger in the capital and the prisons will be fuller, and when the rains are late, like now, people will have to scratch for roots to make a bit of porridge, just the way it's always been here.'

Bray thought, he's saying all the right things to me; but then Shinza paused, and in this room that enclosed them as closely as a cell, there was the feeling, as often happened between them, that Shinza knew what he was thinking: was thinking the same of himself, and said, 'I never thought I would ever do it. Now I have to.'

He said, 'What will I say to you? I'll think it over?'

Shinza gave a sympathetic snort.

'When I've "thought it over" I'll only know what I know already: that I didn't think it would ever be expected of me. Not only by you. By myself.'

Shinza smiled at him almost paternally. 'I suppose we didn't know how lucky we were to get away without guns so far. Considering what we want. You don't expect to get that for nothing.'

'It will be such a very little token violence, Bray; and you won't feel a thing. It will happen to other people, just as the tear gas and the baton charges do.'

163

'But you expect it of yourself?' Shinza was saying . . .
'Yes.'

'Good God, James, remember the old days . . . when the order came from the secretariat that I was to be "apprehended" and you decided it didn't say "arrested" so you could "apprehend" me to tell me about it – ?' They laughed. (pp. 428–430)

The two decisions are one – either that, or the first contained the seeds of the last. In either event, time has described a cycle, and Bray is back at the beginning – or is it a new beginning? The question is not answered with finality, but the reader is invited to scan the evidence, or at least hunt for clues.

These may be found in differences rather than similarities: the whole passage stands in wry juxtaposition to Bray's earlier explanation (to Rebecca) of how he had come to take his stand in colonial times. His explanation is intellectualized and rather pompous, suggestive of *post facto* self-justification, a distortion – no doubt unwilling and unconscious – of reality. It even contains specific reference to the 'dialectic', the significance of which as a clue to real meaning only becomes clear at this much later stage. Now the moment of decision is seen as already past, as never having existed, as perpetually deferred. 'When I've "thought it over", I'll only know what I know already: that I didn't think it would ever be expected of me.' Already the *post facto* self-justification has begun: 'It will be such a very little token violence, Bray'. Again, however, the grammar of differences supervenes: '. . . and you won't feel a thing. It will happen to other people, just as the tear gas and the baton charges do.' At this point Bray at least begins with more self-knowledge: but he is beginning the same kind of thing, a future which is merely an intensification of the past. And this tells us the meaning of his earlier meditation, already mentioned:

But human affairs didn't come to clear-cut conclusions, a line drawn and a total added up. They appeared to resolve, dissolve, while they were only reforming, coming together in another combination. Even when we are dead, what we did goes on making these new combinations (he saw clouds, saw molecules); that's true for private history as well as the other kind. (p. 385)

He thinks in these terms just before he leaves the capital for the last time, after the party congress, and immediately after having arranged for the illegal transfer of Rebecca's funds to a Swiss bank account. The Presidential motorcade sweeps past, and the sight of 'the black profile of Mweta's face rushing away from his focus' provokes him to these consideration, which conclude:

Next time we meet – yes, Mweta may even have to deport me. And even that would be a form of meeting. (p. 385)

But there is to be no further meeting; what Bray has experienced is an intellectual intuition of his own death.

There is another link in this chain of events – since there are three altogether, perhaps the suggestion of the dialectic hovers. The second, which reinforces the speculation of the first and links it with the third, final and climactic one, which is the actuality of Bray's death, takes place on the final journey, after order has broken down in Gala and Bray is taking Rebecca away, to an unknown destination. He, at least, is on his way to fulfil what Shinza has required of him.

His mind was calm. It was not that he had no doubts about what he was doing, going to do; it seemed to him he had come to understand that one could never hope to be free of doubt, of contradictions within, that this was the state in which one lived – the state of life itself – and no action could be free of it. There was no finality, while one lived, and when one died it would always be, in a sense, an interruption. (pp. 464–465)

This is a clearly-defined acceptance of the stage beyond the classic liberal problem of action. It is an intellectual advance for Bray, but it is also an acknowledgment of what is already real and actual: a state of affairs he has helped to bring about before having intellectually resolved the conflict. It leads swiftly to the mystery of death itself.

Bray's death is arbitrary and shocking. As they drive towards the capital, he and Rebecca are stopped by a roadblock, a huge tree-trunk across the road. They get out to try to shift it, and as Bray takes the car jack from under the back seat, he is set upon and beaten to death by a band of men.

Then he was below them, he was looking up at them and he saw the faces, he saw the sticks and stones and bits of farm implements, and sun behind. Something fell on him again and again and he knew himself convulsed, going in and out of pitch black, of black nausea, heaving to bend double where the blows were, where the breath had gone, and he thought he rose again, he thought he heard himself screaming, he wanted to speak to them in Gala but he did not know a word, not a word of it, and then something burst in his eyes, some wet flower covered them, and he thought, he knew: I've been interrupted, then – (p. 469)

Afterwards Rebecca crawls out of the ditch where she has been hiding, and tries to clean his face, taking the shattered frames of his glasses out of his cheek. Then they are found.

Some people came down the road. An old man with safety-pins in his earlobes and a loin-cloth under an old jacket stopped short, saying the same half-syllable over and over. There were little children watching and no one sent them away. All she could do before the old man was shake her head, again, again, again, again, again at what they both saw. The women sent up a great sigh. Bray lay there in the middle of them all. They brought an old grey blanket of the kind she had seen all her life drying outside their huts, and an old door and they lifted him up and carried him away. They seemed to know him; he belonged to them. The old man with the safety-pins said to her in revelation, 'It is the Colonel! It is the Colonel!' (p. 475)

Bray finds synthesis in death; he belongs in Africa, to Africa; he is recognized there. His final echo of the intellectual conclusion towards which he had been working for a long time, from the time of his reawakening, confirms the idea in reality: the shape of his life is different from the orthodox notion governed by the concepts of European liberalism. The demonstration is incomplete, however; one or two revelations have still to be made, even though the central affirmation – 'It is the Colonel! It is the Colonel!' – has taken place.

Up to now the narration has been from Bray's point of view, and he has been the sole centre of consciousness. (His development has been a progression from false to real, in terms of his consciousness; it is never presented as infallible.) With his death the narration passes to Rebecca, and a sense of continuity is successfully evoked.

After a little while she went and sat on the white-washed milestone at the side of the road . . . She watched him all the time. She became aware of a strange and terrifying curiosity rising in her; it was somehow connected with his body. She got up and went over to this body again and looked at it: this was the same body that she had caressed last night, that she had had inside her when she fell asleep.

The basket and his briefcase had been flung out of the car and so were not burned. She picked them up and balanced the briefcase across the basket beside him, to keep the sun off his face.

And more time went by. She sat on in the road. Her shirt was wet with sweat and she could smell it. Sometimes she opened her mouth and panted a little; until she heard the sound, and stopped. She was beginning to feel something. She didn't know what it was, but it was some sort of physical inkling. And then she thought very clearly that the flask was still in the basket and got up firmly and fetched it and poured what was left of the coffee into the plastic cup. As she saw liquid there, it all came back to her with a rush, to the glands of her mouth, to her nerves, to her senses, to her flesh and bones – she was thirsty. She drank it down in one breath. Then for the first time she began to weep. She was thirsty, and had drunk, and so it had happened: she had left him. She had begun to live on. (pp. 474–475)

What is being described here is a rebirth. Rebecca emerges unformed, in some respects, but in possession of formidable knowledge – a sort of new genetic package, a second chance to realize a different potential from that with which she started her first life. The point of this effect is important. Throughout the novel the reader has been carried on a whole body of assumptions about the significant aspects of both the political and the personal life – Bray's assumptions, the assumptions of the upper-class English liberal. Sometimes they have worked, at others proved inadequate. But the reader either shares them or he doesn't, and there is no scope for examining the validity of their origins. Rebecca's rebirth takes her almost immediately and for the first time out of Africa and into Bray's other world, the world that formed him – Europe (and the idea has been subtly emphasized that Bray is a natural cosmopolitan within the European context, not 'just' an Englishman). So she faces, without preconceptions, the basis of his assumptions. This most meaningful 'knowledge', concerning the bald facts of Bray's death, she confirms in the few dreamlike days spent in the capital with her old friends.

With the brandy glasses in their hands they talked about what had happened. Out of that day – yesterday, the day before yesterday, the day before that: slowly the succeeding days changed position round it – another version came into double

167

exposure over what she knew. The men who had attacked were a roving gang made up of a remnant from the terrible riots that had gone on for a week centred round the asbestos mine. A Company riot squad led by white strangers – '*You see*,' Vivien interrupted her husband, 'I knew they'd get round to using those men from the Congo and Mweta wouldn't be able to stop them. I knew it would happen' – had opened machine-gun fire on strikers armed with sticks and stones. The white men dealt with them out of long experience of country people who needed a lesson in the name of whoever was paying – they burned down the village. The villagers and the strikers had made an unsuccessful raid on the old Pilchey's Hotel, where the mercenaries had quartered themselves. Someone had put up those road-blocks, probably with the idea of ambushing the white men (hopeless, they had left already, anyway) . . . It was said that the one who started the hut-burnings was a big German who didn't travel in the troop transports but in his own car.

Vivien said, 'But this was a little Volkswagen, and there was a woman in it.'

'To asbestos miners an army staff car's the same as any other kind. A car's a car.' Neil spoke coldly to her. 'Nobody knows anything, any more, when things get to the stage they are now. I don't suppose Mweta knew they would machine-gun people. Burn their houses over their heads. He just put it in the hands of the Company army, left it to their good sense . . . that's quite enough.'

She offered the information. 'The people who helped us knew Bray. An old man with safety-pins in the holes in his ears. He knew him from before.' (pp. 477–478)

That this is a two-pronged movement towards the completion of Bray's dialectic of life and death is made obvious by the use of the 'double exposure' image. This image suggests confusion, two competing versions of what is true, and is, of course, related to the principle of polarity that permeates the structure. Only here there is a superimposition, so that the conflicting elements – the tensions themselves – tend to coalesce. Thus there is, on one level, no comprehensible or significant difference between Shinza and Mweta, or Rebecca and Olivia, Bray's wife in Wiltshire – or Bray and the German mercenary. But the key word that marks the author's control over the way the passage develops is 'know'. It is about knowledge, without arriving at it: the strikers did not *know* who Bray was, that he was their man; Neil does not know anything except that some things were probably not *knowable* in advance, nor in the particular circumstances – and this kind of knowledge is shown to be academic, explanatory and irrelevant. Rebecca's contribution is more pointed, based on a clear memory of real knowledge: 'The people who helped us *knew* Bray.' In the end, Bray knew something, too: that he had been interrupted. Such knowledge is meant to imply wisdom: tasks are only begun when they seem fulfilled, no man dwells in his promised land, but the plowing-quality of life demands continuous participation until the moment of interruption comes. Withdrawal is betrayal. Neil's academic, historicist, empirical, European-style 'knowledge' comes to nothing, in Africa at any event; and if that is true of Africa, may it not be the case elsewhere?

In other words, what has been at issue in Bray's second life in Africa has been the validation or otherwise of Europe's historic presence in Africa. As Bray's control over himself and his situation has gradually broken down, so the code of values and the historic experience on which it has been based is discredited, because that code and that experience have been responsible for creating the situation itself. But Bray has in the meanwhile begun to live again; uninhibited, this time, by the accumulation of irrelevant tradition, he is also unprotected by it.

The polarity that emerges to prominence in the penultimate section of the book bears out this interpretation. Hjalmar Wentz, the survivor of Europe, who smuggled his wife out of the shadow of the gas chambers, confronts Bray in Gala on the latter's return from a meeting with Shinza in the bush. His daughter, the sexy Emmanuelle, has fled the country with Ras Asahe, the arrogant young broadcaster whose father had been a supporter of Shinza years before; but it is the failure of a coup from the right that has led to Asahe's flight. Hjalmar is having a nervous breakdown; the final straw has an interesting consistency.

'A sign of weakness. It's fatal to show a sign of weakness. She accuses me of weakness. She says I had no authority over the children. But she also blames herself. D'you know why?' Hjalmar began to laugh weakly, unable to help himself. 'D'you know what Margot said?'

His eye was following Olivia's letter as he listened to Hjalmar
. . . you are having a so much more interesting time . . . my poor

169

*dull news . . . I sometimes worry. I wonder where we'll take up
again. Of course I should have come, but the fact that I didn't . . .
shows that it wasn't possible for us.*

'She said, I blame myself. A Jewish father would have had
some authority over his daughter. He would have seen that
she was provided with a proper musical education. He would
have found somewhere better for his children to live than
buried in this place. A Jew would have done better.'

In the appalled silence the weak giggle spilt over, again. 'I
know I'm not well. But that's true – she said it.' The terrible
weak laughter was suddenly a fiercely embarrassed apology –
not for himself, but for his wife.

'Poor Margot,' Bray said.

'I left all the keys, I left the van outside the bar, and I
walked to the main road with my things. She was carrying a
vase of flowers into the entrance and she saw me putting the
keys down.' (pp. 418–419)

Hjalmar and his experience are quintessentially European, like
Bray and *his* – and they simultaneously undergo the same kind of
breakdown: the long-established marital cycle has come off the
rails. Of course, in Bray's case this is much more low-keyed, heavily
modulated; but the ironic purpose of the coincidence is manifest.
Breakdown takes different forms, but in a chaotic age all its forms
have one meaning. The objective fact of coincidence itself bears on
this meaning. Why is the same moment in time employed for the
two identical revelations (what actually takes place in this charged
instant is only, in each case, a report of what has already happened)
in a long novel with plenty of space in it to manoeuvre and with very
little dependence on coincidence as a technical device? Surely the
answer is that the author wants to suggest a particular shape
governed by time, a shape whose nature is external to, and
independent of, human experience and perceptions?

The author is indicating a collapse of the traditional relationship
between the individual and his society. She follows Conrad in
challenging the dominant European vision through the perspective
of the gap between ideology and reality in the colonial (or
immediately post-colonial) situation, as Conrad does in *Heart of
Darkness* and *Nostromo*.

The cycle of return and reawakening that Bray's active life has
undergone thus coincides with a decisive lurch toward the abyss on
the part of European civilization. This was the conclusion towards

which Nadine Gordimer was moving in *The Late Bourgeois World*, a book in which the moral certainties of the characters, and the gestures and affirmations based on them, concealed a profound authorial uncertainty, almost a confusion. In *A Guest of Honour*, on the other hand, the uncertainties and moral groping, the sense of indadequcy and inability to grasp and deal with the complexity of events, constitute the uneven surface of a new underlying certainty, a sense of the shape and direction of things. Nadine Gordimer succeeds in realizing this new certainty not through an experiment on form but through a fairly orthodox traditional novel, which perhaps emphasizes the degree of her success. She works in an area of uncertainty with the common cultural instruments at our disposal and produces a carefully-shaped and unwavering result. European history is plunged into a period of uneasy transience, and the thread linking the polarity between the two men representing the stage immediately past stretches tighter until it snaps. Hjalmar, invited as a matter of course by Bray to accompany him and Rebecca on their journey out of the localized chaos of Gala, surprisingly declines.

Hjalmar sat down on the edge of an old verandah chair whose legs splayed under weight. He said shyly, 'I think I'll stay and keep an eye on things in the house.'

Bray was picking an old label off the box. A small cockroach flashed from beneath, fell to the floor and was caught by his sole. 'I don't know when I'll be back, you know.'

'That's okay. Maybe I'll come down soon. If I get lonely or so. Do you want to take the Orwell?'

'Good lord, keep the books. There's nowhere to put them.'

Rebecca appeared with an armful of children's worn-out sandals. 'What's this about?'

'Hjalmar's decided to hang on a bit.'

'Oh. Have you?' she said, friendly, awkward, to make it seem neither unreasonable nor unexpected.

Hjalmar gave a short laugh – 'It may sound crazy, but you know I want to finish the paving out there under the tree. I hate to leave it half-finished – you know? Then I'll be able to decide the . . . the next thing. Only I must do it first. It's such a mess there with the fruit dropping and the leaves on that uneven ground. When it's paved all you need to do is just sweep if off.' (pp. 459–460)

Bray had once remarked that Hjalmar had a talent for survival, and later he adds the rider that the precocious Emmanuelle has inherited his talent. But when the price of survival is revealed, Hjalmar is shown as an essentially 'linear' character, withdrawing from the complexities of reality into an obsessive concentration on small, single, self-imposed tasks, and the imposition of a meaningless and minuscule order: as a cultural symbol he possesses frightening implications. The civilization of the West lives on, but with inner life (and connections with vital forces) banked down to the lowest embers, while the external manifestation goes on tirelessly, mechanistically and without relevance repeating its little technical tricks and expertises – not even substituting for the living relationship the core of reality it once possessed. Both Hjalmar and Bray, the Europeans, are drawn to the tree, the magnificent, ancient, carelessly fertile, parasite-rotten but vigorous symbol of Africa underneath which Bray has chosen to work in Gala. Thus while Bray, who cannot survive, shows some sort of sympathetic understanding of the tree's meaning, the response of Hjalmar, the survivor, is an etiolated repetition of the empty European habit of tidying up, imposing a meaningless formal order. The implications of this reach out beyond the history of the white man in Africa.

They part, Bray involved with history, and therefore with life, to go to his death; Hjalmar, withdrawn from the meaningful structure of time, to go on smoothing down the ripples of his mind.

What we know about Bray and Europe is placed in perspective by Rebecca. She flies to Switzerland and goes into a bank fitted out with plush solemnity, like a comfortable temple, where Bray had sent her money. In her hotel that evening she finds herself in the lounge together with a honeymoon couple.

A young couple were sitting there, stirring the cream on their coffee and slowly finishing bowls of berries sprinkled with sugar. They murmured to each other in German – something like, 'Good . . .?' 'Oh very good' – and went on dreamily licking the spoons. The girl wore trousers and a sweater with a string of pearls, she was tall and narrow-footed and remote. The man, shorter than she, looked not quite at home in rather smart casual clothes and had a worried little double chin already beginning beneath his soft face. The girl yawned and he smiled. It was the stalemate of conversation, the listlessness of a newly married couple who have never previously been lovers. 'Very good,' he said again, putting his bowl on the tray.

The wine rose to her head in a singing sensation and she

thought of them sitting on politely round a coffee table for ever, he slipped down into fatness and greyness, she never released from her remoteness, while their children grew, waiting to take their places there. She became aware of an ornamental clock ticking away the silence in the room between herself and the couple. (p. 495)

The last image is crucial. Measured time, reduced to an ordered precision, divides her experience from the life of Europe. The Swiss clock in a Swiss hotel lounge and the bourgeois Swiss couple, motionless and apparently sunken into hebetude, are analogues for Hjalmar in Gala; or rather, both are analogues for what has happened to Europe, while Rebecca is on the outside, where the life is, but cut off from it, with a different history, separated by the clock from the experience of Europe.

England, as Bray's birthplace, is, however, the centre. Further confirmation of Bray's speculation about life in time is afforded through Rebecca's perceptions of London.

. . . She went unrecognized here; she was the figure with the scythe.

Yet this was where Bray came from: there were faces in which she could trace him. An elderly man in a taxi outside a restaurant; even a young actor with sideburns and locks. He might have once been, or become, any of these who were living so differently from the way he did. It was as if she forayed into a past that he had left long ago and a future that he would never inhabit. She wandered the bypasses of his life that he had not taken, meeting the possibility of his presence. (p. 497)

Bray is, however, a particular case, and the matter of his 'belonging' is still unsettled. Two clues are given which are suggestive of the full irony of his fate:

One afternoon she was coming out of the supermarket in the suburban shopping street near the hotel when somebody said her name. It came like a heavy hand on her shoulder. She turned. A tall, very slender girl with a narrow, sallow face curtained in straight black hair was leaning casually on a wheeled shopping basket. It was Emmanuelle. 'I thought it was you but it couldn't be – are you over on holiday?'

'My family live in England. I've been here about two weeks.' She held tightly closed her packet containing one pear and one orange; evidence of her solitariness. 'And you – you live round about?'

Emmanuelle's hair wrapped itself across her neck like a scarf, in the wind. 'We're just down the road. Beastly basement flat. But we're getting a big studio next month – if we don't go back, instead.'

'Back? Could Ras go back?'

'It's someone else.'

'I'm sorry – I just thought –'

They stood there talking, two women who had never liked one another much. Emmanuelle's elegant hands mimed a sort of trill of inconsequence along the handle of her basket. 'That's all right. No drama. We're friends and all that. I'm living with Kofi Ahuma – he's just published his first novel, but now his father's in favour again in Ghana, and he can indulge his homesickness. So we may go to Ghana. Are your children with you? We're producing a children's play together – he wrote it and I did the music. It's on at the Theatre Club for the next three days, they might enjoy it.'

'No, they're not here.'

Emmanuelle gave the quick nod of someone who reminds herself of something that hasn't interested her very much. 'Oh my God – you were in that awful accident, weren't you?' She was mildly curious. 'What happened to Colonel Bray – he was beaten up?'

'He was killed.'

'How ghastly'. She might have left Ras but she was still armed with his opinions. 'Of course, he was with Shinza and that crowd. Poor devil. These nice white liberals getting mixed up in things they don't understand. What did he expect?' (pp. 501–502)

We are back to polarities: besides the useless trick of survival, Hjalmar's daughter has inherited from Europe a yawning intellectual emptiness. She is quite unaware that in her second-hand rhetoric she has stumbled upon the crucial question, while at the same time enunciating the grounds of one possible answer. These have been hinted at already: Hitler has been mentioned twice in the book, the first time by Emmanuelle's father, at an independence party, in a discussion with an African doctor, the country's first medical graduate.

Odara laughed. 'But it always comes down to the same thing:

you Europeans talk very reasonably about that sort of suffering because you don't know . . . you may have thought it was terrible, but there's nothing like that in your lives.'

Bray saw Margot Wentz put up her head with a quick grimace-smile, as if someone had told an old joke she couldn't raise a laugh for.

'Well, here you're mistaken,' her husband said, rather grandly, 'we lived under Mr Hitler. And you must know all about that.'

'I'm not interested in Hitler.' Timothy Odara's fine teeth were bared in impatient pleasantness. 'My friend, white men have killed more people in Africa than Hitler ever did in Europe.'

'But you're crazy,' said Wentz gently.

'Europe's wars, white men's killings among themselves. What's that to me? You've just said one shouldn't burden oneself with suffering. I don't have any feelings about Hitler.'

'Oh but you should,' Mrs Wentz said, almost dreamily. 'No more and no less than you do about what happened to Africans. It's all the same thing. A slave in the hold of a ship in the eighteenth century and a Jew or a gipsy in a concentration camp in the nineteen-forties.'

'Well, I had my seventeenth and eighteenth birthdays in the detention camp at Fort Howard, the guest of Her Majesty's governor,' said Odara, 'that I know.'

'Her two brothers died at Auschwitz,' Hjalmar Wentz said; but his wife was talking to Jo-Ann Pettigrew, who offered blobs of toasted marshmallow on the end of a long fork. (pp. 33–34)

The image in the last sentence is perhaps too macabre, suggesting the impersonality of survival, and the irony of transferring European patterns, aspects of a particular survival to Africa, whose present has been largely determined by the destructive elements in European culture; Odara's point is mere political affectation, tinged with a danger of whose presence, let alone the magnitude, of which he is unaware. The comparison he draws, between his own detention prior to independence and Margot Wentz's 'slave in the hold of a ship in the eighteenth century and a Jew or a gipsy in a concentration camp in the nineteen-forties', has just enough surface validity to make its absurdity clear. The level of validity is the continuity of cruelty – European, 'civilized' cruelty – that links

Odara's experience with those evoked by Margot Wentz; but this is swamped in the depths of Timothy Odara's historical egocentrism.

Perhaps there is this link, then, between Odara, a minor character of no intrinsic significance – or, rather, between this episode and the other brief mention of Hitler, later in the novel. On Bray's first return from Gala to the capital, after he has seen Shinza and encountered the young trade unionist who had been illegally arrested and beaten, he spends the evening having dinner with Neil and Vivien Bayley.

> They talked of Bray's work and Bray told an anecdote or two about Gala – how his name had been up at the club for weeks until the bold draper seconded it. Vivien was in conversation with a friend on the telephone; she came back after a while and said, 'Did you know Mweta's going to speak over the radio at midnight? Apparently it's been announced every hour all afternoon.'
>
> Neil opened another bottle of wine. 'The contract's been given to the Chinese. France, West Germany and America have called off the loan. Or they're going to build both dams – the lake one as well. My, my. We can't go to bed.'
>
> Vivien looked at Bray. She said, 'He's tired, he's driven hundreds of miles.'
>
> He was feeling embarrassed for Mweta. Why midnight? Who advised him about such things? Perhaps he didn't know that Hitler used to choose odd hours of the night or early morning for his speeches, entering through the territory of dreams, invading people's minds when blood pressure and nervous resistance are at lowest ebb. 'Certainly midday would be a pleasanter time to report back on his dam.' . . .
>
> At midnight Mweta's voice filled the room. They sat dreamily still, not looking at each other. Vivien's right hand was pressed against the side of her belly to quiet the only movement in the room, stirring there. Mweta announced the immediate introduction of a Preventive Detention Bill. (pp. 154–155)

The link is between Odara's wilful ignorance of history and Mweta's pragmatic brand of ahistoricism; and this illuminates the polarity between Mweta and Shinza: the latter quotes Fanon and brings the history of liberation movements elsewhere on the continent to bear on his political action, while the former is getting the best deals he is likely to be offered by the same businessmen in whose interests the colonial power had ruled and plundered his country.

'Oh we all know about his early Marxist training. His six weeks in 1937. We've heard all about that from him a dozen times. We all know he was the intellectual of the Party while we were the bush boys. We've had all that.' (p. 164)

Mweta is ultimately condemned on the grounds of historical confusion: in the end he has to call in British troops to restore order — and a degree of security to his own tenure of power. At the end of the book the thread linking them has snapped at last, with Shinza in exile in Algiers.

Emmanuelle suffers from the same ahistorical affliction, but in her it is a disease amounting to grotesque deformity. She is in herself an end product, a fusion, combining all the best of what Europe had to offer: her maternal grandfather an emancipated, Germanized professor of physics, her father once courageous enough to risk his life for love and for what he knew to be good in the face of prevailing evil. But all she is left with, in Africa, is a facility for music and the instinct for survival. It is the tragic end of the European liberal line: a pretty and vacuous performing monkey, adept at imitating her lovers' phrases, and agile enough to duck under the blows of Fate. Her background is diametrically opposed to that of Rebecca, also born in Africa but without any such burden of cultural inheritance. Rebecca is learning all the time. She is not only receptive but able to discern and to develop what she accepts, to integrate it with the basic qualities of her being. So Rebecca, neither European nor African, unbound and unconfined by any moral or political frame of reference, is able to absorb, and even embody the most shattering discovery of Nadine Gordimer's longest novel: the non-existence of Europe, or of that idea of Europe in terms of historical and cultural – and moral – significance that has stood sometimes as a consciously-sought goal, sometimes as an objective correlative, but always there, always just outside the reach of her heroes and heroines, just beyond the imaginative frameworks of the lives they lead, the matrix of African reality their creator provides for them. In *The Lying Days* Europe's meaning has to be discovered from scratch; in *A World of Strangers* and *Occasion for Loving* Europe possesses the solidity of moral reference from which the leading characters strive to derive their impulse to action; in *The Late Bourgeois World* the new perspectives that emerge from an awareness of European decay are, like the very awareness, themselves European. In all these works the basis of what I have called moral reference is the Europe of renaissance humanism and romantic liberalism in which the individual is of supreme importance in relation to nature and the community, where the idea of love was apotheosized, the value of the communication between man and man formed into discovery, and the meaning of tragedy understood. This idea of Europe informed the very pattern of Nadine Gordimer's novels, though always from the outside. Bray is a conscious embodiment of this idea; and this is the magnificent justification for saddling him with the burden of narration almost throughout the book. His ambiguities, uncertainties, responses to pressure, and eventual decisiveness in the midst of breakdown, both inner and outer, reflect the growing discovery that he has to make but is spared from absorbing, that the objective meaning of this idea has become ephemeral: its elaborate and ornate structures have turned to mist, dispelled by the African sun.

But Rebecca, who has known Bray as a man (hence the emphasis on physical detail in their relationship) and not as the embodiment of idea or ideal, has been influenced by him. She has received a kind of imprint, so that it has become a matter of instinct for her to seek the real and the healthy in relationships and objects. Rebecca encounters no meaning corresponding to Bray's in London, and her meeting with Emmanuelle, like her confessional session with the Swiss banker, is a confrontation with nothingness, a void where the structure behind the idea might have been anticipated to exist. The only thing that is left is the 'house in Wiltshire':

> She thought of Olivia as an empty perfume bottle in which a scent still faintly remains. She had found one on one of the shelves in the wardrobe of her hotel room: left there by some anonymous English woman, an Olivia. She knew nobody in the city of eight millions. She had nothing in common with anyone: except his wife.
>
> At times she was strongly attracted by the idea of going to see Olivia and his daughters. But the thought that they would receive her, accept her in their supremely civilized tolerance – *his* tolerance – this filled her with resentment. She wanted to bare her suffering, to live it and thrust it, disgusting, torn live from her under their noses, not to make it 'acceptable' to others. (p. 498)

In other words, the strictly personal continuity that exists between Bray and herself has nothing to do with Europe or

England. The house in Wiltshire might provide a structure of values that would 'tolerate' her suffering, but not one that would validate it in any permanent moral or human sense. Thus again, where continuity or at least contact with a mighty and potent scheme of values might have been expected, none can exist because the scheme no longer does.

Of course it is possible that Nadine Gordimer has, herself, never quite understood, what she boils down to the 'house in Wiltshire'; she doesn't really come to grips with it, and quickly turns it into a symbol of things past. Rebecca, the new person, reborn into the old society, is unlike her predecessors Helen Shaw and Jessie Stilwell in the author's fiction: she shows little curiosity to discover the nature of what they would have regarded as a rightful part of their heritage from which they had been unfairly excluded. So Wiltshire, Bray's past, what made him, remain mysterious, readable only in what became of him.

The final ironic twist occurs in the closing paragraph of the book, and bears full blast on the nagging question of knowledge that underpins the presence of the Europeans in Africa.

> Hjalmar Wentz also put together Bray's box of papers and gave them over to Dando, who might know what to do with .them. Eventually they must have reached the hands of Mweta. He, apparently, chose to believe that Bray was a conciliator; a year later he published a blueprint for the country's new education scheme, the Bray Report. (pp. 503–504)

This links the structure together in important ways and places. First, it comments on the passage quoted earlier in which Vivien, Neil and Rebecca talk about Bray's death (pp. 477–478) where, for all the bright knowingness that the young Bayleys possess, they are unable to achieve true knowledge, or come near to an understanding of the nature of knowledge – which has so much to do with their presence in Africa.

It also seals the limits of possibility on this level of knowledge, deadening the echoes set off by Dando in the following passage:

> He was talking of Bray. 'The thing is, of course, all our dear friends abroad will say he was killed by the people he loved and what else can you expect of them, and how ungrateful they are, and all that punishment-and-reward two-and-two-makes-four that passes for intelligent interpretation of events.

179

That's the part of it that would rile him. Or maybe amuse him. I don't know.'

Vivien's beautiful controlled voice came out of the dark. 'I wish we could know that James himself knew it wasn't that, when it happened.'

'Of course he knew!' Roly spoke with the unchallengeable authority of friendship on a plane none of the others had shared. 'He's got nothing to do with that lot of spiritual bed-wetters finding a surrogate for their fears in his death! He knew what's meant by the forces of history, he knew how risky the energies released by social change are. But what's the good. They'll say 'his blacks' murdered him. They'll go one further: they'll come up with their guilts to be expiated and say, yes, he certainly died with Christian forgiveness for the people who killed him, into the bargain. Christ almighty. We'll never get it straight. They'll paw over everything with their sticky misconceptions.' (p. 479)

Dando 'knows' more than he admits: he has made Rebecca aware that he knows of Bray's illicit transfer of her money to Switzerland, for instance. Perhaps he has a hand in Mweta's final gesture, since Hjalmar handed Bray's papers on to him. But even his admission of inadequacy, his unconscious invocation of the source of the kind of knowledge his culture is supposed to possess *par excellence* ('Christ almighty. We'll never get it straight'), even this falls short of what Bray had really learnt, and what is confirmed, not only structurally, by the ending.

. . . human affairs didn't come to clear-cut conclusions a line drawn and a total added up. They appeared to resolve, dissolve, while they were only reforming, coming together in another combination. Even when we are dead, what we did goes on making these new combinations (he saw clouds, saw molecules); that's true for private history as well as the other kind. (p. 385)

This is true of Africa and Europe (or Europe-in-Africa); but is also a formulation distinctly out of the main stream of the European novelistic view of time, linked as it almost invariably is with particularist, individualistic, liberal-'meliorist' ideas. The whirling of the molecules cancel out, rather ruthlessly, the liberal European universe, the reality that Jessie and Helen hungered after so keenly; and this is utterly confirmed, beyond doubt, in the last lines of the

180

book, in 'The Bray Report'. The huge, ironic question remains – what is the nature of the continuity between Europe and Africa, then, in the post-colonial age: the Bray Report, or white mercenaries in Katanga?

So in a rather subtle manner, in *A Guest of Honour* Nadine Gordimer not only topples the burden of the great myth of the metropolitan culture that has always been a problem in her work; she also digs away at the foundations of the fictive monument which that myth has had erected to it, and undermines one of the major struts of the structure of the English realistic novel. Of course, this is not the same thing as saying she has found her African feet, or given the novel in Africa an indigenous foundation; but she has written something that contains the seeds of a conscious rejection of those aspects of Europe and the West in general that the West itself considers most central to its tradition, and an essential cultural export – or neo-imperialist imposition. An idea of history radically removed from the conventional Western one at least opens the possibilities of a new interpretation of African experience, of the imaginative realization of Tom Stilwell's project in *Occasion for Loving* – a new history of Africa that is not a history of colonization, but of life. It may be significant that South American writers of fiction have also chosen the sensitive territory of time as prime target for attacking an imperialist past. The relationship of Borges or Gabriel Garcia Marquez to European culture is just as tortuous and ambivalent as Nadine Gordimer's, and perhaps they have a common starting point.

In any event, Nadine Gordimer has developed through her career as a novelist to a point which has eluded both her nearest South African contemporaries, Abrahams and Jacobson. At various stages in his career, each has performed tricks, perilously similar to the other two: in terms of immediate conscious preoccupation, Jacobson's *The Beginners* is Miss Gordimer's *The Lying Days* is Abrahams' *Tell Freedom*; Jacobson's *The Evidence of Love* is Nadine Gordimer's *Occasion for Loving* is Abrahams' *The Path of Thunder*; Abrahams' *A Night of Their Own* is Nadine Gordimer's *The Late Bourgeois World*; both *A Wreath for Udomo* and *This Island Now* (Abrahams) have close bearing on central aspects of *A Guest of Honour*. But Abrahams and Jacobson both live in exile, are both, perhaps with increasing reluctance, Europeans, citizens of the Western world. Nadine Gordimer is the only one of the three to have realized an autonomous creative self, as free as she would desire to be of a culture and a tradition whose relevance she sees as severely limited and in any event distorted and impotent; and she has done it with both feet on South African soil. This is one compelling reason why she is the most important of the three as a South African, or an African, writer.

6   The Conservationist

Nadine Gordimer's most recent novel is also her most complex in design and technique. *The Conservationist*[1] appeared in 1974, three years after the major statement of *A Guest of Honour*. It was preceded by a rather subdued and even disappointing volume of short stories called *Livingstone's Companions* (1972)[2], which collects pieces published over a span of seven years.

Enough thematic links exist between these three works for them to constitute a unified, if uncompleted, phase in Nadine Gordimer's career. The most important of these is the concern with the white man's relationship with the indigenous realities of Africa. The focus in *Livingstone's Companions* is necessarily fragmented, by contrast with the steady grandeur of *A Guest of Honour*; magnified slivers of the theme are presented, their imperfections much enlarged, like the pores in the breasts of serving wenches in Gulliver's Brobdingnag. The authoress's awareness of the continuity of this theme in South African fiction is made explicit in a story called 'The Bride of Christ' (*Livingstone's Companions*, pp. 156ff.), in which the central character is a sixteen-year-old girl, daughter of progressive, rationalistic Jewish parents whose moral position in relation to South African politics is unexceptionable – except, perhaps, in terms of the crucial problem of action. They are faced by a new kind of problem, however, when their daughter writes to them from school that she wishes to be confirmed in the Christian faith. The literary-historical context of the story is supplied through the heroine's first name, which is that of the first heroine of South African fiction – Lyndall.

In *The Story of an African Farm* Olive Schreiner's Lyndall is a young girl of sufficiently powerful personality and intellect to declare for herself on manners and morals, to differentiate herself

---

[1] *The Conservationist* (Jonathan Cape, London, 1974).
[2] *Livingstone's Companions* (Jonathan Cape, London, 1972).

sharply from her background in these matters and thus, at a great price, to establish her individuality. Her characteristic mode is one of rejection, her ultimate aim the perfect Romantic affirmation: and she will have nothing to do with social convention or the outward forms of religious observance. To her successor, however, both of these are important: but though *her* characteristic behavioural impulse is toward affirmation, in action each affirmative evokes its corresponding negation, and the final result is doubt. The original Lyndall endured a situation of uncreated consciousness, in which the meaning of Europe in Africa was not questioned – by Europeans. Nor was it by any means fully or properly understood by them; but it had an objective status, nonetheless. Thus the first step towards consciousness is necessarily a negation of the self-evident. The contrast between this and the fully-articulated nature of Lyndall Berger's historical context is illustrated with a sort of tired clarity in an early exchange between Mrs. Berger and Lyndall, in which the mother tries to respond honestly to her daughter's (to her) bizarre and threatening decision.

> '... Of course there are Anglicans and Catholics and Methodists who don't preach brotherhood and forget it when it comes to a black face. But the fact is that they're the rarities. Odd men out. The sort of people you'll be worshipping Christ with every Sunday are the people who see no wrong in their black "brothers" having to carry a pass. The same sort of people who didn't see anything wrong in your great-grandparents having to live in a ghetto in Galicia. The same people who kept going to church in Germany on Sundays while the Jews were being shovelled into gas ovens.'
>
> She watched her daughter's face for the expression that knew *that* was coming; couldn't be helped, it had to be dragged up, again and again and again and again and again – like Lear's 'nevers' – no matter how sick of it everyone might be. But the child's face was naked.
>
> (*Livingstone's Companions*, p. 168)

Lyndall's unresponsiveness relates, among other things, to European events, European judgments, and European values – the interaction of European ideas and African realities, the European past and the African present. For her, in direct contrast with her predecessor, the need to conform, to unlearn the known about the meaning of Europe in Africa, is paramount. So *her* first step towards the goal of security is along the road of conformity; she affirms her faith in the surface patterns whose value is self-evident to her peers. But her evasion of reality leads to conflict and guilt, and in the end nothing can be affirmed.

> '. . . Don't feel much like dancing,' the girl added, off-hand, in a low voice to her mother, and the two faces shared, for a moment, a family likeness of doubt . . .
>
> (*Livingstone's Companions*, p. 181)

But Lyndall goes to her party instead of to church, the first Easter after being confirmed; and either way the grid of reality, of a fully-articulated social system, traps her into conformity without the possibility of affirmation. The landscape of the African farm has been built up, made urban and industrial in imitation of Europe, and the result for the individual is restriction, not freedom.

The Conservationist is also a story of an African farm. Its action is located on one; and on one level Nadine Gordimer has super-imposed her contemporary highveld landscape onto Olive Schreiner's nineteenth-century Karroo. The patterns of similarity and difference are instructive. In both, black people toil patiently close to the soil, seemingly unconscious of usurpation; and in both strong-willed whites seek a coherence through domination, through a projection onto reality of an internal intellectual environment; in both they fail, though for different reasons, and their failures have different meanings. Mehring, the industrialist who is also the conservationist, is an alternative version of Bray, the liberal hero of *A Guest of Honour*: Mehring does not see himself as a guest. He is indigenous, and his Europeanism is (like Lyndall's) stripped of the complexities of conscience, pared down to a perfection of pragmatism. Despite his freedom from doubt, however, he is, like Bray, a white man in Africa in the second half of the twentieth century, and thus an embodiment of an alien culture, of a particularly expressive form of dominance, of the organization of reality through action as the product of contemplation – and always in danger of rejection by the local soil. He is at the opposite end of the continuum from Waldo in Schreiner's *African Farm*. Waldo's failure to impose order through the intellect on the environment leads to his peaceful absorption by it.

Another important link that draws together Nadine Gordimer's recent work is a preoccupation with betrayal. This constitutes a cut-off point from the affirmative ending of *The Late Bourgeois World* or stories like 'Some Monday for Sure'. In her most recent phase Miss Gordimer considers the intensities of different kinds of political and cultural pressures on ordinary people, and concludes that they are too heavy to be sustained. Thus in *A Guest of Honour* Bray betrays Olivia and certain class and cultural traditions; Mweta betrays his revolution and his friend Shinza; in the two directly political stories in *Livingstone's Companions*, 'Open House' and 'Africa Emergent' betrayal is the central theme – betrayal, under pressure, of beliefs, ideals and friends. In these two stories, however, there is a variation from *A Guest of Honour* in the ontological treatment of the theme: the authoress is interested in the problem of personal responsibility, and thus refuses the option of a Conradian universal pessimism. In both stories it is 'liberal' white characters whose confusion about their roles and identities in South Africa causes them to betray their relationships, both political and personal, with black friends. In 'Open House' Frances Taver is 'on the secret circuit for people who wanted to find out the truth about South Africa', prominent visitors who knew 'that there *were* still ways of getting to meet Africans, provided you could get hold of the right white people'. Frances Taver is one of these whites.

> Had been for years. From the forties when she had been a trade union organizer and run a mixed union of garment workers while this was legally possible, in the fifties, after her marriage, when she was manager of a black-and-white theatre group before that was disbanded by new legislation, to the early sixties, when she hid friends on the run from the police – Africans who were members of the newly-banned political organizations – before the claims of that sort of friendship had to be weighed against the risk of the long spells of detention without trial introduced to betray it.
>
> (*Livingstone's Companions*, p. 140)

She arranges a lunch party for a visiting American political journalist, a Kennedy liberal who wants to meet 'a few ordinary, articulate people' (p. 142) – he means black people. But there are not many available in the days of instant repression, and the situation she creates is, to her, highly artificial and embarrassing – the 'clean' black lawyer complaining bitterly at the harassment he must undergo from the security police when he applies for a travel document, because he took over the clientele of a colleague who was sent to prison for six years for political activity; the stupid young journalist who tries to interest the American in a play he is writing 'right out of township life'; and the cynical entrepreneur, aware of the rules of the game but only half-willing to play it, combine to distort the reality she has known to be impossible to present. After the party she finds a note left by a friend, a banned black activist who has had to go 'underground' and who visits her very occasionally, when he knows it is safe; she thinks of him as a 'vision strayed from' her youth. (p. 141)

> Someone had left a half-empty packet of cigarettes; who was it who broke matches into little tents? As she carried the tray into the deserted kitchen, she saw a note written on the back of a bill taken from the spike. HOPE YOUR PARTY WENT WELL.
> It was not signed, and was written with the kitchen ballpoint which hung on a string. But she knew who had written it; the vision from the past had come and gone again.
> (*Livingstone's Companions*, p. 149)

The horrible irony of the situation is clear to her, even though she absolves her friend from ironic intention in the note he has written: she realizes that the fulness of his knowledge would preclude facile judgment on his part. But what of the 'knowledge' presented by herself and absorbed by the American political journalist? She accepts responsibility for the distortion, and overcomes reluctance to telephone him to explain. The conversation is not a success: she has deferred it until almost sure that he'd left, and her surprise at finding him causes one awkwardness among many. In the end there is no effective communication.

> The urgency of her voice stopped his mouth, was communicated to him even if what she said was not. . .
> He understood, indeed, that something complicated was wrong, but he knew, too, that he wouldn't be there long enough to find out, that perhaps you needed to live and die there, to find out. (p. 151)

Thus awareness of responsibility for betrayal is no help in communicating reality. Frances Taver has said to the journalist, " 'I don't want you to be taken in . . . by anyone" '; she includes herself in the category, but this, of course, the American can not understand.

One of the ironic effects generated by this story is that while the blacks at the lunch party are all, in their different ways, imitation white men, the man who stays away is a 'real' one – a Forsterian liberal in his delicacy of perception, in his refusal to judge his betrayer. In the final story in the collection, 'Africa Emergent', however, this neat grid of European cultural perception and moral judgment does not fit. The black man who is at the focus of the white narrator's perception is inaccessible to/the normal tools of liberal scrutiny.

The story's opening statement concentrates the readers' attention on the theme of betrayal.

> He's in prison now, so I'm not going to mention his name. It mightn't be a good thing, you understand. Perhaps you think you understand too well; but don't be quick to jump to conclusions from five or six thousand miles away: if you lived here, you'd understand something else – friends know that shows of loyalty are all right for children holding hands in the school playground; for us they're luxuries, not important and maybe dangerous. If I said, I was a friend of so-and-so, black man awaiting trial for treason, what good would it do him? And, who knows, it might draw just that decisive bit more attention to me. *He'*d be the first to agree.
>
> (*Livingstone's Companions*, p. 233)

Two layers of difficulty of communication are suggested: the one between narrator and reader, insider and outsider in relation to the given situation; but the second emerges with more force later in the story and refers to communication within the situation, between those for whom the show of loyalty is a forbidden luxury. If the narrator knows he will not be understood by his remote metropolitan audience, he is even more immediately aware that he does not understand the men at the centre of the story he tells – a black sculptor who gets a scholarship to study in the United States, is refused a passport, leaves on a one-way exit permit, and drowns himself in New England, and a close friend of the sculptor, a black actor on the fringes of an inter-racial drama group in Johannesburg, who *is* given a passport to take up *his* scholarship, and returns, alive, having used the return half of the sculptor's air ticket to do so. He is faced with the suspicion of his 'progressive' white friends, of being a police spy: a house he lives in is raided by the security police, every adult in the establishment except for himself is charged with attending a secret meeting of a banned political organization.

> *He* was the only one who remained, significantly, it seemed too impossible to ignore, free. And yet his friends let him stay on in the house; it was a mystery to us whites – and some

blacks, too. But then so much becomes a mystery where trust becomes a commodity on sale to the police.

> (*Livingstone's Companions*, p. 246)

The narrator and the central character drift apart, in the general atmosphere of suspicion and the particular tension over the latter's failure to repay a loan.

> As for the friendship, he'd shown me the worth of that. It's become something the white man must buy just as he must buy the co-operation of police stool pigeons. Elias [the sculptor] has been dead five years; we live in our situation as of now, as the legal phrase goes; one falls back on legal phrases as other forms of expression become too risky.
>
> And then, two hundred and seventy-seven days ago, there was a new rumour, and this time it was confirmed, this time it was no rumour. *He* was fetched from his room one night and imprisoned. That's perfectly legal, here; it's the hundred-and-eighty-day Detention Act . . .
>
> . . . Heaven knows – those police spy rumours aside – nobody could have looked more unlikely to be a political activist than that cheerful young man, second-string, always ready to jump up and turn over the record, fond of Liberace jackets and aspiring to play Le Roi Jones Off-Broadway.
>
> But as I say, we know where he is now; inside. In solitary most of the time – they say, those who've also been inside. Two-hundred-and-seventy-seven days he's been in there.
>
> And so we white friends can purge ourselves of the shame of rumours. We can be pure again. We are satisfied at last. He's in prison. He's proved himself, hasn't he?

> (*Livingstone's Companions*, pp. 247, 248)

Various points about communication and betrayal emerge from the way the story ends. The last paragraph in particular, with its emphatic first-person – third-person interchange, suggests the impossibility of comprehension between the groups that compose the human setting; and yet the whites, from habit of history, must always judge the others – and in making that judgment, betray themselves again.

In all of Nadine Gordimer's first five novels the central characters were driven by a painful need to purify their perceptions, to understand themselves and the way they functioned within their historic moment. The structural consequence of this dynamic principle was in each case a pattern of radiations outward from the

Nadine Gordimer

perceiver to the facts of the world around; the hero's definition of
the world around him was active and progressive. And, of course, in
each case the hero was somehow marginal to the main current of
white behaviour in South Africa: the old story of the morally
imperative but historically irrelevant enactment of European
romantic liberalism on an alien stage was presented each time.

In *The Conservationist*, however, Nadine Gordimer creates her
first Newtonian hero. Mehring the super-pragmatist is formed by
his environment. What he regards as ineluctable realities lead him
to certain patterns of response which he considers relevant. The
superficial outcome is, naturally, very successful. Mehring is an
enormously wealthy industrialist, a self-made man (in an ironic
sense, since, as we have suggested, his basic behavioural principle is
a passive one). But a principal structural dimension of this book is
the continuous interaction between surfaces – different surfaces of
consciousness, of inner and outer reality, of the forces of nature
themselves. And the reader is presented with the collisions between
Mehring's pragmatic apparatus of self which he uses for dealing
with the world, and a whole range of dimensions of reality whose
existence or force he has not accounted for.

The technique of interaction between surfaces is deployed in the
book's opening scene. Mehring, industrialist and weekend tax-loss
farmer, arrives at his farm one Sunday morning in autumn.

Pale freckled eggs.

Swaying over the ruts to the gate of the third pasture,
Sunday morning, the owner of the farm suddenly sees: a
clutch of pale freckled eggs set out before a half-circle of
children. . . . There is pride of ownership in that grin lifted
shyly to the farmer's gaze. The eggs are arranged like marbles,
the other children crowd round but you can tell they are
not allowed to touch unless the cross-legged one gives
permission . . .

The emblem on the car's bonnet, itself made in the shape of
a prismatic flash, scores his vision with a vertical-horizontal
sword of dazzle. This is the place at which a child always
appears, even if none has been in sight, racing across the field
to open the gate for the car. But today the farmer puts on the
brake, leaves the engine running, and gets out. One very
young boy, wearing a jersey made long ago for much longer
arms but too short to cover a naked belly, runs to the gate and
stands there. The others all smile proudly round the eggs . . .

190

The eggs are a creamy buff, thick-shelled, their glaze pored
and lightly speckled, their shape more pointed than a hen's,
and the palms of the small black hands are translucent-looking
apricot-pink. There is no sound but awed, snuffling breathing
through snotty noses.

He asks a question of the cross-legged one and there are
giggles. He points down at the eggs but does not touch them,
and asks again. The children don't understand the language.
He goes on talking with many gestures. The cross-legged child
puts its head on one side, smiling as if under the weight of
praise, and cups one of the eggs from hand to hand.

Eleven pale freckled eggs. A whole clutch of guinea fowl
eggs. (pp. 8–9)

Ostensibly, the most intense interaction takes place in the passage
where Mehring tries verbal communication with the children. The
perspective is one of emphatic objectivity: the reader is removed
from proximity to the scene, and the effect is of a sound film with
the soundtrack temporarily expunged. The absolute absence of
communication clearly amounts to a form of interaction, the
meaning of which prefigures the much larger process that takes
place between black and white surfaces throughout the novel. The
incomprehension is made more striking (through hindsight)
because this is the first encounter between these surfaces in the
book.

But other prefigurations of similar interactions occur. The
multiple value of the emblem on Mehring's car's bonnet is one.
Itself eggshaped, its metallic sterility is contrasted with the
potential fertility of the guinea fowl eggs. The 'vertical-horizontal
sword of dazzle', reminiscent of a cross, and also, surely, of the
parameters for aiming in the telescopic sights of a gun, suggests
Mehring's 'European' mode for perceiving his African environment. The arrangement of the eggs like marbles ties this encounter
between Mehring and the children to his relationship with his own
son – which is, in turn, effectively symbolised by the barren glass
egg-substitute, a marble, that Mehring has found and intends
absent-mindedly to give his son, who is far past the age for playing
with marbles. Thus an interaction between generations is also
suggested, and a pattern of potentially considerable complexity
begins to emerge.

The interaction between white and black 'surfaces' connects
tightly with, and perhaps leads into other themes of interaction

within the pattern. Nadine Gordimer proceeds with this in the opening chapter. Mehring, the farmer, goes off to seek the 'chief herdsman' to complain about the kraal children taking the guinea fowl eggs.

> Suddenly he sees the figure of the black man, Jacobus, heading for *him*. He must have come out of the road behind the lucerne and is lunging across the field with the particular stiff-hipped hobble of a man who would be running if he were younger. But it's *he* who's looking for Jacobus; there's a mistake somewhere – how could the man know already that he is wanted? Some semaphore from the kraal? The farmer gives himself a little impatient, almost embarrassed snigger – and continues his own progress, measuredly, resisting the impulse to flag the man down with a wave of the hand, preparing in his mind what to say about the guinea fowl. (p. 10)

The words 'There's a mistake somewhere' reverberate along the dimensions of interaction between groups of people throughout the book. The precise local significance of the phrase also serves as a tone-setter.

> Each is talking fast, in the manner of a man who has something he wants to get on to say. There is a moment's pause to avoid collision; but of course the right of way is the farmer's. – Look, Jacobus, I've just been down at the third pasture, there –
> – I'm try, try to phone last night, master –
> But he has in his mind just exactly how to put it: – The children are taking the guinea fowl eggs to play with. They must've found a nest somewhere in the grass or the reeds and they've taken the eggs. –
> – There by the river ... you were there? – The chief herdsman's lips are drawn back from his decayed horse-teeth. He looks distressed, reluctant: yes, he is responsible for the children, some of them are probably his, and anyway, he is responsible for good order among the dependants of the farm workers and already the farmer has had occasion to complain about the number of eggs they are harbouring (a danger to the game birds).
> – It's not as if they needed them for food. To eat. No, eh? You've got plenty of fowls. They're just piccanins and they don't know, but you must tell them, those eggs are not to play

192

games with. If they find eggs in the veld they are not to touch them, you understand? Mustn't touch or move them, ever. – Of course he understands perfectly well but wears that uncomprehending and pained look to establish he's not to blame, he's burdened by the behaviour of all those other people down at the kraal. Jacobus is not without sycophancy. Master – he pleads – Master, it's very bad down there by the river. I'm try, try to phone you yesterday night. What is happen there. The man is dead there. You see him. – And his hand, with an imperious forefinger shaking it, stabs the air, through chest-level of the farmer's body to the line of willows away down behind him. (pp. 10–11)

The technique of compression whereby the entire interchange with its vast range of concern is crammed especially into the last paragraph suggests not only the complexity of the relationship involved but also the whole area inhabited by error, by the 'mistake somewhere'. The one extreme by which the area of interchange (and error) is bounded is represented by the farmer's concern with the guinea fowl eggs. The other is the matter of life and death which concerns Jacobus. Of course, this constitutes a precise expression of what the farm means to each of the protagonists.

The depth and complexity of the possibility (and actuality) of misunderstanding is based on this fundamental difference. From the time Mehring perceives his version of the 'mistake' the narration jerks through a minefield. Mehring's announcement that he has just been down at the third pasture leads Jacobus to assume that he has seen the corpse: thus Jacobus must impress on Mehring that he has not been idle, that he has tried to telephone him. But Jacobus is mistaken, too, of course.

The rest of the passage, except for the last sentence, is rendered through Mehring's perceptions, which produces the shock of revelation, when Jacobus eventually pierces the network of preconception and error with his news. It also has the effect of illustrating the distance between Mehring's version of reality and what is actually happening. Mehring assumes that Jacobus's preoccupation must be identical with his. He reaches the extreme of irrelevance in his judgment that 'Jacobus is not without sycophancy' an instant before his standards of relevance are overridden by reality.

The imagery of the passage is consistent with this approach. Mehring's preoccupation with the eggs is trivial in itself, not only because of the contrast with the dead man. The intensity of his preoccupation with the eggs is undermined by Nadine Gordimer's implied insistence on his manifest unawareness of their symbolic value in any universal system – that is, in any system outside his own, closed, pragmatic, one. And the sentence 'Mustn't touch or move them, ever. –' is double-edged in its application – the children know well enough not to touch or move a corpse – and prefigurative of the symbolic power of the dead man and different relationships with his presence throughout the book. The sentences that follow, leading with increasing pace to the inevitable explosion of shock, render Mehring's coded perceptions of Jacobus's behaviour. But Mehring's omnipotence falls very far short of thought-reading. His version of reality is severely circumscribed not only by stereotype but by the nature of his own role within it. What seems, initially, to be a super-pragmatic approach on the perceptual and interpretative levels has actually a perilously narrow – and shrinking – base. In the end his 'objectivity' declines into total illusion, and his universe becomes Laputan, a pragmatic fantasy. But this is a process, and we are still somewhere near the beginning.

If we test Mehring's version of reality at this stage by comparing his reliability as a narrator with that of the object of his perceptions, Jacobus, we are able to appreciate how thin the crust of truth is on which Mehring's apparently objective mode of perception rests.

– The Dutchman can take the pick-up and break the light at the back and scratch the door. Yes. –

– What kind of man is that? Like a stray dog running back. Where's his child? His woman? he doesn't seem like a rich white man. – Dorcas's husband stood among them and followed the figure with the eyes of a town-dweller; on Saturdays and public holidays farm labourers worked but he did not.

– Oh he's got a son. He comes here sometimes. –

– 'Terry.' His son said he doesn't want to be called master – he told Jacobus, didn't he? You mustn't call me Master Terry. He just wants us to call him by his name. – Izak gave his young laugh.

Jacobus dismissed irrelevancies, dropping his voice although he knew his words, even if audible at this distance, wouldn't be understood. – Does it break the tractor if I take it to the shop? – ...

They are raking down cattle feed from the bunker silo. A

great show of industry – no one looks up except a visitor (the
constant stream of Saturday and Sunday visitors, drunk and
sober) who is gossiping with them. He must have imagined it,
composed out of the cadences of their language what was
somewhere in his mind, but did he hear the name 'Terry',
quite distinctly, it seems to him, as he passed? Very unlikely.
It was some other word that has a similar sound. The round
lid of the dustbin outside the kitchen door lifts like a cymbal in
his hand (the letter drops into the mess of burnt mealie-meal
and potato peelings giving up a smell of fermentation) and
clangs closed. (p. 74)

The passage is tightly meshed into the pattern. On its own it provides
the necessary contrast in perceptual modes. Mehring has received a
letter from his sixteen-year-old son, Terry, from boarding school,
in which the latter expresses various progressive views and
announces his determination not to serve in the South African
army. Mehring, who has read the letter on the farm, is
characteristically, and obsessionally, worried about where to throw
the (organic, but only slowly-decaying) fragments of paper after he
has irritatedly torn it up. Miss Gordimer shows how the Newtonian
perceptual system carefully evolved by industrial civilization (in
Mehring's case an exceptionally advanced product of the process)
constructs for itself impenetrable barriers beyond which the very
existence of perceptual events is denied in the teeth of the evidence.
The black men cannot be imagined by Mehring to exist as thinking
beings within the area of mental activity that he occupies.
Therefore they did not mention his son's name. And the dangerous
path of illusion trodden by the anti-imaginative perceptual mode is
revealed – though not to its possessor.
    A powerful thematic image which occurs rhythmically in the text
is used to convey the essential nature and meaning of the way
Mehring experiences reality. It exists not only as the key element of
Mehring's perceptual make-up, but also in relation to modes
employed by the African and Indian groups which are depicted
in the novel.
    Its form is developed directly from the constituent paradigms of
modern industrial society, whose values Mehring worships and
embodies in his behaviour. The author gives metaphoric shape to
the basic frame of life in this society, and what emerges is the
unattractive and imprisoning pattern of deeply-scored straightline
grooves, parallel and crossing at right angles to one another. In

grid

other words, a grid. The precision and appropriateness of this metaphorical shape in the narration will emerge. In order to explicate the force of the grid within the novel as a signification of South African reality it will be necessary to approach it gradually, through the narrative.

The police have dealt with the corpse Jacobus has discovered with charactistic brutality: summoned by Mehring over the telephone, they descend on the farm in the person of a white sergeant and some black constables on the following day, question the black employees, and unceremoniously bury the body where it lies, without ceremony or coffin. When Mehring hears about this from Jacobus on his next visit to the farm at the weekend, he is derisive and angry; but beyond another telephone call to the local police station, he does nothing about it. The police sergeant explains that the mortuary van hadn't been available, and promises that the body will shortly be removed. But the promise is not kept.

In the jagged symmetry of the novel's structure, Mehring reappears at the farm some weeks later, after a brief business trip to Japan. It is a Sunday; he lies on the grass and momentarily he dozes off.

> . . . remembering a point he ought to have made clear in Tokyo, making a mental note to make a note of it. . . His presence on the grass becomes momentarily a demonstration, as if those people on the other side of the world were smilingly seeing it for themselves: I have my bit of veld and my cows . . . Perhaps he has dozed; he suddenly – out of blackness, blankness – is aware of breathing intimately into the earth. Wisps and shreds of grass or leaf stir there. It is the air from his nostrils that moves them. To his half-open eye the hairs that border it and the filaments of dead grass are one.
>
> There is sand on his lip.
>
> For a moment he does not know where he is – or rather who he is; but the situation in which he finds himself, staring into the eye of the earth with earth at his mouth, is strongly familiar to him. It seems to be something already inhabited in his imagination.
>
> At this point his whole body gives one of those violent jerks, every muscle gathering together every limb in paroxysm, one of those leaps of terror that land the poor bundle of body, safe, in harmless wakefulness. The abyss is no deeper than a

doorstep; the landing, home. . . . He rolls on to his side, where
he has the impression the reeds facing him hide him as drawn
curtains keep out day. The sense of familiarity, of some kind
of unwelcome knowledge or knowing, is slow to ebb. As it
does, it leaves space in his mind; or uncovers, like the retreat
of a high tide, carrying away silt. (p. 37)

The passage takes its departure from the structural principle of
interaction. Much of the action is internalized, within the
increasingly closed-in world of Mehring's perceptions; but there
are at this stage still viable lines of connection, and three parties are
operational here. They are Mehring, the world of international big
business that he inhabits so confidently, and the blacks on the farm.
In terms of interaction between white and white, or at any rate
within the range of normal contact connoted by the phrase 'those
people on the other side of the world', Mehring's presence close to
the farm's earth is a validification of his claim – a claim that
establishes his individual existence in his own eyes.

At this moment, however, the author juxtaposes two levels
of interaction, and in doing so reveals the fundamental tension
between them. Significantly, she places these levels in a repre-
sentational relationship of some intricacy: thus Mehring's
conscious, waking mind reflects his interactions within the white
world, while his subconscious, while he sleeps, stands for the
interaction between white and black. That the latter is an area of
great vulnerability for him is delicately but decisively indicated,
and one view of the structural dynamic of Mehring's character
emerges at this point: it may be seen as a struggle for the discovery
and assertion of identity between a fully-elaborated conscious
perception of the world, which accepts phenomena at their face
value and proceeds skilfully and instrumentally to deal with them
from there: and a subconscious whose experience of reality is
located only within the fundamental paradigms of birth and death,
and is therefore without a sufficient accumulation of defences
against the potent ambiguities of Mehring's real situation – that is, a
reality constituted at a deeper than surface level. For let us consider
who Mehring is. We know little of his background. He is born in
South-West Africa, or Namibia; the problem of naming places the
ambiguity of his existence, of his historical belonging, at its very
beginning. He is English-speaking, but not of English stock,
apparently; his surname resembles a common Afrikaner one –
Meiring – but is not identical. And if his parentage is ultimately

German, it is not a meaningful factor in his life. Brothers or sisters he does not possess, or they aren't mentioned in the text. He is long divorced from his wife, who lives in New York with her new family. He has one son, who is at boarding school and with whom he finds it impossible to communicate. His one-time mistress, <u>Antonia</u>, exists in flashbacks, as a continuous source of frustration and irritation for him; she is a political exile, living in England, and he has had no contact with her for some years. An elderly German couple whom he maintains on a remote South-West African farm were once valuable to him, when he was a boy; they seem to have filled something of a parental role, but this, too, is hinted at rather than described.

Thus Miss Gordimer <u>tricks her reader into accepting a hero who is at once somebody and nobody: a powerful, attractive, thinking man who at the same time has forgotten where he comes from, is uncertain as to who he is, and has no clear idea of where he is going.</u> This seeming dichotomy between an efficient idea of the other and an inadequate one of self, can only be temporary, and in due course it resolves into disintegration all around. It constitutes a critique of a modern, 'post-ideological' version of the rationalist or Newtonian idea of man which Blake attacked so energetically. So Mehring's subconscious fights for liberation against an imposed, imprisoning patterning of experience, rendered through the metaphor of the perceptual-experiential grid; and although its victories are at this stage occasional, they are profoundly disorientating. The imagery in the passage quoted indicates the disruptive power of such incidents.

Mehring's physical position, 'staring into the eye of the earth with earth at his mouth', mirrors that of the dumped dead man, covered uncaringly with earth. It is clearly this specific situation, relating to this person known only in death, which is 'something already inhabited in imagination'. And the return to a semblance of perceptual balance from this hit-and-run terrorist attack by the forces of his own imagination (which are in the process of forging a decisive alliance with the natural environment) is depicted in images redolent of catastrophe: 'violent jerks', 'paroxysm', 'leaps of terror'. Thus his struggle between the subversive imagination and the ordered perception is all-embracing. <u>In his seeming balance, in the pragmatic competence with which he encounters reality, Mehring is a divided individual, a man without a past or future.</u> The significance of Nadine Gordimer's repeated use of words like 'grid' and images suggestive of an artificial and restrictive patterning of reality now begins to emerge.

Later on in the same day Mehring is visited by a neighbour, a local Afrikaner farmer, a patriarch who brings with him his son, daughter-in-law and grandchildren. Their purpose is to ask to borrow Mehring's small pick-up truck which he keeps at the farm, to transport some building materials. But first they must complete the conventional courtesies of a conservative agrarian community; they drink Mehring's brandy, converse about weather, and crops. Afterwards the patriarch talks about his hobby, which is 'The – history – of – the – Afrikaner' (p. 48). When they have gone, Jacobus asks Mehring to employ another 'boy' to help with the cattle; Mehring refuses. This exchange also is carried out on well-established and familiar lines, the formal conventions that exist between white master and black servant. The section concludes in a manner which reveals the extent of Mehring's dependence upon a particular way of perceiving and experiencing.

> The well-regulated demands and responses between the Boers and himself, the usual sort of exchange between his black man and himself have re-engraved the fine criss-cross of grooves on which his mind habitually runs. The empty space that was clear in him this afternoon is footprinted over, it exists no more than does a city pavement under the comings and goings of passing bodies that make it what it is. He recognizes with something like pleasure the onset of the usual feeling he has on Sunday night – a slight anticipatory impatience to set off for the city. Just as on Sunday morning he is ready to get out of it. The rhythm of these alternating feelings is simple and dependable as the daily cognisance of peristaltic activity that presages his bowel movement, along with the after-breakfast cigarette. (p. 54)

Thus the antagonism is made explicit between two levels of experience: one bound up with the farm (though the event in itself is a pretty regular feature of South African life – the almost casual murder for wages in a black slum 'township' and the dumping of the body) and the other with Mehring's routine existence. The use of urban images in the passage quoted helps to locate the polarities of the tension. It also points up the nature of Mehring's 'routine' mode of perceiving and experiencing, by associating it with the concrete of city pavements and an eagerness to return to the city from the farm.

On Mehring's next recorded visit to the far, some weeks later, he brings with him the unread letter from his son at boarding school.

Four hundred acres. But like an old horse, he . . . Everything has its range. Even the most random-seeming creatures are shown by studies to have a topography of activity from which they never really depart, although they may appear to casual observation to weave and backtrack aimlessly, almost crazily, free. From the flat to the car to the office, from tables to beds, from airports to hotels, from city to country, the track like the etching something (worms? ants?) has left on this tree trunk amounts to a closed system. No farther. Wherever he sets out for or from, or however without direction he sets out to roam, on his farm, it's always here that he ends up. Down over the third pasture at the reeds. Peaceful, of course. They don't come down here any more, for some reason or other; not even the piccanins. He is here alone; there is a sensation he can't place, it's as if, sitting down, he has taken a (non-existent, since he hasn't been wearing one) hat off . . . A shallow grave of stones is under his eye for a few seconds of absent lack of recognition – of course it's not the grave, there is no grave: the pit where sheep were roasted in the summer. (p. 69)

He has come to this spot to read the letter, which is for him an angry and unsettling experience, because his adolescent son elaborately rejects his values and makes thoughtless demands: he does not wish to serve his compulsory nine months in the South African army when he finishes school, he does want to visit his mother in New York at the end of the year, but for the winter holiday he will hitch to South-West Africa, to stay with the elderly German couple whose role in Mehring's early life is presented enigmatically but seems to have been, in some way, parental.

'. . . Don't send an air-ticket or the train-fare. I'll hitch.'
Oh, fine, okay, cast off the things of this world for those jeans with the hems carefully cut ragged and take your begging bowl on the road to South-West Africa. No one's going to know that the old couple who're waiting to anoint the little lordling's feet at the other end are living on a pension from your father. (p. 71)

Thus the pattern of Mehring's life experience emerges, and again it contradicts the appearance of power and freedom he manifests. He rejects the very quality of freedom – and the words he associates with it – 'almost crazily' (p. 67) – shock the reader into a realization of the extent of his insecurity. This insecurity drives him to bind others to himself – Emmy and Kurt, the elderly German couple, for example – so that he can comprehend the whole universe within his mechanistic vision. Whenever he encounters a particularly direct threat to this vision – his son's rejection of his values, for example – he falls back for comfort on an explicit reiteration of his conception of human behaviour as something restricted, following the metallic bars of a grid. Of course, what he fails to realize about this 'truth' he has succeeded in imposing upon himself is that where he thinks himself most free is precisely the area of most powerful and ineluctable restriction – he is caught by the earth of 'his' African farm.

Thus, months later, when his son has visited the farm very briefly after his holiday in Namibia, Mehring returns him to the airport on his way back to boarding school. Then he sets out for his flat in town, with a subsequent social engagement in mind.

> He will be back in town within half-an-hour on the expressway but where the overhanging signs of different exits present him with an alternative he simply glides off, maintaining speed without hesitation, as if that were his intention all along, to the lower lane on the right. That road dives under the highway he has left, literally dodges – it is overhead a moment – the road to town. He's on the way back to the farm, that's where he is. The car is making for the farm. It's done now. These great new roads have no provision for the retracing of steps. Once you're on course, you're on; that's it. So he drives without let or hindrance (as the phrase goes) as one can only on an expressway, without distraction or interruption, a mechanical hare set streaking along its appointed lane of track. (p. 147)

The narrative viewpoint is Mehring's; he is in the position of one who enjoys an illusory sense of freedom through accepting that he is entrapped within a predetermined system. He is, of course; though it isn't the one he thinks it is. Thus his situation is essentially and pervasively ironic. It is the farm that is exercising control over his movements. In this sense it is notable that there is little difference between Nadine Gordimer's African farm and that of her predecessor Olive Schreiner. In both cases the white masters are subject to the Appollonian illusion of the possibility of control over their environment, even if it is a rather passive kind of control, through a recognition of necessity: and in both cases what cannot be recognized is the harsh truth of the antagonism, power and eventual triumph of the environment (symbolized by the farm) over them.

Mehring's chosen images for his perception of the human situation are again metallic and concrete, yet the force of determinism that is exerted on him comes from the farm, which he sees in terms of his obsession with ecology, conservation and the balance of nature. The ironic contrast points up the extent of his misperception, of the contradictions inherent in his vision.

Thus his motives are complex and unclear to himself. Why did he really buy the farm, in the first place? Is it a good place to bring a woman to, or will farming prove a fulfilling hobby as well as worthwhile because of tax deductions that can be claimed against tax losses?

A good deal of the action takes place in Mehring's memory, and Nadine Gordimer uses a technique of what might be called simultaneous projection rather than flashback. All Mehring's perceptions of the past are framed within a firm fictive present, a definite locality, usually the farm. The dominant strain in these memories is an intricate, argumentative, angry and one-sided dialogue conducted between Mehring and Antonia, his former mistress, who had to leave South Africa some years before because of her left-wing political activities. His internal disputes with her connect with events on the farm, his paternalistic and suspicious treatment of the blacks who live on it and work for him (as they did in the time of previous owners), his relationship with his adolescent son – in short, with most of his perceptions of and relationships with the world. Her position is the precise opposite of his – idealistic, committed to political action and the possibility of bringing about change. But it is to him she had to turn when, inevitably, events proved too strong for passionate conviction and the security police arrested and interrogated her: she asked him to find a respectable, non-political lawyer to obtain her right to escape.

So she is exiled in London, in the fictive present of the book; she appears only as the subject of Mehring's angry self-interrogatory introspection. To her, or the memory of their illicit and furtive relationship, their political arguments in bed between love-making, Mehring refers events that occupy the fictive present: and the intensity of the argumentative self-justification mirrors the intensity of Mehring's need for her. This, of course, is both conscious (though unadmitted) and unconscious; Mehring as Newtonian man-of-action is one part of a duality, and some of his inadequate functioning may be explained by his inability to recognize or admit the need to be complemented by someone who is his opposite, so to speak. Without contraries, said Blake, is no progression; the problem is for the contraries to relate in some way to one another. Mehring refuses to relate effectively to Antonia, just as he fails to relate to the blacks on 'his' farm. They, too, are in the position of 'contraries'; but the possibility of interacting in a complementary manner with them is not even remotely present to Mehring's perceptions. Of course, there *is* an effective level of contact with them: Mehring works together with the blacks on his weekend visits to the farm, mending a broken pump or fencing cow pastures, just as he made love with Antonia. But he cannot see that in relation to the South African farm, they possess precisely what he lacks: continuity, tradition, authority, a family structure, moral values enforced, casually but effectively, by religious practice – just as Antonia possesses what he lacks in relation to the world at large: compassion, loyalty, the capacity for sacrifice – no matter in how flawed or partial a manner.

The actual movement of fictive present time in the book is signal-led by events significantly beyond Mehring's Appollonian control. The first is the discovery on the farm of the murdered man, and his subsequent riteless burial by the uncaring police. Then Solomon, one of the 'boys' who lives and works on the farm, is called out of his room one night by two men, taken away from the farmworkers' dwellings, beaten up and left for dead in the veld, where he is discovered the next day by Jacobus, and taken to hospital. He survives, after lying unconscious for some days.

During the same winter the farm is attacked by veld-fire, and even the reeds which grow by the river-side (a symbol of the farm's unending fertility coming from the underground watersource) are consumed – which has not happened since Mehring bought the farm, though it has been swept by veld-fires every winter but one. The unusual extent of the fire is clearly a link in the chain which begins with the finding of the corpse and continues with the attack on Solomon. The last paragraphs of the section describing the latter event make the connection clear.

The men to whom money was owed sent henchmen to lure Solomon out at night and beat him up. He did not know who they were – two among thousands, over in the location and the shanty town, ready to do at someone's bidding what they did to him; he knew why it was done.

But the children did not go to the third pasture. They stopped one another, hung back: there is something there. No one had seen it; it had frightened one of the little ones. Which one? Who? – Something there. –

They did not remember any more what there was there, down under the reeds. What Solomon had found, months ago, in the third pasture; still there. (p. 86)

These words are immediately succeeded by the section dealing with the effects of the fire and Mehring's reactions, and in the children's confusion, out of which a local myth is to emerge, the connection between the first two links in this temporal chain is forged. Thus the action in the fictive present flows from the finding of the corpse, through the attack on Solomon, to the unusually severe veld-fire; then Mehring's son Terry makes his only direct appearance when he visits the farm for half a day between his holiday in Namibia, as he by this time calls it, and returning to boarding school. The visit coincides with a ceremony on the farm: Solomon sacrifices a goat to appease his ancestors, and the wife of Phineas, another of the farmworkers, undergoes an initiation ceremony to become a diviner. Which of the two events – Terry's visit or the ceremony – has the more significant connection with the farm's reality is clear.

People started arriving on Saturday night. The old women from the location who came to the farm for weeding in summer must have heard about it, and they walked over on Sunday morning. There were Solomon's brother's people, from across the vlei. That crazy woman seemed to have asked some people of her own; they behaved almost as if it were her goat that was going to be killed. Anyway, they brought a lot of beer. The goat was led into the yard where everyone was already gathered except her followers, who were still at their singing and clapping in Phineas's room. It was happy to be out of the dark of the barn and pulled determinedly towards the cabbage leaves some woman had left from her cooking, breaking a chain of droppings like a broken string of shiny black beads. In the instant of straining for the leaves it was thrown on its right side by many hands. Solomon's brother stabbed it over the aorta. It took quite a few minutes to die; the noise it made seemed to be muffled out gradually, as if

some invisible weight were descending on the creature. At last
– quite soon – it made no sound.

Solomon heard what there was to hear but did not see. He
stood as he had been instructed by people there who knew
about these things, facing away, with a friend who worked
with his brother for the bus company. The friend spoke
conversationally to the air – Here is your beast, Bengu, father
of Solomon, Nomsa, mother of Solomon. It is to say we give
thanks that you have cared for him. May God protect his
child –

No one among the crowd was paying any attention; already
the men were gathered over the dying goat, everyone was
animated by the thought of meat and wanted to get on with
the skinning and the cutting up so that cooking could begin.
(pp. 162 – 163)

The relaxed and low-keyed diction (which is narrated from a point
of view identified with Solomon) and the climactic absence of
climax in the description of the ceremony, indicate a sense of
community as well as an effortless association with the locality.
These people belong organically in this place, even when historical
change deflects the course of tribal, agrarian life and some work in
town for bus companies, or in factories, or as domestics. They come
and go casually, without displaying any traumatic sense either of
separation from or identification with their African farm.

The sound of a party drew comers across the vlei. It went on
all through the afternoon and almost through the night;
people came and people went, long after the meat was
finished, people slept and people woke. Jacobus was there like
everybody else, as drunk as everybody else. There was
nothing to worry about; the farmer and the young one had
been and gone early in the day. Once or twice Jacobus
remembered the irrigation but could not remember whether it
was turned off or not; then he no longer remembered what it
was that bothered him. (p. 163)

The 'tempo of pleasure, of excess, that regulated everyone's blood'
is unbroken even by the necessity to worry about white approval.
Thus the day's 'white' and 'black' events are juxtaposed, from the
effusive greeting Terry as feudal heir presumptive is given by
Jacobus in the morning to the community festival in the evening
and night – an inclusive experience from which Mehring, who *has*,

after all, returned to the farm after dropping Terry at the airport, is shut out.

Terry's visit in the morning is characterized by a tone of unease, from his inability to respond appropriately to Jacobus's greeting when he arrives to the mutual inability to communicate that exists between his father and himself. The latter is given deft symbolic emphasis when Mehring finds a book called 'Eros Himself', which is 'An Anthology Compiled and Published By the Campaign for Homosexual Equality' in his son's rucksack. Mehring is staggered; later he recollects his own youthful sexual initiation in the same part of South-West Africa. But no communication takes place. The unease which surrounds the whites in their comings and goings is thus effectively contrasted with the continuity of black experience in this focusing in time of their simultaneous presence on the farm, which represents, of course, the South African totality.

It is Jacobus who points out the increasing uncertainty of Mehring's movements that begins (or at least becomes evident) about this time. He is uncertain about holding the ceremony at the weekend, because that is when Mehring comes to the farm. When teasingly challenged by his fellow-workers to allow the feast 'instead of working on Monday or Tuesday' he responds: You never know when he comes these days. (p. 162)

It is impossible for Mehring to say what force attracts him across the lines of his prized grid with increasing frequency towards the farm. He begins to ignore social engagements among his fellow-financiers and their families in their luxurious suburban homes. He cannot account for his impulsive turning off the main road to town from the airport when he leaves Terry that afternoon.

He will be back in town within half-an-hour on the expressway but where the overhanging signs of different exits present him with an alternative he simply glides off, maintaining speed without hesitation, as if that were his intention all along, to the lower lane on the right. That road dives under the highway he has left, literally dodges – it is overhead a moment – the road to town. He's on the way back to the farm, that's where he is. The car is making for the farm. It's done now. These great new roads have no provision for the retracing of steps. Once you're on course, you're on; that's it. So he drives without let or hindrance (as the phrase goes) as one can only on an expressway, without distraction or interruption, a mechanical hare set streaking along its appointed lane of track.

There is the usual sort of Sunday gathering he was expected at – people would begin to turn up only in an hour or so from now, but he remembers the invitation or rather obligation as if it were something he has already missed. (p. 147)

The trance-like impersonality of Mehring's perception of his choice and his acceptance of his arbitrary-seeming change of direction as something determined outside his own range of conscious activity possesses potent symbolic implications which extend to the whole white group in its Appollonian embodiment. Mehring's thought-images are connected with the motorway, the classic product of high-technology civilization (and also a traditional symbol in certain kinds of literature about Africa for Western 'progress' – see Joyce Cary's *Mr Johnson* as well as Chinua Achebe's *Arrow of God*); but it seems the road betrays its own Appollonian master by presenting him with the illusion of choice.

In reality, Mehring has no choice. Just as the train of events which begins (for the sake of historic convenience, in the symbolic framework of the novel) with the murder of the black man on the farm and his hugger-mugger burial, leads to Solomon's need to exorcise his bad dreams and appease his ancestors with sacrifice, so it also includes the gradual breakdown of regularity and order in Mehring's grid-tight world. The unappeased spirit of the murdered man is the symbolic analogue for the underlying displacement of Mehring and his group, in the land they consider their own, but have acquired by force and by ignoring not only the prior claims of other groups, but also their obligations as fellow human beings towards those other groups. To put it baldly, the spirits of the farm are offended by the man improperly buried on their property, (or the victim's own spirit claims the consideration due to him) and they bring about an insistent magnetic pull, making Mehring deviate further and further from the lines of his own grid and come closer and closer to the farm, until his own energies are entirely subjugated to those of the land he thinks he owns. The power which the energies of the farm come to exert over Mehring's consciousness is demonstrated at once, immediately after the description of the festival of the black workers. Mehring, at the farm, engages in one of his extended, irritated internal dialogues with his exiled lover, the liberal Antonia. Mehring is entranced by the farm's

207

recovery from fire with the first rains of summer. In particular the wild Orange River Lily is abundant: *crinum bulbispermum*. Mehring interrupts his one-sided dialogue to consider the plants:

> *Crinum bulbispermum.* The bulbs of many species contain alkaloids and some have medicinal value. (He keeps the book now on the sideboard in the house.) Perhaps that's why the boys seem to have gone round clumps of the plants instead of ploughing them in, over here, and in other places where they occur on the edges of the mealie fields! Fortunately the piccanins don't pick flowers (they're not interested in such things) but he does remember last year seeing some woman from the kraal digging up roots. Jacobus ought to be told that medicine or no medicine, these bulbs mustn't be taken. (p. 166)

Mehring's attention is more and more compelled by the material life of the farm, while his responses grow correspondingly more obsessional and less relevant to the real nature of the phenomenon which involves him. The extent of the mistakenness of his attitude to the earth and its inhabitants is fully revealed here in his conception of the relationship between man and the land. Total 'conservationism' plus mechanistic cultivation denies the bridge of a *human* dependency; and of course it is the black people on the farm – those whom he doesn't *see* as human – who are therefore denied this living interdependency relationship. The contrast is made at this point with telling force between the two relationships with the land that he possesses: the one from which he derives his sustenance – the mining of pig-iron, and his obsessional 'hobby' – tax-loss farming.

In his running reverie, immediately following his mental note to tell Jacobus to stop the farmworkers picking the therapeutic bulbs of *crinum bulbispermum*, he remembers one of Antonia's characteristic questions: 'What *is* pig-iron? No, I'm serious.' (p. 166.) The contrast is, of course, between the ruthless despoliation of the earth involved in tearing pig-iron out of it, and the pointlessness of preserving an impossible and artificial projection in a farming operation which sustains no-one, by denying a relevant dimension of human dependence on natural growth in favour of an abstract and sterile fad.

By this time nearly all Mehring's internal monologues have become duologues with the absent Antonia, a process which mirrors ironically his steadily increasing isolation from people in the real world of the present. Even in her absence, however, Antonia is an uncomfortable companion. She has perceived the sentimentality which is an underlying component of his relationship with the African farm, because she is capable of understanding the historical dimension, and sees that his relationship rests on a false claim. The land without its indigenous inhabitants only half exists.

> I don't have anyone hanging around here, thank God, if you walk about this place on your own, I can tell you, you see things you'd never see otherwise. Birds and animals – everything accepts you. But if you have people tramping all over the place –
>
> – All to yourself. You've bought what's not for sale: the final big deal . . . That bit of paper you bought yourself from the deeds office isn't going to be valid for as long as another generation. It'll be worth about as much as those our grandfathers gave the blacks when they took the land from them. The blacks will tear up your bit of paper. No one'll remember where you're buried. (p. 167–168)

Finally Antonia pinpoints the ultimate direction of Mehring's life:

> – I can hear it. 'He's in love with his farm,' they'll say. But you don't want them to come out and play at milkmaids. Perhaps you'll really believe it's love. A new kind. A superior kind, without people . . . (p. 168)

Thus Mehring's relationships gradually fail him. When his son goes to America to spend Christmas with his mother, he doesn't return, in order to avoid serving in the South African army. Before that a business associate, whose wife has designs on Mehring and whose teenage daughter Mehring lusts after, commits suicide because of a financial scandal. Mehring avoids the funeral, not only because of his (by now) inevitable preference for the farm but also any assertion of a natural human relationship repels him by this time.

Christmas itself is, for Mehring, a time of isolation, of avoidance of the social pleasures of his circle. Miss Gordimer exercises her satirical bent on Johannesburg high society (as she has done before, notably in *A World of Strangers*) in describing the various invitations recorded on Mehring's telephone answering device, in his absence. But the point that emerges concerns Mehring's almost total isolation, his inability to communicate with his peers.

Some people are intimidated by the machine and couch their messages in telegraphese, as if paying so much a word. Others are cut off just when they are getting into conversational stride – they forget or do not know the span of the recording does not take into consideration how much you may still have left to say. The machine simply stops listening.

Just as he gives no answer. He takes no part in the conversation. He sits with his head tipped back in a long chair, but not negligently. If it were not for the drink in his hand, anyone looking in on the closed-up flat where the owner is away on holiday would take the attitude to be one of a doctor or other disinterested confidant, reliably impersonal. (p. 191)

Mehring's silence is an aspect of the pathology of the situation. It is, moreover, cognate with that of another character:

Tracing his consciousness as an ant's progress is alive from point to point where it is clambering over the hairs of his forearm, he knows he is not the only one down at the reeds. He doesn't think of him, one of them lying somewhere here, any more than one thinks consciously of anyone who is always in one's presence about the house, breathing in the same rooms. Sometimes there arises the need to speak; sometimes there are long silences. He feels at this particular moment a kind of curiosity that is in itself a question: from one who has nothing to say to one to whom there is nothing to say. Falling asleep there he was not alone face-down in the grass. There are kinds of companionship unsought. With nature. Nature accepts everything. Bones, hair, teeth, fingernails and the beaks of birds – the ants carry away the last fragment of flesh, small as a fibre of meat stuck in a back tooth, nothing is wasted. (p. 190)

The juxtaposition of these two passages suggests the continuity of Mehring's silence with that of the dead man buried on the farm; by this time the interrelatedness of their fates is obvious. Miss Gordimer's resource to a pararational (suprarational) system for expressing this continuity may be related to the growing conviction evident in her recent work of the failure of Western values, particularly those which are meant to remind Western man that his technological superiority does not imply moral superiority over other groups. Thus Mehring becomes 'one who has nothing to say' because nothing of value remains to be articulated in the value system of his culture. Paradoxically, this brings him into a closeness of communion which would otherwise be impossible with the one 'to whom there is nothing to say'. But of course, even in silence, Mehring must, compulsively, interpret: 'There are kinds of companionship unsought. With nature. Nature accepts everything.' This reverse-Romantic Westernism is, of course, mere perversion in the context of local realities, as subsequent events show. It is a coded response, a kick of the reflex from the body of the dead culture: at this stage it is enough to be aware of it as a clichéd and easy evasion of the most fundamental responsibilities that exist between man and man. Nature does not accept everything – particularly not the hypostatic extraction of conscious man from the frame.

Thus the dead man's presence is progressively more and more pervasive, and Mehring's inability to communicate with living human beings springs from his unrealizable need to communicate with a dead one.

This need pushes him blindly into that far outpost of isolation where consciously-controlled fantasy begins to resemble hallucination. His New Year is spent sleeping alone on the verandah of a roofless outhouse on the farm, amid the carousals of the farmworkers. His fantasy, which is on one level a massive attempt at self-justification to the liberal Antonia, takes the form of a manly intimacy with Jacobus, a night spent with him, seeing the New Year in over a shared bottle of whisky. Even at the height of fantasy, however, Mehring's well-trained, relentless Western mind never ceases to interpret, to make marginal comments – and, in doing so, to betray itself.

> – How long you been here? –
> No, not how long he's worked for me; how many years on this place is what I mean. Jacobus was in residence when I bought; he had worked for the previous owner, or perhaps it was only on some neighbouring farm: boundaries mean little to them, when they say 'here', (p. 194)

Again:

> – You think we're strong enough to finish the bottle? –
> And of course he laughs. Everyone knows how much of their own brew they can put away. It's a feast or a famine with them; they gorge themselves when they can and starve when they have to, that's their strength. (p. 196)

And so on. The lofty tone of patronage is never absent; and the denial of the possibility of real communication emerges as something beyond Mehring's control. His super-pragmatism fails him in this apparently simple human situation. And his vulnerability is further revealed by a sudden turn in the imagined conversation:

> But we are getting along fine. We're laughing a lot; I would always recognize him by his laugh, even if his face is hidden by darkness. – D'you remember at all what he looked like? That time, Jacobus? You must have turned him over, seen the face, surely? When you took the sunglasses and the watch, all that stuff. Would you know it if you saw him again – were shown a photograph, the way the police should have done, for identification. – (pp. 197–198)

The Indian family that runs the general dealers' store near to the farm (the location – the juxtaposition of the two is reiterated of constant necessity, a symbol of its own context) completes the book's governing emblem of group interaction. It is engaged in constant vigilance against the hostility of both white and black, but especially the former. Blacks –servants–live within the wire-fenced fortress-compound. Whites don't. Mehring refuses to pose as the fictitious owner to enable the family to get around the provisions of the Group Areas Act. But Terry is friendly with them. (Terry also names one of Mehring's bulls 'Nandi', 'after the Hindu God he saw on the temple in Durban'.) What differentiates the Indian group from Mehring and his world (and draws it closer, paradoxically – or so it seems – to the Boer family depicted) is the presence within it of a meaningful structure of relationships, including a system of human values based on an acceptance of authority and of the instinctive and over-riding importance of continuity. What distinguishes the Indians from the Boers is the relative density of their population – four generations already inhabit the house and shop, forbidden by law to expand their territory, almost forbidden to remain where they are. They relate most closely, however, to their customers, the blacks: they exist symbiotically, unconsciously. Each accepts the other as part of the landscape, organic to it.

Thus the Indian group has a peculiar importance within the structure of a novel which mirrors the complex balance between groups in South African society. And the only instance of effective unselfconscious communication between members of different groups in the book takes place between Izak, Jacobus's son, and

Jalal, one of the Indians, a youth of Izak's age. Izak cycles from the farm to the shop, where he sees Jalal painting the metal struts which hold up the rainwater tank. Jalal wears the peace emblem on a leather thong around his neck; and when he has finished painting the struts, he climbs onto the platform on which the tank itself rests. Izak watches him.

> When he looked up again a band of brown was begun round the top of the tank. It was not a very large tank, shaped like a barrel, and by standing on his toes – the red rubber soles of his sandals showed – the Indian could reach up the brush to the rim. He was going to paint the tank after all? No. When he had eased himself all round it and finished the top band, he squatted and with some difficulty, because squatting took up more room than standing on the platform, made the same band, the width of the paint brush, round the bottom. Now he was starting to write – no, draw something on the belly of the tank, where it faced Izak and the road. Izak began to pass remarks and show off, gently, not going too far, laughing. – What are you doing? What's that you're making there? It's a face! What is this? *Ag* come on, man –
> The Indian only shook his head again slowly; he knew what he was doing.
> – What thing is it? –
> When the sign was gone over a second time to thicken the outlines, he drew himself aside from it and turned the dark glasses once again: – Don't you see? –
> The outline of an egg, standing upright, was divided inside by four lines, or rather one vertical line that half-way down sub-divided, branching off a shorter line to either side at an angle . . .
> Izak knew that egg. He saw it on the motorbikes. Even on shirts. It was smart. People wore it like you wear Jesus's cross. It was, he saw now, what was shiny hanging at the end of the chain on the Indian's bare chest. But he did not know what it really meant, as he knew the cross and also the six-pointed star that the people of the Church of Zion had on their flag. – It looks nice there. – (pp. 203–204)

At this point, the tentative and fragile communication between the two contemporaries has already ceased, and perhaps the significant point of closure exists where Jalal changes his mode from the practical-painting the struts, during which time the two chat competently about rust, asbestos and how the job might have been done better – to the symbolic, where he begins to work on the peace sign, a defiant and futile gesture in itself, as he will understand. That Izak perceives it as an egg relates to the persistent symbolic value of eggs and egg-like objects made of other materials throughout the book. It also connects Jalal with Terry, who buys his mother an alabaster egg while he is in Namibia. The egg symbolism seems to work, crudely speaking, as follows: black people relate to real eggs without ascribing sentimental or cult value: Mehring sees them as objects within his obsessional ecological scheme, perfect in a solipsistic universe, producing baby guinea fowl, perhaps, but for the edification of the solitary perceptual controller of that universe: Terry buys his mother an alabaster or glass egg-shape whose value is purely decorative – and in those terms pretty unexceptional: Jalal conceptualizes his egg as defiance against the wicked present and hope in a better future: and the circle closes with the failed communication of this conceptualization between Jalal and Izak, age-mates and members of oppressed groups, so that the egg fails to unite or to transcend the fragmentation that characterizes group relationships in South Africa. The potentially fruitful connection between Jalal, Izak and Terry is thus never made, and when flood strikes the area some time later, the struts are damaged and the peace sign is in danger, as Mehring puts it to himself, of ending up 'face-down in the mud'. (p. 234)

The particular distinction between Jalal and Terry emerges at this point, too. In his attempt to reach out to a relevant value system, Jalal feels hampered by his involvement in the very thing that Terry lacks – a significant human context, a continuous family structure with an explicit value system. The point is, of course, that the Indians are equivocal as inhabitants of the South African farm although, unlike the whites, they are not afflicted by the fantasy of possession, neither are they rooted, like the blacks: and this emerges clearly in the ambivalent relationship that exists between these two groups.

Although they are mutually dependent on each other, the dimension of the relationship is almost solely economic, and as we see from the preceding quotation, cannot flower on the human level. The inability of the indian value structure to fertilize the system of eggs that stand for potential human fruition in the novel comes from the fact that this structure is a hothouse plant, crowded within the walls and behind the dog-guarded fence of the house –

and that is the point of the claustrophobic warmth evoked in the descriptions of the family – the eldest son lying in bed with a cough, with his young wife, her bosoms overflowing with milk for their baby, in the bedroom so trousseau-crammed that movement is difficult – or Jalal's retreat when challenged by his father for painting the peace symbol on the water tank:

He shouted as if he and his father were alone . . .
– So the police are going to come and say you're a communist, we're communist Koolies, that's what's going to happen, ay? – That's the hammer and the sickle up there, *you* say – they've told you – *you* and *they* say –
His temper and his nerve flew apart under his own words. He took a hammer to the coloured photograph of himself smiling on the day he got his matric results that hung with all the wedding pictures in the sitting-room. He was smashing himself. – *They* know – *you* believe – Suddenly aware – urgent as an alarming internal spasm prefacing uncontrollable diarrhoea – that tears were about to come, he burst through the dark passage that led from shop to house and shut himself in the room he shared with brothers.
They were at school. There was no key but he pushed the corner of a bed across the door as he had done at other times. He heard his mother breathing on the far side and making small polite noises in her throat. But she would hang about, afraid actually to speak. He lay on his bed and smoked. There were no tears. He thought where he might go. To cousins in Klerksdorp. His mother's aunt in Lichtenburg. An uncle and cousins in Standerton. Even Dawood's wife's people near Durban. Plenty of places. To work in the same kind of shop and hear the same talk.
His mother smelt the cigarette and almost soundlessly, although she was of majestic size, turned away, down the narrow passage. (p. 206)

Jalal is surrounded by family, tradition, continuity – smothered by it, in precise contrast to Terry. Of the three young men, however, only Izak is at ease within the hierarchical continuum of the generations – and this, of course, is a function of his group's relationship to the landscape of the South African farm.

The tenuousness of family relationships in the 'English' group is brought home immediately at this point, by an international telephone call which Mehring does answer, from New York. His former wife announces that Terry, who has gone to visit her at Christmas, will be staying, in order to avoid being drafted into the South African army. Mehring's external isolation closes around his inner intensity of need, and his precarious balance is rendered through a dual consciousness of the world.

The last fifty pages deal with Mehring's accelerating isolation, to the point where he ceases to be what he was. The isolation is conveyed through an intensification of this fantasy life – he is not at home to answer telephone calls, so he fantasizes about the identity of a caller from abroad who might haved been Antonia. The real caller, of course, is Terry, and the call signals a further break in a relationship, and not the renewal which Mehring needs but is incapable of. Thus the narrowing vector of Mehring's grasp on the concrete in human relationships, already concentrated solely on his son, disappears; the blacks on the farm are not, for him, human beings, and what was at best an inner dialogue with the absent Antonia becomes a cracked record of insistent, repetitive, self-justification. He loses his opportunity to tell Terry – to convey in the terms of normal human discourse – the preoccupation of his isolation:

> He's thought of something he could have said to the boy, anyway. Sticking out of the open windows of the car are the shaking heads of two young saplings, one on either side. Their roots, each in a big fist of soil carefully gloved in packing and plastic, are on the back seat of the Mercedes. The trees I told you I was going to plant – remember? – they've been delivered by truck but I don't trust the nursery with these beauties. You know what they are? Spanish chestnuts. Specially imported variety. A hundred rands each. My present to myself. God knows how they'll do, but I'm going to have a go. Have you bought yourself roast chestnuts in the street? That's the best part of the bloody miserable New York winter. (p. 208)

Mehring's expertise in the matter of inner dialogue – talking to himself – has drowned his ability to communicate with others. The trees, of course, are an attempt to communicate in another way. But the attempt is spurious because of the spuriousness of Mehring's claim to the land – the African farm – where he will plant them. And the foreignness of the trees crosses the symbolic t's. The intensity of his isolation combines with the inner confusion of his motives when he calls the trees 'My present to myself'. If that *is* what they are, why the concern at having failed to tell Terry about them? Clearly the trees are meant to outlast Mehring, to provide continuity of his own line in a particular sphere, just as he has hoped Terry would do. But that place, too, is a present he has made to himself, without the real owners' consent, and so his possession of it is another illusion.

In the paragraphs that immediately follow, Miss Gordimer moves in for the kill, with an intensified reiteration of the mechanistic grid-imagery that characterizes and entraps Mehring's existence.

> The road is so familiar that it exists permanently in his mind like those circuits created when electrical impulses in the brain connecting complex links of comprehension have been stimulated so often that a pathway of learning has been established . . . He could drive it in his sleep; sometimes does; he awakens in the middle of the night in town and for a moment thinks he is at the farm . . .
>
> How many times has he gone to and fro, ironed out the path of the first time he went to look at the place and decided it was a good buy. Scoring a groove over and over again, ineradicable. If there is a first purpose there will also one day be a last. It will probably be something like – something not more than a new grease-trap for a drain that Jacobus's asked for, or a supply of drench for the cows. That's the reality of the place, my dear; keeping it up. (pp. 208–209)

Whether there was ever a clearly-conceived 'first purpose' doesn't matter any more. The kind of last purpose he imagines to himself possesses a diminished significance in relation to virtually any other imaginable one. But the statement is significantly conditional – '*If* there is a first purpose' – was there one? In terms of the political significance of white occupation in Southern Africa, or of the personal meaningfulness on the individual existential level of Mehring's life, the only purposes that exist are intermediate, relative, insignificant. His life and the grid have merged.

And the remaining portions of the book bear this out fully. The events related bear an intensified symbolic burden, but the pace and rhythm, which together constitute a major achievement of consistency, maintain the nagging, irritating near-monotony, their sense of being unanchored in the world of sequential time (and, where Mehring is the perceiver, certainly not in any transcendental realm). Mehring plants his imported chestnut trees (or, rather, he

217

supervises, the blacks dig) while he conscientiously explains to Jacobus what chestnuts are, Miss Gordimer coldly lancing the hoary pretension about the white's educating mission to the black:

– Ah, is coming fruits, that's nice. And now is plenty, plenty rain, is going grow quick. –

– Not fruit, nuts. You know what that is? –

It is difficult to find an accurate comparison for chestnuts. None of them is likely ever to have seen an almond or walnut tree, although these grow in people's gardens in town. Groundnuts – those they know, a common crop not here but in the middle- and low-veld; but groundnuts grow attached to the plant's roots.

– Yes I know nuts. –

– Peanuts, you know peanuts. Well, something like that only these are very big, they're big as small new potatoes, and they grow in bunches on the tree. –

– Big like potatoes! –

–I think I can taste that nuts next year. –

That wily character knows he is exaggerating, he may not speak the language but he understands the conventions of polite conversation all right.

– Oh it will be many years before these have any nuts. You and I will be old men, Jacobus. –

– Well, is all right. Is all right, when Terry can get them, when he can marry and bring them nice for his wife, his little children? –

The farmer stands over them while they dig. It's necessary because there must be no skimping . . . (this earth has come all the way from Europe). . .

. . . Whatever else they may or may not be able to do, they know how to dig. . . . The cross-section of close-packed soil laid bare has its layers of colours and textures stored away. Broken in upon, the earth gives up the strong muthy dampness of a deserted house or a violated tomb. At one layer roots frayed by the spades stick out like broken wires. He leans down to tug at one – the young trees must not have to compete for nourishment with the root system of some other growth. But the roots don't yield, and he can't see where they can come from . . .

All the colours of the layers are mixed up, now, there will be a fault – negligible, on the natural scale – where the two

small trees now stand like branches children have stuck in the
sand to make a 'garden' that will wither in an hour. (pp.
210–213)

The detached irony with which Miss Gordimer presents the
situation, essentially comic, of the unconscious white overlord
being manipulated by the altogether aware black serf so that the
former is denied possession of anything valuable, while the latter
retains his vital grasp on his land, his life gives way suddenly to an
echoing hollowness when Jacobus becomes sincere, in evoking from
within his own value system the promise of natural continuity. Of
course Terry won't inherit the fruit of the trees. And from that
point the symbolic alienness that characterizes the whole business
of planting the European trees – playthings, bearers of luxury fruit
– in the African soil assumes a pervading emphasis. The soil
surrounding the roots comes from Europe – Mehring and his
whites, if they possess roots at all, still locate their origins in Europe.
The local root system won't budge even though damaged by the
holes dug for European soil and trees – and Mehring's inability to
'see where they come from' represents the final blindness of the
European in Southern Africa to the reality of the blacks among
whom he lives, upon whom he depends. In the end the whole
history of white settlement in Africa is reduced to 'a fault –
negligible, on the natural scale': and what is more, Miss Gordimer
prefigures a future in which 'All the colours . . . are mixed up, now'

The steady movement of the passage from satirical lancing of
Mehring's pretensions into predictive foreboding is maintained
until the end of the chapter. Quantities of rain have been falling,
and Mehring goes away from the scene of the tree-planting to
inspect 'his' property, and approaches the third terrace where the
still unappeased black man lies improperly buried.

Upon higher ground he hears himself crashing through them
as if he were coming towards himself, about to come face to
face with . . . It could only be one of them – a farm worker,
that is, a familiar black face among black faces, up here. (p.
214)

But it isn't anyone – tangible. And then Mehring's foot sinks into
the soft mud, and he panics:

It has already seeped in over the top of the boot and through
the sole and holds him in a cold thick hand round the ankle.
A soft cold black hand. Ugh . . . He pulls and pulls; down
there, he's pulled and pulled. It's absurd; he's begun to giggle

with queer panicky exasperation.
And then he's been let go. That's exactly how it feels:
something lets go – the suction breaks. (p. 215)

Mehring's perceptions are excited. As we have seen, his isolation
has steadily increased, to the point where it is almost complete.
Why? The two facts clearly function together; but what do they
relate to outside the closed system they create for Mehring? There
are two levels here analogously interrelated and interdependent.
Symbolically and personally, Mehring fails in his human obligation
to the black man whose body is found on 'his' land, thus offending
whatever gods or spirits – or value system – that possess the
dominant influence, however concealed. Historically, the whites
who Mehring represents have failed in their confrontation with the
blacks and their land to understand the latter or themselves, to
discharge their obligations whether political or moral. This larger
system, in fact, *causes* the smaller one in which Mehring is enclosed;
and it is *symbolized by* the smaller one. Thus, just as Mehring is
isolated in personal terms from his local white world, so the white
group he represents is cut off – morally, politically, in terms of
habits of thought – from its roots, its past, its cultural cognates
abroad. And Mehring is meanwhile drawn closer and closer to the
final confrontation with the ineluctable presence the independent
reality of whose existence he has tried so hard – and so successfully –
to remain ignorant of.

Then Miss Gordimer lets loose a richly allusive (and over-
intense) stream of symbolic description, as the weather of the novel
takes a significant turn for the worse. Freak rains set in: their source
is the Mozambique Channel (and it would be unfair to deny Miss
Gordimer's writing before events in Portugal had suddenly begun
to indicate fresh directions, her degree of prophetic insight) and
floods result. The farm is partly flooded and the road that connects
it with Johannesburg is swept away. The telephone lines come
down, too. So the farm and its black inhabitants are cut off from the
city and its white 'owner'. Although parts of the farm are severely
flooded, Jacobus assumes control and triumphs.

> Jacobus's gumboots leaked ... The telephone would not
> serve him, either. He spent long periods in the house turning
> the handle; the thing was dead, it was not merely the refusal of
> the white man at the other end to take any notice. At last he
> went from the telephone through the rooms of the house in a
> way he had never done before; he opened the cupboards as

possessions must be sorted after a death, putting objects aside
like words of a code or symbols of a life that will never be
understood coherently, never explained, now . . . He found a
pair of gumboots that must have belonged to the son, too;
they were all right . . .

He drove Phineas and Solomon, Witbooi, Izak and
Thomas hard about the reconstruction and repair necessary
on the farm. A calf had wandered off and drowned, but only
one; the other one hundred and forty-nine of the herd were
intact. A cow calved and developed mastitis and he had found
the right medicine for that, in the house, and filled up the
syringe and injected it the way he had seen the vet do. He had
had the lucerne and teff that was on the flooded side of the
barn moved to the verandah of the house, where the drainage
was good . . . He would get everyone busy soon digging the
irrigation canals free of the muck that blocked them. (pp.
224–225)

The prose rhythm differs from the characteristic brittle tension of
Mehring's introspection: its relaxation reinforces the sense of
natural order evoked by Jacobus's actions – the automatic delicacy
with which he makes his way through the potential complexities of
the situation confronting him – acting without a white man's
authority, taking steps that affect a white man's property.

While Mehring cannot get to the farm during this time, his
nemesis literally surfaces to meet him, in a manner reminiscent of
the ancestors in Soyinka's *Dance of the Forests*. Undisturbed by fire,
the body of the black man surfaces because of the flood, its shallow
covering of soil washed away; Mehring discovers it on his first visit
after the flood, after his patronizing acknowledgement of (and
mental reservations about) his serfs' achievements.

He feels an urge to clean up, nevertheless, although this
stuff is organic: to go round collecting, as he does bits of paper
or the plastic bottles they leave lying about. He has been so
busy tidily looking he hasn't noticed Jacobus has turned back
and is coming straight up the third pasture through the
shallow pools and mud and is almost upon him again.

Jacobus is in a hurry. He's running, as far as this can
describe the gait possible in such conditions, over such
terrain, stumbling and sliding, lurching, slipping. There's the
sensation that the eyes of the old devil are already fixed on him
before they can be seen, before the face can be made out.

221

When it is near enough to separate into features he becomes strongly and impressively aware that there is something familiar, something that has already happened, something he knows in their expression.

Jacobus is panting. His nose runs with effort and a clear drip trembles at the junction of the two distended nostrils.

Jacobus is going to say, Jacobus is saying – Come. Come and look. – (p. 232)

Thus the circumstances of first and last meeting are structurally balanced. Again Mehring is preoccupied by his obsessional desire for tidiness, order, 'conservation'; again Jacobus is the intermediary between Mehring and reality but this time Mehring fears an additional burden of self-knowledge, which is almost entirely unconscious. His conscious perceptions remain bounded within the walls of the white South African world view: as Jacobus comes closer Mehring notes with Apollonian attention to detail (and the critical revulsion that underlies the common perceptual response of most whites to blacks in the situation) the distasteful clinicalities of Jacobus's appearance. Mehring's own deep, all-embracing involvement – responsibility, even – in the reality behind that appearance is something that he, tragically (for himself but perhaps also for all those who inhabit the African farm) is incapable of bringing to consciousness. In technical terms the gradual increase in the detail available to Mehring's eyesight before the emotional response of disgust slips out seems to indicate a whole series of choices available to Mehring – he may judge either way, any way, throughout the infinite multitude of instants which compose his increasingly clear perception of the approaching man. And in the end he loses all these opportunities and responds – judges – in terms of habit, stereotype and external appearance – in terms of the grid. This final failure of human function, to break free, indicates Mehring's negative readiness to be claimed by whatever forces the dead man represents – the offended spirits of the land, the ancestors, the real owners.

Mehring's reaction to the discovery reflects the ambivalence of his psychic state. Seen from the western, European, Appollonian point of view, the fact that he is so extremely upset by seeing the corpse reflects his demoralization. But this is not the only point of view available; and it is possible to argue that Mehring, having been drawn, unconsciously (though, ironically, through his own insistence on relating to the land of the farm), into an entirely different conceptual framework, reacts appropriately. For one thing, and most strikingly, perhaps the most prominent effect rendered in terms of a thematic image is that Mehring is dislodged from the defining grid which has held his life in its mechanistic pattern. Enough has been said about the grid-imagery as defining an industrial-technological perceptual style and life pattern. Mehring drives back from the farm after encountering the decaying corpse: his inner monologue burns him on a short fuse:

> – A stink to high heaven. It was not final; the only thing that is final is that he's always there. It was never possible to be alone down there. (p. 236)

> A stink to high heaven: the burned willows have grown again and the reeds have become thickets of birds, the mealies have stored sweetness of lymph, human milk and semen, all the farm has flowered and burgeoned from him, sucking his strength like nectar from a grass straw –
> *An awful moment looking at a green light and not knowing what it means.*
> Jeers of horns are prodding at him. Blank. (p. 237)

Thus it is clear that the shock of confrontation with his brother's neglected corpse, as it were, has jerked him clear of the metallic framework of the everyday routine of industrial society. Miss Gordimer infuses his inner monologue at this point perhaps a little richly; but the connections she establishes in doing so are vital to the political and historical statement she has to make. His dislocation is recorded, symbolically, as he sits in his powerful car, protective and aggressive at once, itself constituting the supremely symbolic statement of the society of which he is a product. (The moment is analogous, as we shall see, to Helen Shaw's insight of horror in the location riot in Miss Gordimer's first novel, *The Lying Days*, when Helen, too, is shut in a powerful car, but immobilized by a natural force going beyond what the car stands for. The analogy becomes pointed as we see the difference in direction taken by Helen and Mehring from their respective moments of dislocation.)

> A shudder of tremor comes up the back of his neck to his jaw and he jerks to engage the gear. Unnerving; but it happens to everyone now and then. The single syllable chatters away crazily at his clenched jaw. No, no. No, no. He has not waited

to hear more. Let them do what they like with it, whether or not the word was 'nose'. (p. 237)

The rhythm is sufficient to indicate Mehring's loss of control in directions which have been crucial to him – first, what 'happens to everyone now and then' is *not* what has happened to him, except on the most fundamental level of the horror of human relations in South Africa – and even there, realization has been forced on him in a way it is seldom forced on others; and secondly, his abandonment of responsibility to the blacks for something that happens on the farm – 'Let them do what they like with it' – again suggests the force by which he has been dislodged even from the chosen aspects of his customary framework.

> Everything at the intersection which he is now crossing like any other competent driver who's had a dozen cars in his lifetime and to whom the wheel in his hands is second nature, asserts the commonplace and ordinary reassurance of what are the realities of life . . . Nothing has happened. Good god, tomorrow he will settle a dispute with the Industrial Council, and he has decided to turn down another directorship . . . As much money as he needs and knows what to do with, what's more. The road back is commonplace and familiar enough to bring anyone down to earth. The white working man knows he couldn't live as well anywhere else in the world, and the blacks want shoes on their feet – where else in Africa will you see so many well-shod blacks as on this road? There is a bus-stop for them (beer cartons strewn) and here ten yards on, a bus stop for whites employed round about; just as counting sheep puts you to sleep so ticking off a familiar progression of objects can be used to restore concentration. (pp. 237–238)

The effort he makes to restore his perceptions to their Newtonian, regulative framework is a conscious one, and the enterprise is vital to his survival. It develops into a familiar litany, a verbalization of the grid, in the well-known justification of white domination on the grounds that it gives economic advantages for the blacks. But the dent in his orbit persists, and against the inclination of his own routine convictions he picks up a hitch-hiker, a tart in her twenties, equivocally white, to whom he has once before given a lift, (in the rain, together with her garrulous grandfather).

Mehring's disorientation is so thorough that he easily succumbs to her seduction of him. They park the car in a concealed spot off the road and the book moves rapidly to its thoroughly ambiguous climax. Is Mehring physically attacked and robbed by the burly young Afrikaner (himself symbolic of white South African manhood) who is concealed at the spot? Or does he make his escape in the Mercedes, leaving the girl (whom he suddenly fears to be coloured, a police 'trap' inciting whites to transgress the Immorality Act)? The penultimate chapter ends:

> No no, what nonsense, what is there to fear – shudder after shudder, as if he were going to vomit the picnic lunch, it's all coming up, coming out. That's a white tart and there was no intent, anyway, report these gangsters or police thugs terrorizing people on mine property, he's on a Board with the chairman of the Group this ground still belongs to . . . No, no, no. RUN.
> – Come. Come and look, they're all saying, What is it? Who is it? It's Mehring. It's Mehring, down there. (p. 250)

The whole constellation of 'white' fears emerges from Mehring's consciousness at this moment – the tart must be white or else the legal question of intent becomes relevant; the irony of the objection to 'police thugs' 'terrorizing', and the solid emphasis (about the only solid thing in Mehring's feelings) on property, complete the ironic picture of a group living within a complete misperception of its surroundings. One is conscious that this is Meyring's only sexual encounter located both within the fictive present and on African soil, as it were. And, of course, the chapter ends with the (at least) imaginative identification (by Mehring himself) of Mehring with the dead black man on the African farm – the discovered corpse. The orderly confusion of Mehring's Appollonian scheme has been reduced to the chaotic truth. And the final chapter, two pages short, returns to and confirms the real world.

> Witbooi offered to make a coffin. They used a tarpaulin in the meantime, weighted with stones from that place where the whites once cooked meat. Izak helped saw the planks at the work-shop near the house; Alina brought tea and porridge and stayed to talk, but not loudly, because of what it was the two men were hammering together. Jacobus had phoned the farmer in town at his office and asked for money for the wood. It was granted without questioning or difficulty . . . the farmer didn't want to hear about it. He was leaving that day for one of those countries white people go to, the whole world is theirs.

He gave some instructions over the phone; Jacobus must look after everything nicely. (p. 251)

The situation depicted is one of community, co-operation, dignity, respect, pervaded by a sense of order. The only jarring notes are the (by now pretty meaningless) 'instructions' – the white man's only mode of discourse. The funeral is celebrated with due propriety and solemnity, and the African farm claims (and is claimed by) its own.

The one whom the farm received had no name. He had no family but their women wept a little for him. There was no child of his present but their children were there to live after him. They had put him away to rest, at last; he had come back. He took possession of this earth, theirs; one of them. (p. 252)

The last paragraph of the book stresses the continuity in relation to the land which mere possession does not confer; it is what cuts sharply between white and black, and makes the life of the Indians so intolerably, waveringly ambivalent.

The Conservationist is a novel of faith, or belief. Mehring, the 'new man', dweller in the global village, latest product of countless years of evolution, supremely pragmatic, in control of his environment, beyond religion or politics, and related illusions, possessed of apparently total knowledge – lacks the wisdom of faith, and inevitably, collapses as a result. This is a culmination of the major process evident in Miss Gordimer's work, since, say, *The Late Bourgeois World*. In her last three novels she has depicted, in her leading male characters, the collapse of the romantic hero – an event of enormous importance in Western culture. In *The Late Bourgeois World* the romantic rebel found final irrelevance, geographic as well as historic, at the bottom of Table Bay. Max van den Sandt's beliefs – his political and personal faith – perished with him. The same may be said of Bray in *A Guest of Honour*, though, of course, Bray's heroism is in the liberal democratic rather than the romantic rebellious mould. But both men have represented attempts within the Western tradition to synthesize faith and belief in politics and personal relations into a workable system of life.

Mehring represents the stage after these failures – man unfettered (from one point of view) by the limitations that belief systems impose, and thus, apparently, in an altogether enviable state of total control combined with total freedom – the veritable Apollonian apotheosis. Politics mean nothing to Mehring because faith and belief are obsolete tools as far as he is concerned. But the result is, in a sense, a surprise. Miss Gordimer has not shared tendencies fashionable among some of her famous contemporaries – Doris Lessing, for example – towards a mystical key to the complexities of experience unaccountable in various rationalistic systems. But she *does* demonstrate with great conviction what is lost by the death of faith in Western culture. It is precisely the spontaneous and easy continuity of the traditional community that Mehring lacks. Continuity in *time* and *place* on the African farm ensure the Africans' inheritance: isolation in time and place – their virtual negation as human paradigms – annihilate Mehring's claim.

Thus, in terms of the structure of this novel, Mehring's position in relation to the blacks on 'his farm' may be seen as a matter of distance. In their possession of what he lacks – a working system of belief, a faith in that system and in the pattern of personal relations generated by historic circumstance within their group, a living connection between the two – they are utterly remote from him. Perhaps the most astonishing results of this (since the context is, after all, a novel by Nadine Gordimer) is the virtual abolition of politics – or, perhaps, its reduction to its simplest basis of faith or the lack of it. In this respect, of course, Mehring is both right and ultimately altogether wrong.

7 Conclusion

Nadine Gordimer is the most important South African writer since Olive Schreiner. In an age when political exile is often a mark of respectability for the creative artist, she chooses to stick to her post in the face of a situation of moral, cultural and political repression that is frightening in its intensity. She continues to record the realities of South African life with the sensitivity and dedication that mark everything she writes; but the conception of the novelist's task that appears in her work does not stop at that of the faithful recorder.

Nadine Gordimer is also a passionate interpreter of South African reality. The perspective of her interpretation has evolved over the years and changed. At the beginning of her career it tended to embody the main assumptions of the European liberal moral tradition, though even then these assumptions were not granted the status of unquestioned validity. She came to see them later as components of a larger historical reality, rather than as definitive standards of judgment; and her interpretation of South African life thus achieved a new dimension, unprecedented in any South African fiction, of accuracy and insight.

In establishing this new appreciation of Southern African reality as not a European phenomenon, not subject to the rules and criteria of a code of judgment evolved within a different scale of experience, Nadine Gordimer has subjected the governing notions of European liberalism, as these are conventionally expressed in fiction, to the most appropriate (and stringent) form of critical scrutiny – by embodying them within her novels. In particular, she has focused on the central problem of the moral status of action, through an extensive creative probing of what has happened to the conventional liberal hero, rooted in romantic ideology and subjected to the post–Darwinian (and post-Auschwitz) doubts of contemporary technological civilization.

Her conclusion, that heroic action on the liberal-romantic scale

228

possesses a distorted significance in the context of the post-colonial realities of the 'third world', works in both directions, because it illuminates the moral situation within the metropolitan culture at the same time as discovering the ground rules for moral action in the local culture. Through her explicit challenge to most of the European conventional (and conventionally experimental) conceptions of the function and meaning of time, both for the individual and the history of a group, she becomes a pioneer in the crucial task of establishing a new South African historiography. No group can understand its present or its future (or itself) without first coming to terms with and understanding its past. By liberating the South African past from European conceptions – whether of the moral status of action, of heroism, of the shape or function of time – Nadine Gordimer shows in her novels the way to a fresh understanding of the combination of processes and events that shaped South Africa's reality. Since that reality, and its future course, constitute one of the most crucial test cases for the moral experience of the twentieth century, the importance of Nadine Gordimer's work is evident.

By placing South African reality firmly within the context of the post-colonial experience of the 'third world' Nadine Gordimer has located her own work within that context as well. She has moved from being a European writer born in exile, to a writer inhabiting and understanding a reality once organically related to and dependent on Europe, but now essentially separated from it. Thus, as an African writer, she is in the same literary category as Borges or Marques as South Americans, in relation to their respective 'metropolitan' cultural roots. And as an African novelist writing in English, there can be little doubt that Nadine Gordimer occupies the leading position in her chosen field.

Bibliography

This is a brief and incomplete guide to Nadine Gordimer's fiction. It includes her novels and those of her short stories that have appeared in collections. It also includes one work of literary criticism, but its scope does not extend to the large amount of polemical writing in the forms of essays, journalism, occasional criticism, introductions to books and so forth that Nadine Gordimer has produced.

Face to Face (Johannesburg, Silver Leaf Books, 1949) short stories.
The Soft Voice of the Serpent and other stories (London, Gollancz, 1953) short stories, largely overlapping with *Face to Face*.
The Lying Days (London, Gollancz, 1953) novel.
Six Feet of the Country (London, Gollancz, 1957) short stories.
A World of Strangers (London, Gollancz, 1958; Harmondsworth, Penguin, 1962; and London, Jonathan Cape, 1975) novel.
Friday's Footprint (London, Gollancz, 1960) short stories.
Occasion for Loving (London, Gollancz, 1963) novel.
Not for Publication (London, Gollancz, 1965) short stories.
The Late Bourgeois World. (London, Gollancz, 1966) novel.
A Guest of Honour (London, Jonathan Cape, 1971) novel.
Livingstone's Companions (London, Jonathan Cape, 1972) short stories.
The Black Interpreters (Johannesburg, Ravan Press, 1973) criticism.
The Conservationist (London, Jonathan Cape, 1974) novel.
Selected Stories (London, Jonathan Cape, 1976) a collection of works that have already been published in earlier books.

Index